The EVERYTHING
Indian Cookbook

Dear Reader:

Namaste, I salute the divine in you! Welcome to the wonderful world of Indian cooking. Let me guide you as you begin your journey exploring the spice continent, a journey that will make the exotic simple and the unknown familiar.

I present to you simple recipes from all over India. Designed with the beginner in mind, these recipes are easy to prepare and use simple ingredients and cooking methods. They will give you a taste of the wide variety of ingredients and food preparation styles that come together to form Indian cuisine. From the lap of the Himalayas in the north to the coast of southern India, from the Ghats of western India to the eastern Bay of Bengal, I present to you a multitude of flavors.

All the recipes have been tested and come with easy instructions and handy tips. I hope that you will enjoy preparing them as much as I have enjoyed writing them.

May you always be blessed with great meals,

Monica Bhide

The EVERYTHING® Series

Editorial

Publishing Director	Gary M. Krebs
Managing Editor	Kate McBride
Copy Chief	Laura MacLaughlin
Acquisitions Editor	Bethany Brown
Development Editor	Karen Johnson Jacot
Production Editor	Jamie Wielgus

Production

Production Director	Susan Beale
Production Manager	Michelle Roy Kelly
Series Designers	Daria Perreault
	Colleen Cunningham
Cover Design	Paul Beatrice
	Frank Rivera
Layout and Graphics	Colleen Cunningham
	Rachael Eiben
	Michelle Roy Kelly
	John Paulhus
	Daria Perreault
	Erin Ring
Series Cover Artist	Barry Littmann

Visit the entire Everything® Series at everything.com

THE
EVERYTHING®
INDIAN COOKBOOK

300 tantalizing recipes—
from Sizzling Tandoori Chicken
to Fiery Lamb Vindaloo

Monica Bhide

Adams Media
Avon, Massachusetts

An Everything® Series Book.
Everything® and everything.com® are registered trademarks of F+W Publications, Inc.

Published by Adams Media, an F+W Publications Company
57 Littlefield Street, Avon, MA 02322 U.S.A.
www.adamsmedia.com

ISBN: 1-59337-042-3
Printed in the United States of America.

J I H G F E D C B

Library of Congress Cataloging-in-Publication Data
Bhide, Monica
The everything Indian cookbook / Monica Bhide.
p.   cm.
(An everything series book)
Includes bibliographical references.
ISBN 1-59337-042-3
1. Cookery, Indic. I. Title. II. Series: Everything series

TX724.5.I4.B55 2004
641.5954–dc22

2003020367

This book is available at quantity discounts for bulk purchases.
For information, call 1-800-872-5627.

Contents

Dedication

Dedicated to my dear friend Beth Lipka. You will always be in our hearts. We miss you.

Acknowledgments

To all my friends and family for their amazing support.

To my husband Sameer and my son Jai for their love, my mom and dad for their amazing support and recipe advice, and my in-laws for their love and support.

To my agent Lisa Ekus, Steven Shaw of Egullet.com, Marcy Claman, and ichef.com for their unwavering faith in me.

To my dedicated testers, led by Anna Nielsen: Arti Bahl, Kent Villard, Yvonne May, Anjali Kumar, Anu Duggal, Shivani Mahendroo, Maya Nair, Saroj Nair, Meghana Bhave, Vrinda Deval, Aroop Gosh, Boaz Coaster, Elie Nassar, Mary Rachich, Susan Koch, Foster Rockwell, Christine Traini, Lydia Ketkar, Protima Jadhav, Pooja Bavkar, Mike Lipka, Sandy Turba, Ruchi Saigal, Anu Rohatgi, Sonia Kohli, Simon Majumdar, Mike and Debbie Smith, Prasad from Thali, and Javad Maftoon.

To Lavina Melwani for the delicious Sindhi Kebab recipe.

To Swati Elavia for her guidance on the menu-planning section, and Shiela Malik for her great pickle and dessert recipes.

To my researchers: Neerja Mishra, Puneet Agarwal, Shirley Taur. My tasters: Smita, Neal, Priya, and Shree Gondhelkar; Jeannie and Jim Thomas.

The amazing editorial team at Adams: Thank you!

Introduction

▶ A COUNTRY OF MORE THAN 1 BILLION PEOPLE, with over a dozen languages, 800 recognized dialects, and several religions, India is as diverse as it gets! The geography of India is extremely varied, with mountains, beautiful rivers, vast deserts, and extensive plains. This allows for a wide array of crops, flowers, wildlife, and climates—all of which are reflected in the diverse food culture of the country.

India's cuisine has been influenced greatly by the multitude of invaders throughout the country's history; the Mughals, Turks, Europeans, and Portuguese all left their mark. By adding their own cooking styles and ingredients, they provided a rich diversity, resulting in a unique cuisine. What holds this diverse cuisine together are the aromatic and flavorful spices. The art of Indian cooking is in blending the spices so that they are in perfect harmony in each dish.

The diverse Indian landscape provides a variety of fruits and vegetables. In addition, the abundant coastline provides a lot of seafood. Each region in India is known for its own distinct cuisine—largely influenced by the physical and social environments. In each region, however, food is served in a similar way—all together, as opposed to the Western way of serving food in courses. Tables are also jazzed up with condiments like pickles and chutneys, adding pizzazz to any meal. Regardless of the region you are in, Indians are known for their incredible hospitality. Northern Indian cooking is rich in meats, nuts, and amazing breads. The cuisine of western

India is simpler, focusing on rice and lentils. The eastern coastline is blessed with abundant seafood, which is reflected in the cuisine of the region. Southern India is famous for its legendary pickles and chutneys.

Religion also influences the cuisine a great deal. There are sects of Indians who don't eat any root vegetables, the Muslims do not eat pork, and the Hindus do not eat beef. There are special ingredients used to prepare religious meals, specifically for the purposes of breaking "fasts."

Indian cooking categorizes foods into six tastes—sweet, sour, salty, spicy, bitter, and astringent. A well-balanced Indian meal contains all six tastes. This is accomplished, in part, by accompanying the dishes with a wide variety of condiments.

The Everything® Indian Cookbook is all you need to start making fabulous Indian feasts in your own kitchen.

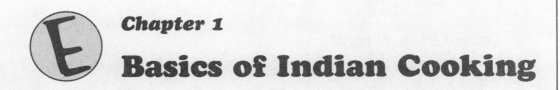

Chapter 1

Basics of Indian Cooking

Before you get started, there are a few things you need to know about the techniques and ingredients used in Indian recipes. This chapter covers the basics of what you should know to get started cooking delicious Indian meals.

Essential Techniques

It is important to understand a few simple cooking techniques before you begin your journey into the world of Indian cooking. These techniques can be used individually in recipes, but more often they are used in unison. By understanding the principles behind each technique, you can ensure the success of your recipes.

Dum (Steaming)

This refers to cooking the food in its own steam. You will notice that many recipes direct you to cover the cooking pot with a lid and reduce the heat to complete the cooking process. This is the modern-day version of dum—it helps the dish retain its aroma and helps the flavors seep in. In olden days, the lid of a cooking pot was sealed to the pot using wheat flour dough, thus ensuring that the steam would not escape. This pot was then placed on hot charcoals, and the dish was allowed to cook.

Tadka or Baghar (Tempering)

Tempering is the process of seasoning a dish with hot oil seasoned with spices. This can be done at the beginning of the recipe or at the end, depending upon the dish. It involves heating the oil until it is almost smoking, reducing the heat, and then adding the spices. The spices begin to sizzle and change color, indicating that they are cooked; then either more ingredients are added to it or the tempered oil is poured over a completed dish.

There are a couple of things to keep in mind with this process. When you add spices to hot oil, they will sizzle and splatter, so be prepared to remove the skillet from the heat immediately or have the additional ingredients on hand so you can add them quickly. Do not add any water to this seasoning; this will cause it to lose its flavor and potency. Also note that when you are adding spices to the heated oil, you should add them one at a time. Begin with the whole spices, then add the herbs, and then the powdered spices.

Bhunao (Sautéing)

This is the mostly commonly used cooking technique in Indian cooking. This technique requires sautéing ingredients over medium to high heat while constantly stirring. In the recipes where sautéing is required, you can add a bit of water to the ingredients to keep them from sticking to the pan. This technique allows the ingredients to release their true flavors. To ensure that the ingredients are fully cooked, continue to sauté until the fat begins to separate from the spice mixture or the masala that is being cooked.

Tandoori Cooking (Grilling)

Traditionally, roasting in the Indian kitchen was done in clay ovens called *tandoors*. All the recipes in this book have been modified to suit your grill or oven. Just remember: If a recipe calls for a dish to be marinated prior to grilling, make sure to follow the recipe's directions as to how long it should be marinated to ensure that the marinade is able to exude its flavors. Discard any remaining marinade per the recipe directions.

Talina (Deep-Frying)

Another key cooking technique used in Indian food is deep-frying. Traditionally, a deep vessel, similar to the Chinese wok, is used to heat the oil. You can use a deep fryer if you wish. Although some people like to reuse oil used for deep-frying, it is best to use fresh oil each time you deep-fry. The key to deep-frying is to let the oil return to frying temperature between fried batches. Also, do not use large quantities of oil to deep-fry—the quantity should be just enough to immerse the ingredients, usually about 1 or 2 inches of oil is enough.

ALERT!

Safety is important when you are deep-frying, so please take appropriate precautions when using hot oil. Make sure the deep fryer or wok is not easily accessible to children.

Essential Ingredients

It's important to become familiar with the common ingredients, their usage, and their necessity in the cuisine. Once you have mastered these basic ingredients, you can begin to improvise on the recipes.

Basic Spices and Spice Mixes

Spices are used in Indian cooking to provide a myriad of flavors. They can be used whole, ground, toasted, rarely raw, individually, or as mixes. Chapter 2 introduces you to some basic spice mixtures that are used throughout the book. I would advise you to prepare these as needed (not in advance) to ensure that you get the best flavor each time.

Many Indian grocery stores now sell some of these spice mixes pre-made. These can be a real time saver if you are in a pinch. If you buy premade mixes, be sure to check the manufactured dates on the packages. Spices are covered in more detail later in this chapter.

Ginger-Garlic Paste

A mixture of minced ginger and garlic, this paste is used in many recipes in this book. I have provided a recipe for you to prepare this at home. Again, if you are in a pinch you can buy premade ginger-garlic paste at your local Indian grocer. This paste keeps for months if refrigerated. Ginger-garlic paste cooks quickly and can burn, so watch it carefully when you cook with it.

Oils

Traditionally, Indian cooking uses ghee, or clarified butter, as a cooking medium. Most of the recipes in this book have been prepared using any light vegetable oil of your choice. Ghee is used in some dishes to provide a unique nutty flavor to the dish. In some eastern Indian states, mustard oil is used as a cooking medium. This oil is very pungent and should be heated to a smoking point before using (to reduce its bitterness).

Olive oil is not used in traditional Indian cooking because it causes the spices to lose their individual flavors. Also, many Indian dishes require cooking at a very high heat, and olive oil tends to burn easily.

Souring Agents

Indian dishes have a balance of many flavors—hot, sour, sweet, salty, spicy—all in one recipe. Common souring agents are tamarind, lemon or lime juice, vinegar, tomatoes, and even yogurt. Tamarind and lemon juice can generally be substituted for each other in the recipes here, except in the recipe for Tamarind Chutney (see page 224). When a dried (as opposed to wet) souring agent is needed, *amchur* or dried mango powder is often used.

Tenderizers

Traditional Indian cooking uses raw papaya and yogurt as meat tenderizers. I have used plain yogurt in the recipes in this book.

FACT

There really is no such term as *curry* in the Indian language and no spice mix called "curry powder." Each region has its own special mixes and spices that are blended together to form "curries," or sauces.

Thickening Agents

You will notice the use of yogurt, chickpea flour, onions, and nut pastes in a number of recipes. These are traditionally used as thickening agents. They add a lot of body to sauces in Indian dishes.

Cooking with Spices

Using spices in Indian cooking is a 3,000-year-old tradition. Ancient Indian texts focused primarily on three characteristics of spices—their medicinal properties, their ability to act as food preservatives, and their ability to season food. Ayurveda, the ancient Indian art of healing, teaches that food plays an essential part in one's health and sense of well-being. For food specifically, it says that you should have sweet, tangy, salty, and hot all in the same meal or at least in the day; this helps balance out your sense of taste. Spices provide all of these flavors.

Combining Spices

Spices also add depth and complexity to food. They can be added individually or in "mixes." Use the spice mix recipes provided in this book or create your own. There really is no one right spice mixture—if it tastes good to you, it is the right mix! Many Indian grocery stores sell premade spice mixes that can be a real time saver if you are in a bind.

The secret to making perfect Indian dishes is in the spices. Understanding the flavors that they provide, at what point in the cooking process to add them, and in what order to add them is at the heart of Indian cuisine. Most spices need to be cooked before they are eaten to help release their flavors. There are a few that can be used raw, but raw green cardamom or cloves, for instance, are often used as a garnish.

Guidelines for Preparing Spices

If you are using oil or ghee (clarified butter) to cook your spices, ensure that the oil is hot before you add the spice. Hot oil has the ability to retain the flavor of the spice. If your oil is too cold, the spice will not release its flavor. Ghee is often used in India, as it has the ability to be heated to very high temperatures. It also retains spice flavors a lot better than oils.

If you need to roast spices, first make sure that you use a totally dry skillet—no oil or water. Second, ensure that the skillet is hot before you add the spices. Spices cook very quickly and can easily burn, so you must constantly stir and be ready to remove them from the heat as soon as they brown and you can smell their fragrance.

Be careful when making substitutions. Coriander powder, for instance, cannot be substituted for fresh coriander, or cilantro, and saffron cannot be substituted for turmeric. If you are unsure about a spice, check the glossary of this book for more information. You can use ground spices for whole spices in some cases, but just remember that whole spices have a much stronger flavor. Taste to adjust seasoning as necessary, being careful not to overspice.

As you begin to gain an understanding of spices, their flavors and characteristics, and begin to cook some of the recipes in this book, I have one piece of advice: Follow the recommended steps and spice quantities the first time. As you gain more experience with the spices and are able to determine how to balance the amount of spices to add to a dish, you can improvise as you like.

Finally, make sure that you have all the spices ready to go before you start cooking. In many recipes the spices need to be added in quick succession and you will not have time to go looking for them in the middle of the cooking process. Remember, spices tend to burn easily, so having them at the ready will make the process easier. If your spices do burn, toss them away and begin again. There is nothing worse than the taste of burned spices!

Basic Indian Spice Pantry

Every Indian spice pantry needs to have the bare essentials to start cooking Indian meals. Make sure your shelves are always stocked with the following spices:

- Salt
- Red chili (whole and powder)
- Turmeric
- Coriander (whole and powder)
- Cumin seeds
- Mustard seeds
- Bay leaves
- Cinnamon
- Cloves
- Black peppercorns
- Asafetida
- Green and black cardamom
- Carom seeds (also called *ajowan* or *ajwain*)
- Mango powder
- Tamarind pulp
- Dried fenugreek leaves

Grinding and Storage Guidelines

Make sure that your spices are fresh—this is the golden rule of Indian cooking. Replace your spices at least once a year. How should you test freshness? Use your nose. If you open a package of spices and cannot smell the aroma, the spices have lost their potency and should not be used. Even for the mixed masala or spice mixtures, you will notice a difference in smell (and flavor!) if you prepare them fresh when you need them.

For grinding spices you can use a couple of different tools. You can use a mortar and pestle or a coffee grinder. (If you are using a coffee grinder, buy one to use just for the spices, since it will take on the smell of the spices.)

The best place to store the spices is in a cupboard or a drawer away from direct sunlight. If you can, use glass or clear plastic jars—this way you can see how much spice you have left. Also never use a wet spoon to remove spices from a jar. This will keep them fresh longer.

If you live in a very hot area, you can store your spices in the refrigerator to keep them fresh longer. Just make sure that you are using airtight jars.

What You'll Need

Indian cooking does not really require any specialized utensils. For most of the recipes, you can use your standard cooking pots and pans, measuring cups, and wooden spoons. Following is a list of the commonly used equipment for the recipes in this book:

- **A deep pan:** A dutch oven or a deep sauté pan can be used. To make the cooking process easier, use nonstick pans. In India a traditional cooking vessel like this is called a *karahi* and is similar to a wok.
- **Food processor:** This is a real time saver in the kitchen, perfect for mincing, chopping, and grating.
- **Blender:** Wonderful for making chutneys, drinks, and soups.
- **Sieve:** A sieve is perfect for draining whey and straining.

- **Spice grinder/coffee mill/mortar and pestle:** Use any one of these to grind dry spices.
- **Slotted spoon:** A metal spoon that is perforated is perfect for deep-frying.
- **Deep fryer/deep pan:** Either one can be used for deep-frying, with appropriate safety precautions.
- **Griddle:** A nonstick griddle is perfect for making Indian breads.

CHAPTER 2
Basic Recipes (Mool Vidhi)

Warm Spice Mix
(Garam Masala Powder)

Yields 2 tablespoons
Prep Time: None
Cook Time: 10 minutes

You can vary this recipe a bit—experiment with various spices until you find the combination that works for you.

8 cloves
4 teaspoons cumin seeds
3 green cardamom pods (whole)
2 black cardamom pods
  (whole)

1 (2-inch) cinnamon stick
2 teaspoons coriander seeds
1 teaspoon black peppercorns
1 bay leaf
Pinch of grated nutmeg (optional)

1. Heat a small skillet on medium. Add all the spices except the nutmeg, and dry roast the spices, stirring constantly. After about 5 minutes, the spices will darken and begin to release a unique aroma.
2. Remove the skillet from the heat, then add the nutmeg. Transfer the spice mix to a bowl and allow to cool for about 5 minutes.
3. Using a spice grinder, grind the spices to a fine powder. Store in an airtight jar. The spice mixture will keep for up to 3 months.

Indian Cheese
(Paneer)

Yields approx. 1 cup
Prep Time: None
Cook Time: 15–20 minutes, 2 hours to set

An extraordinary source of protein, paneer is one of the most versatile Indian ingredients. It keeps for about 1 week, refrigerated.

2 lemons, juiced

8 cups whole milk

1. Bring the milk to a boil in a large pan over medium heat. Line a sieve with several layers of cheesecloth. Set aside the sieve in a clean, dry sink.
2. Once the milk has reached the boiling point, remove the pan from the heat. Add the lemon juice slowly. The milk will begin to form a curd cheese. Using a wooden spoon, stir the mixture until all the milk has curdled, about 1 to 2 minutes. You will see the curd cheese, which is white, separating from the whey, a cloudy-looking liquid.
3. Pour the mixture into the cheesecloth-lined sieve to drain off the whey. When the cheese has cooled (about 20 minutes), fold the corners of the cheesecloth and squeeze to remove any remaining whey. To make the *paneer* firm, put it between 2 large plates and place something heavy (such as a large pot of water) on top to weigh it down. Once it has set for about 2 hours, remove the cloth.

Ginger-Garlic Paste
(Adrak Lasan Ka Paste)

2 serrano green chilies (optional)   1/2 cup garlic cloves, peeled
1/2 cup fresh gingerroot, peeled   1 tablespoon cold water

1. Remove the stems from the green chilies.
2. Place all the ingredients in a food processor and purée to form a smooth paste. Add no more than 1 tablespoon of water to help form a smooth consistency.
3. Store the paste in an airtight jar in the refrigerator. The paste will keep for up to 2 weeks in the refrigerator.

Yields 1 cup
Prep Time: 5 minutes
Cook Time: None

To freeze convenient portions of this paste, scoop 1-tablespoon portions into ice trays, freeze, and transfer to a container or plastic bag.

Tandoori Spice Mix
(Tandoori Masala)

1/2 teaspoon carom seeds   1/2 teaspoon dried fenugreek
1 tablespoon Warm Spice Mix   leaves
   (see recipe on page 12)   1/4 teaspoon dried mango
1/2 teaspoon ginger powder   powder
1/4 teaspoon black salt

1. Place the carom seeds in a resealable plastic bag and pound with a rolling pin.
2. Combine all the ingredients in a bowl and mix thoroughly. Transfer to an airtight jar and store.

Yields 4 tablespoons
Prep Time: 2 minutes
Cook Time: None

This recipe is quintessential in North India. You can also try adding red chili to it.

Chaat Spice Mix
(Chaat Masala)

Yields 3 tablespoons
Prep Time: None
Cook Time: 5 minutes

This zesty spice mix is sprinkled over dishes once they have been cooked, adding a very tangy flavor.

1 tablespoon cumin seeds
1½ teaspoons dried mint leaves
¼ teaspoon black peppercorns
¼ teaspoon carom seeds

Pinch of asafetida
1 teaspoon ginger powder
1 teaspoon dried mango powder
1 teaspoon black salt

1. Heat a small skillet on medium heat; dry roast the cumin seeds, mint leaves, black peppercorns, and carom seeds for about 2 minutes, until fragrant. Remove from heat and mix in the asafetida, ginger powder, dried mango powder, and black salt.
2. Grind all the ingredients using a mortar and pestle or a spice grinder.
3. Store in an airtight jar for up to 3 months. Sprinkle over salads or cooked dishes.

Hung Yogurt
(Dahi)

Yields 1½ cups
Prep Time: None
Cook Time: 2 hours to drain

Yogurt has a wonderful creamy texture that holds during the cooking process, and it provides a cooling effect during spicy meals.

2 cups plain yogurt

1. Line a sieve with several layers of cheesecloth. Place the yogurt in the sieve and suspend over a bowl.
2. Let any liquid drain into the bowl, then discard the liquid. Tie the ends of the cheesecloth to form a pouch. Weigh it down using a few cans in a plastic bag as weight. Let it sit for about 2 hours to allow any remaining liquid to drain out.
3. Remove the cheesecloth. Transfer the yogurt to a container. Cover and refrigerate for up to 2 weeks.

Clarified Butter
(Ghee)

½ pound unsalted butter

1. Heat a heavy pan over low heat. Add the butter, allowing it to melt. Once the butter has melted, increase the heat, bringing the butter to a boil. The fat will start to separate and the butter will begin to foam.
2. Reduce the heat and simmer for about 15 minutes. Watch carefully, as it may burn. The milk solids will start to settle at the bottom, and the liquid butter will float to the surface. When the liquid butter becomes amber in color, remove from heat. Allow the liquid to cool to room temperature.
3. Strain the amber liquid into a jar; discard the remaining sediment.
4. Cover the jar and store, refrigerated, for up to 6 months.

Yields about ½ cup
Prep Time: None
Cook Time: 25 minutes

This butter lends a nutty taste to Indian cooking. Use sparingly, as it is high in fat.

Whole-Milk Fudge
(Khoya)

4 cups whole milk

1. In a heavy-bottomed pan, bring the milk to a boil, stirring constantly. As the quantity of milk starts to reduce, scrape any dried milk off the sides of the pan. Continue to cook until it reduces to the consistency of mashed potatoes.
2. Remove from heat and let cool. Transfer to a heat-resistant container. Store covered in the refrigerator for up to a week.

Yields about ⅓ cup
Prep Time: None
Cook Time:
30–40 minutes

To save time, you can also buy powdered Khoya at your local Indian grocer.

Fried Onions
(Barista)

4 cups vegetable oil
1 pound red onions, peeled
   and thinly sliced

1. In a deep pan, heat the oil until it is almost smoking. Reduce the heat to medium, and wait about 30 seconds.
2. Add the onions a few at a time and deep-fry until they are golden brown and crispy. Transfer the onions onto a paper towel to absorb the extra oil. Continue until all the onions have been fried.
3. When the onions have cooled off for about 10 minutes, roughly pound them with a rolling pin. Store in a jar for up to 2 months.

Roasted Saffron
(Kesar)

¼ teaspoon saffron threads
2 tablespoons whole milk

1. Warm the milk over low heat until it is warm to the touch (but not hot).
2. In a dry skillet, dry roast the saffron threads over low heat until fragrant, less than 1 minute. Remove from heat.
3. Put the milk in a small bowl and add the saffron threads. Use immediately.

❄ **Caution!**

Don't try to substitute another spice for saffron. The aroma and flavor of this sophisticated spice cannot be duplicated.

CHAPTER 3

Starters and Snacks (Shurat)

Cucumber Cup Coolers
(Kheere Ki Katori)

Serves 4–6
Prep Time: 15 minutes
Cook Time: 10 minutes

These edible cups stuffed with a creamy garlic yogurt are so easy to make. Amaze your friends with this delight.

2 medium seedless cucumbers, peeled
½ teaspoon cumin seeds
½ cup yogurt, whipped
1 clove garlic, peeled

1 serrano green chili, seeded
1 teaspoon fresh lemon juice
Table salt, to taste
2 sprigs fresh cilantro, stemmed

1. *To make the cucumber cups:* Cut the cucumber crosswise into 1-inch pieces. Use a melon baller to scoop out the insides. Leave a ¼-inch border on the sides and the bottom. Set the cups upside down on a plate lined with paper towels to drain. Refrigerate.
2. Heat a skillet over medium heat. Add the cumin seeds and dry roast them until fragrant, about 1 to 2 minutes. Stir constantly to prevent the seeds from burning. Let them cool and then roughly pound them.
3. Using a hand blender or a mixing spoon, blend together the cumin seeds, yogurt, garlic, green chili, fresh lemon juice, and salt. Transfer the yogurt mixture to a mixing bowl.
4. Finely chop the cilantro. Add it to the yogurt mixture.
5. When you are ready to serve, place all the cucumber cups on a serving platter. Spoon the yogurt mix into each cup. These can be made ahead and refrigerated until ready to serve.

❋ Cumin Seeds

Easily the most popular spice in Indian cooking, cumin seeds are known for their digestive powers. Cumin is never used raw. It is always either dry roasted or added to hot oil before other ingredients are added.

Spiced Crunchy Okra
(Chatpati Bhindi)

1½ pounds okra, rinsed and dried
1 teaspoon red chili powder
½ teaspoon Warm Spice Mix (see recipe on page 12)
1 teaspoon dry mango powder

3½ tablespoons chickpea flour
2 cups vegetable oil
1 teaspoon Chaat Spice Mix (see recipe on page 14)
Table salt, to taste

Serves 4
Prep Time: 10 minutes
Cook Time: 15 minutes

For a spectacular presentation, create a "nest" using the okra and nestle grilled shrimp or Chicken Tikka (page 24) in it.

1. Remove the stems from the okra. Cut each piece lengthwise into 4 pieces. Lay out the pieces in a large, flat dish; set aside.
2. In a small mixing bowl, mix together the red chili powder, spice mix, and dry mango powder. Sprinkle this mixture over the okra. Toss well to ensure that all the pieces are covered with the spice powder.
3. Sprinkle the chickpea flour over the okra. Toss again to ensure that each piece is lightly and evenly covered.
4. In a deep pan, add the vegetable oil to about 1 inch deep. Heat the oil over high heat until smoking, about 370°. Reduce the heat to medium-high. Add some of the okra and deep-fry until well browned, about 4 minutes. Remove with a slotted spoon and place on a paper towel to drain. Continue until all of the okra is fried. Let the oil return to its smoking point between batches.
5. Sprinkle the spice mix on the okra. Toss well and season with salt. Serve immediately.

❊ Buying Okra

Okra is commonly known in India as "ladies finger." When you buy okra, check for freshness by trying to snap the end. If it snaps, the okra is fresh. If it just bends, it is old. Before you cut up okra for any recipe, make sure that it is completely dry. The gummy liquid that appears when you cut it will disappear once the okra is cooked.

Fenugreek-Flavored Meatballs
(Methi Ke Kofte)

Serves 4
Prep Time: 10 minutes
Cook Time: 10 minutes

Serve these bite-sized
meatballs with
Mint-Cilantro Chutney
(see page 224).

½ pound ground lean lamb
1 small onion, minced
1 tablespoon dried fenugreek
    leaves
¼ teaspoon Ginger-Garlic Paste
    (see recipe on page 13)

2 teaspoons Warm Spice Mix
    (see recipe page 12)
2 teaspoons fresh lemon juice
Table salt, to taste
2 tablespoons vegetable oil
Red onion rings, for garnish

1. Preheat oven to 500°, or turn on the broiler.
2. In a mixing bowl, combine all of the ingredients *except* the oil and
   red onion rings. Mix well, using your hands.
3. Divide the mixture into 8 equal parts and roll into balls. Using a
   pastry brush, brush the meatballs with the oil. Place all the meatballs
   on a baking sheet in a single layer.
4. Place the baking sheet under a hot broiler or in the oven and cook
   for 8 to 10 minutes, turning frequently until the meatballs are well
   browned on all sides and the meat is completely cooked through.
5. Garnish with red onion rings and serve hot.

❈ Dried Fenugreek

*Dried fenugreek leaves, or kasoori methi, add a wonderfully powerful
aroma to dishes. These dried leaves are not interchangeable with
fenugreek seeds. Fenugreek seeds, a powerful, bitter spice, are used
in pickling and for some curries.*

Indian Cheese Manchurian
(Paneer Manchurian)

1½ tablespoons rice flour or
   corn flour
1½ tablespoons all-purpose
   flour
¼ teaspoon white pepper
   powder
¼ teaspoon table salt

1 teaspoon Ginger-Garlic Paste
   (see recipe on page 13)
Water as needed, at room temperature
Vegetable oil for deep-frying
½ pound Indian Cheese (see
   recipe on page 12), diced

Serves 4
Prep Time: 5 minutes
Cook Time: 10 minutes

These appetizers are
so flavorful in them-
selves that they do
not need any
dipping sauce.

1. Combine the corn flour, all-purpose flour, pepper, salt, and Ginger-Garlic Paste in a medium-sized bowl. Mix thoroughly and add just enough cold water to make a thin batter. (A few tablespoons of water should be enough, but add more if needed.)
2. In a deep pan, heat 1 to 2 inches of vegetable oil to 370° on a deep-fry thermometer. To test the temperature, you can add a drop of the batter; if it rises to the top immediately, your oil is ready to use.
3. Dip a few pieces of the Indian Cheese in the batter, turning to coat all sides; add to the hot oil. Deep-fry until golden brown in color (turning them in the oil to prevent them from sticking together).
4. Remove the cheese from the oil using a slotted spoon and drain on paper towels. Let the oil return to temperature and continue this process until all the Indian Cheese is fried. Serve hot.

☀ Deep-Frying Made Easy

When deep-frying, make sure that the ingredients are all cut the same size to ensure even cooking. Add small quantities of the ingredient to the oil. This maintains the oil's temperature. Try using fresh oil—it will improve your final product!

Sweet Potatoes with Tamarind
(Shakarkhandi Ki Chaat)

Serves 4
Prep Time: 10 minutes
Cook Time: None

Serve this with Fresh Lime Soda (page 41).

4 small sweet potatoes
1½ tablespoons Tamarind Chutney (see recipe on page 224)
¼ teaspoon black salt
1 tablespoon fresh lemon juice
½ teaspoon cumin seeds, roasted and roughly pounded

1. Peel the sweet potatoes and cut them into ½-inch cubes. Cook in salted water to cover for 5 to 8 minutes or until just fork-tender. Drain and let cool.
2. Put all the ingredients in a bowl and toss gently. Scoop the sweet potatoes in equal portions into 4 bowls. Stick a few toothpicks into the cubed sweet potatoes and serve.

Sweet and Spicy Fruits
(Phal Ki Chaat)

Serves 5
Prep Time: 5 minutes, plus 20 minutes to chill
Cook Time: None

This dish can also be a healthy low-fat lunch, but with a lot of flavor. Serve this with Fresh Lime Soda.

½ small apple, peeled and diced
Handful of seedless grapes
1 small banana, sliced
½ small pear, peeled and diced
½ small mango, peeled and diced
1-inch slice watermelon, peeled and diced
Juice of ½ lemon
1 tablespoon chopped cilantro (optional)
¼ teaspoon black salt
1 teaspoon Chaat Spice Mix (see recipe on page 14)

Mix together all the ingredients in a bowl. Toss to ensure that the fruits are evenly coated with the spices. Chill for about 20 minutes, then serve.

Indian Cheese Tikka
(Paneer Tikka)

1 cup plain yogurt
1 tablespoon vegetable oil
½ teaspoon turmeric powder
1 teaspoon Warm Spice Mix
    (see recipe on page 12)
¼ teaspoon cumin powder
1 teaspoon Ginger-Garlic Paste
    (see recipe on page 13)
Table salt, to taste

2 cups Indian Cheese (see
    recipe on page 12), cubed
    (about ¾ by ½ inch)
1 onion, quartered and layers
    separated
1 tablespoon vegetable oil
1 teaspoon Chaat Spice Mix
    (see recipe on page 14)

Serves 4
Prep Time: 10 minutes,
plus 1 hour to marinate
Cook Time: 8 minutes

Try substituting tofu in
place of the Indian
Cheese (paneer) for a
different flavor.

1. In a mixing bowl, combine the yogurt, vegetable oil, turmeric powder, spice mix, cumin powder, Ginger-Garlic Paste, and salt; mix well.
2. Add the Indian Cheese and onions to the marinade, cover, and refrigerate for about 1 hour.
3. Preheat the broiler. Thread the cheese and onions alternately onto skewers. Broil about 4 inches from the heat for 5 to 8 minutes or until done, turning and basting once with oil. When the onions start to char around the sides, the *Paneer Tikka* is ready.
4. Serve warm, sprinkled with Chaat Spice Mix and accompanied by Green Chili Chutney (see recipe on page 236).

❄ Secret Behind Wooden Skewers

If you like to use wooden skewers, soak them in water for about 30 minutes before use. This will prevent them from burning during grilling.

Chicken Tikka
(Murgh Ka Tikka)

Serves 4
Prep Time: 5 minutes,
plus 5–6 hours
to marinate
Cook Time: 15 minutes

Punjabi Onion Salad
(page 66) and Mint-
Cilantro Chutney
(page 224) nicely
complement this dish.

¾ cup Hung Yogurt (see
recipe on page 14)
1 tablespoon Ginger-Garlic
Paste (see recipe on
page 13)
1 teaspoon fresh lemon juice
1 tablespoon vegetable oil
½ teaspoon, or to taste, red
chili powder
Table salt, to taste

½ teaspoon Tandoori Spice Mix
(see recipe on page 13)
¼ teaspoon Warm Spice Mix
(page 12)
1 pound skinless, boneless
chicken breasts, cubed
2 tablespoons melted butter,
for basting
Lemon wedges, for garnish

1. To make the marinade, combine the Hung Yogurt, Ginger-Garlic Paste, lemon juice, oil, red chili powder, salt, and the spice mixes in a mixing bowl; mix well. Add the chicken cubes. Cover, and let marinate in the refrigerator for 5 to 6 hours or overnight.
2. Heat oven to 400°.
3. Thread the chicken onto skewers and baste with the melted butter. Place the chicken on a baking sheet and roast in the hot oven for about 5 minutes. Turn once and baste with any remaining butter. Roast for another 10 minutes or until golden brown and the juices run clear.
4. Serve hot, garnished with lemon wedges.

✺ Gingerroot

Ginger is a rhizome native to India and China. Its name comes from a Sanskrit word, which translates to "a body with horns." In addition to its many healing powers, it is said to be quite the aphrodisiac!

Chinese Indian Chili Chicken
(Mirchi Wala Murgh)

2 tablespoons Ginger-Garlic
   Paste (see recipe on
   page 13)
2½ tablespoons soya sauce
1 tablespoon vinegar
1 teaspoon red chili powder
½ teaspoon sugar
½ teaspoon table salt

2 fresh seranno green chilies,
   seeded and minced
1-2 drops red food coloring,
   optional
1 pound boneless, skinless
   chicken, cubed
2 tablespoons vegetable oil

> **Serves 4**
> **Prep Time:** 10 minutes,
> plus 3 hours to marinate
> **Cook Time:** 15 minutes
>
> This dish packs a
> punch, so make sure
> you have something
> cold and sweet
> nearby like Fresh Lime
> Soda (page 41).

1. To make the marinade, combine the Ginger-Garlic Paste, soya sauce, vinegar, red chili powder, sugar, salt, green chilies, and red food coloring (if desired) in a mixing bowl or sealable plastic bag. Add the chicken pieces and mix well. Cover and marinate in the refrigerator for about 3 hours.
2. Heat the oil in a large skillet on high. Add the marinated chicken pieces, shaking off any excess marinade. Discard any remaining marinade. Stir-fry for about 5 to 7 minutes, until the chicken is cooked through. You can add 1 or 2 tablespoons of water if the mixture starts to stick or dry out. Remove from heat. (Depending on the type of chicken you select, your cooking times might vary slightly.)
3. To serve, place equal portions of the chicken on 4 appetizer plates. Serve hot.

※ Hot Oil Is a Must
The most common mistake that people make with this recipe is not heating the oil to a high enough temperature before adding the chicken. Hot oil retains the flavor of spices much better than cold oil.

Semolina Pancakes
(Rava Uthapam)

Serves 4
Prep Time: 20 minutes
Cook Time: 15 minutes

This mild recipe is perfect for a Sunday morning breakfast. Serve these with tangy Tamarind Chutney (page 224).

1 cup coarse semolina or plain cream of wheat
1 cup plain yogurt
Salt, to taste
Water at room temperature, as needed
¼ teaspoon baking powder
¼ teaspoon carom seeds

¼ small red onion, peeled and finely chopped
1 small red bell pepper, seeded and finely chopped
½ small tomato, seeded and finely chopped
2 tablespoons vegetable oil

1. Combine the semolina, yogurt, and salt in a medium-sized mixing bowl; mix well. Add ¼ to ½ cup water to reach the consistency of pancake batter, ensuring that you do not have any lumps in the batter.
2. Add the baking powder. Set aside for about 20 minutes.
3. In a separate bowl, create the topping. Mix the carom seeds, onions, bell peppers, and tomatoes.
4. Heat a griddle on medium-low. Add a few drops of oil.
5. Ladle about ¼ cup of batter into the center of the griddle. It should have the thickness of a regular pancake. As the batter starts to cook, bubbles will begin to appear on the surface.
6. Add a small amount of topping to the pancake, while it is still moist. Press down gently with the back of your ladle. Add a few drops of oil around the sides of the pancakes to keep it from sticking.
7. Flip the pancake over and cook the other side for about 2 minutes. Remove the pancake from heat and place on a serving platter. Continue this until all the batter is used up. Serve warm.

Mixed Vegetables with Bread Rolls
(Mumbai Ki Pav Bhajji)

1 cup cauliflower florets
¼ cup diced carrots
¼ cup diced green bell pepper
¼ cup chopped French beans
6 tablespoons butter
1 small red onion, peeled and chopped
2 small tomatoes, chopped
1 tablespoon Ginger-Garlic Paste (page 13)
2 serrano green chilies, chopped

1 teaspoon red chili powder
¼ teaspoon turmeric powder
½ teaspoon table salt
4 medium boiled potatoes, peeled
8 square bread buns, cut horizontally
Minced cilantro, for garnish

Serves 4
Prep Time: 10 minutes
Cook Time: 30 minutes

If you like, you can add 1 tablespoon of commercially available pav bhajji masala. It provides a distinct aroma.

1. In a small amount of salted water, cook the cauliflower, carrots, bell peppers, and French beans together until soft. Drain, discard the water, and set the vegetables aside.

2. In a large skillet, melt 4 tablespoons of the butter over medium heat. Add the onions and sauté until transparent. Add the tomatoes and cook until the tomatoes soften, about 3 to 5 minutes. Add the Ginger-Garlic Paste and the green chilies. Use a potato masher or the back of a spatula to mash the mixture. Continue cooking until you see the oil separating from the sides of the tomatoes.

3. Add the red chili powder, turmeric powder, and salt; sauté for 1 minute. Add all the cooked vegetables and the potatoes. Continue to cook, stirring, for another 3 to 4 minutes. If the mixture starts to dry out, add 1 tablespoon of water. Remove from heat and transfer to a serving bowl.

4. Return the unrinsed skillet to the stove. Turn the heat to low. Butter the buns with the remaining butter. Place the buns buttered sides down on the skillet. Toast both sides until slightly crispy and golden brown. Remove from heat.

5. Serve the buns alongside the *bhajji*. Garnish the *bhajji* with cilantro.

Tapioca Delight
(Sabudana Vada)

Serves 4
Prep Time: 15 minutes, plus 3 hours to soak
Cook Time: 15 minutes

Serve this alongside the tangy Tamarind Chutney (page 224).

1 cup tapioca
2 medium potatoes
2 serrano green chilies, minced
2 sprigs cilantro, stemmed and minced
Table salt, to taste
¼ cup roughly ground unsalted peanuts
1 tablespoon fresh lemon juice
Vegetable oil for deep-frying

1. Cover the tapioca with water and soak for about 3 hours. Leave some room in the bowl for expansion as the tapioca soaks up the water. After 3 hours, drain off any remaining water.
2. While the tapioca is soaking, peel and cut the potatoes into ½-inch cubes and boil in salted water to cover for 5 to 8 minutes or until just fork-tender. Drain and mash.
3. Put the drained tapioca in a mixing bowl and add all the other ingredients *except* the oil. Mix thoroughly with your hands.
4. Lightly oil your hands and form about ¼ cup of the mixture into a ball, then flatten it into a small patty. Continue lightly oiling your hands and making patties until you have used up all the mixture.
5. Fill a deep pan with 1 inch of oil and heat on medium. Add 1 patty at a time and cook until golden brown on each side, about 2 minutes per side. Remove the patties from the oil and drain on a paper towel. Serve hot.

❋ Too Hot?

If you find the green chilies are too hot for your taste, remove the seeds before you cook with them. You'll get the flavor, without the heat. One word of caution though, wear gloves when you deseed the chilies.

Flour Savories
(Marwari Sawali)

2 cups white all-purpose flour
  (maida)
3 tablespoons Clarified Butter
  (see recipe on page 15)
¾ teaspoon carom seeds

½ teaspoon black pepper
Pinch of baking soda
Table salt, to taste
Oil for deep-frying

Yields 20 pieces
Prep Time: 30 minutes
Cook Time: 15 minutes

Try serving these delightful chips alongside Raw Mango Chutney (page 235).

1. In a large, flat bowl, mix together the flour, butter, carom seeds, black pepper, baking soda, and salt. Add just enough water to knead into a stiff dough. (To use a food processor, place the flour, butter, carom seeds, black pepper, baking soda, and salt into the bowl fitted with the steel blade. Pulse a few times to mix the ingredients and then process briefly until the mix looks like coarse cornmeal. Gradually add water through the feed tube until the mixture just begins to stick together. Turn out onto a very lightly floured surface and knead a few times until the mixture forms a dough.) Let the dough rest, covered, for 30 minutes.

2. Divide the dough in half, and roll each portion into a log about 5 inches long. Slice each log into 10 pieces. Roll out each portion into a small disk a little thicker than a potato chip and about 4 inches in diameter. Prick each piece all over with a fork.

3. Heat the oil in a deep pan to 380° on a deep-frying thermometer. Fry 3 to 4 disks at a time (be careful not to overcrowd the pan). They are ready when they are light golden brown and a little puffy.

4. Remove the disks with a slotted spoon, and drain on a paper towel. Let the oil return to temperature. Continue until all the disks are fried. Serve alongside your favorite chutney.

Corn Fritters
(Maki Ke Pakore)

**Yields about 8
golf ball–size fritters**
Prep Time: 15 minutes
Cook Time: 20 minutes

Particularly alluring in the monsoon season, these appetizers are a perfect accompaniment to evening tea.

1 cup corn kernels (fresh or frozen)
2 slices white bread, ripped into small pieces
½-inch piece ginger, peeled and grated
1 serrano green chili, minced
Table salt, to taste

¼ teaspoon red chili powder
1 teaspoon minced cilantro
Juice of ½ lemon
2 tablespoons chickpea flour
Pinch of baking powder
4 tablespoons water, at room temperature
Vegetable oil for deep-frying

1. To make the batter, combine all the ingredients *except* the oil in a mixing bowl. Mix well, adding enough water to coat all vegetables.
2. In a deep pan, add the oil to about 1 inch depth. Heat the oil on high until smoking, then lower the heat to medium. Press a spoonful of the mixture between 2 spoons to get a nice compact fritter. Use 1 of the spoons to push the fritter into the oil. Add a few spoonfuls at a time, ensuring that the balls do not stick to one another. Be careful not to overcrowd the pan. Fry the fritter until golden brown, about 4 minutes.
3. Use a slotted spoon to remove the cooked fritters from the oil. Transfer to a paper towel to absorb the extra oil. Skim any loose bits from the oil and discard. Continue until you have used up all the mixture.
4. Serve immediately with your choice of chutney.

❈ Bhutta, Makka, Maki, or Corn
Corn is very popular in India. The most popular way to eat corn is to grill it. Grill corn on the cob and sprinkle it with lemon juice and a little Chaat Spice Mix (page 14).

Pork Tikkas
(Pork Ke Tikke)

1 cup Hung Yogurt (see recipe on page 14)
1 small onion, peeled and minced
1 tablespoon Ginger-Garlic Paste (see recipe on page 13)
1 teaspoon Warm Spice Mix (see recipe on page 12)

¼ teaspoon red chili powder
¼ teaspoon turmeric powder
Table salt, to taste
1 pound lean boneless pork, cubed
1 tablespoon oil

Serves 4
Prep Time: Overnight to marinate
Cook Time: 15 minutes

Your guests will devour these succulent tikkas. Serve them along with chilled Saffron Lemonade (page 43).

1. In a bowl (or resealable plastic bag), mix together all the ingredients *except* the oil. Cover and refrigerate overnight.
2. Thread the pork onto skewers. (If you are using wooden skewers, soak them in water for 30 minutes so that they don't scorch or burn.) Discard any remaining marinade.
3. Cook on a hot grill to desired doneness (about 12 minutes for well done). Turn once during the cooking process and baste with oil. Serve hot.

❈ Hung Yogurt

Yogurt is used as a tenderizer in meat dishes and provides a perfect base for marinades. It is "hung" to drain out the whey and give it a creamier consistency.

Crunchy Bread Fritters
(Dabel Roti Ke Pakore)

Serves 4
Prep Time: 35 minutes
Cook Time: 25 minutes

A wonderful variation to this recipe is to make a chutney sandwich, dip the entire sandwich in the batter, and then deep-fry.

4 slices of white bread, crust removed
1 cup chickpea flour
Table salt, to taste
¼ teaspoon red chili powder
⅛ teaspoon carom seeds
1 teaspoon vegetable oil
Approximately ¾ cup warm water
Oil for deep-frying

1. Cut each slice of bread into 4 equal-sized pieces; set aside.
2. To make the batter, mix together the chickpea flour, salt, red chili powder, carom seeds, and the vegetable oil. Begin adding the warm water a little bit at a time. Beat well to ensure that there are no lumps. The batter needs to be thick. Let the batter rest for about 20 minutes.
3. Heat about 1 inch of the oil in a deep pan to 350° on a deep-fry thermometer. Dip each bread piece in the batter, let the excess batter drip off, and place the bread into the hot oil. Add a few pieces at a time. Reduce the heat to medium. Fry the fritters, turning them in the oil until they are golden brown on all sides.
4. Using a slotted spoon, remove the fritters from the oil and place on a double layer of paper towels to drain. Place in a warm (200°) oven. Let the oil return to temperature and continue until all the fritters are done. Serve hot.

❋ Chutney Sandwiches

These could not be easier to make. Select your favorite chutney. Butter a slice of bread. On another slice of bread, slather on as much chutney as you desire. Cover with the buttered slice. Serve along with Spicy Papaya Salad (page 56).

Spiced Broccoli
(Chatpati Broccoli)

1 cup broccoli florets
1 tablespoon Ginger-Garlic Paste (see recipe on page 13)
1 tablespoon chickpea flour
¼ teaspoon dried mango powder

½ teaspoon coriander powder
¼ teaspoon, or to taste, red chili powder
Table salt, to taste
Vegetable oil for deep-frying

Serves 4
Prep Time: 15 minutes to marinate
Cook Time: 20 minutes

Broccoli is a relatively recent addition to the Indian cuisine. It is seasoned and deep-fried here for a crispy snack.

1. In a bowl, toss the broccoli florets with the Ginger-Garlic Paste and chickpea flour. Ensure that the florets are evenly coated. Let the florets marinate for 15 minutes.
2. In a small bowl, mix the dried mango powder, the coriander powder, red chili powder, and salt; set aside.
3. In a deep pan, heat about 1 inch of the oil to 350° on a deep-fry thermometer. Add a few pieces of broccoli at a time. Deep-fry until the florets are pale brown in color, about 3 minutes. Remove the broccoli with a slotted spoon and place on a paper towel to absorb the extra oil. Let the oil return to temperature. Continue until all the florets are fried.
4. Place all the florets on a serving platter and sprinkle with the prepared spice mixture. Serve immediately.

※ Chickpea Flour—Not Just for Dinner
To this day, many Indian beauty books promise that chickpeas can help you achieve flawless skin. The secret is a facemask made of chickpea flour, turmeric powder, and water.

Puffed Rice Mix
(Bengali Jhal Muri)

Serves 4
Prep Time: 25 minutes
Cook Time: 10 minutes

Puffed rice loses its crispness once it is exposed to air. Store in an airtight container.

2 small potatoes
½ pound puffed rice
½ cup canned chickpeas, drained and rinsed
1 serrano green chili, seeded and chopped (optional)
¼ cucumber, peeled and chopped
1 small tomato, seeded and chopped

½ teaspoon cumin seeds, roasted and roughly pounded
¼ teaspoon Chaat Spice Mix (see recipe on page 14) (optional)
1 tablespoon mustard oil (optional)

1. Peel and cube the potatoes. Boil the potatoes in a large pot until they are tender. Drain off the water and let the potatoes cool to room temperature.
2. Mix together all the ingredients in a large bowl. Serve immediately.

Indian Cheese Cubes
(Khatti Paneer Chaat)

Serves 4
Prep Time: 5 minutes
Cook Time: None

A number of souring spices are added to the paneer (Indian Cheese) here, giving it a wonderful tangy taste.

8 ounces Indian Cheese (see recipe on page 12), cubed
2 tablespoons minced cilantro
½ teaspoon grated gingerroot
2 tablespoons fresh lemon juice

1 teaspoon dried mango powder
1 teaspoon dried pomegranate powder
½ teaspoon black salt

Mix together all the ingredients in a bowl. Serve immediately. This can also be refrigerated for a few hours before serving.

Potato Cutlets
(Aloo Ki Tikki)

4 small potatoes
2 serrano green chilies, minced
4 slices white bread
Table salt, to taste
¼ teaspoon black pepper
    powder

1 tablespoon minced cilantro
¼ cup crumbled Indian Cheese
    (see recipe on page 12)
6 tablespoons vegetable oil

> **Serves 4**
> **Prep Time:** 40 minutes
> **Cook Time:** 20 minutes
>
> Leave out the green chilies if you like your cutlets mild. Serve these with the Mint-Cilantro Chutney (page 224).

1. Boil the potatoes, then peel and mash them. Mix in the green chilies.
2. Soak the bread in water. Remove the bread and squeeze out all the water. Add the bread to the potato mixture and knead well. Add the salt, pepper, cilantro, and the Indian Cheese; mix well.
3. Divide the mixture into 8 equal portions. Rub a little bit of oil in the palms of your hands and flatten each portion into small disks.
4. Heat the oil in a skillet. Add the disks (or *tikkis*) 1 at a time. Fry for about 2 minutes on each side or until they turn golden brown. Remove the *tikkis* from the oil and place on a paper towel to drain off excess oil. Continue until all the *tikkis* are cooked. You can keep these warm in a warm oven. Serve hot.

✳ Easy Potatoes

A really easy way to "boil" potatoes is to microwave them! Simply prick the potato all over with a fork. Microwave for about 12 minutes, and your "boiled" potato is ready.

Onion Rings
(Pyaz Ke Pakore)

Serves 4
Prep Time: 25 minutes
Cook Time: 30 minutes

You can also make pakore with your choice of other vegetables like cauliflower, spinach, eggplant, or even green chilies.

1 cup chickpea flour
Table salt, to taste
1/4 teaspoon red chili powder
1/4 teaspoon cumin seeds, roasted and roughly pounded
Pinch of baking powder

1 teaspoon vegetable oil
Approximately 3/4 cup warm water
2 medium-sized red onions, peeled and thinly sliced
Oil for deep-frying

1. To make the batter, mix together the chickpea flour, salt, red chili powder, cumin seeds, baking powder, and the vegetable oil. Add the warm water a little bit at a time. Beat well to ensure that there are no lumps.
2. Add the onions to the batter and make sure that they are well coated.
3. Heat about 1 inch of the oil in a deep pan to 350°. Add a few onion rings at a time to the hot oil. Reduce the heat to medium. Fry the onion rings, turning them in the oil until they are golden brown on all sides, about 2 to 3 minutes.
4. Using a slotted spoon, remove the onion rings from the oil and place them on a double layer of paper towels. Continue until all the onion rings are done. Serve hot. If you wish to serve them later, keep them warm in a 200° oven.

❋ Which Onion to Use

Indian onions are much stronger in taste than their American counterparts. I suggest using mild red onions. If you enjoy a stronger flavor, try white Vidalia onions, which are available in local grocery stores. If your onions are too bitter and you want to make them sweeter, soak them in cold water with a few tablespoons of salt for about 30 minutes. Drain, rinse well, and then use as desired.

Pomegranate Chaat
(Anardana Ki Chaat)

¼ cup fresh raspberries
¼ cup seedless grapes
1 cup fresh pomegranate seeds
¼ cup fresh blueberries
¼ cup canned mandarin
  oranges, drained

1 tablespoon fresh lemon juice
1 tablespoon chopped cilantro
1 teaspoon Chaat Spice Mix
  (see recipe on page 14)

Serves 4
Prep Time: 5 minutes,
plus 20 minutes to chill
Cook Time: None

Serve this with Fresh
Lime Soda (page 41)
or Fizzy Rose Drink
(page 40).

Rinse the fresh berries in cool water and drain. Mix together all the ingredients in a bowl. Toss to evenly coat the fruits with the spices. Chill for about 20 minutes, then serve.

Spicy Potato Snack
(Aloo Chaat)

4 medium potatoes
1 cup sprouted mung beans
  (bean sprouts)
2 tablespoons Mint-Cilantro
  Chutney (see recipe on
  page 224)

1 tablespoon Tamarind Chutney
  (see recipe on page 224)
¼ teaspoon Chaat Spice Mix
  (see recipe on page 14)
Table salt, to taste
1 tablespoon chopped cilantro

Serves 4
Prep Time: 5 minutes
Cook Time: 5 minutes

Try serving these
topped with sesame
seeds, bread crou-
tons, and minced
green chilies. For a
variation, pan-fry the
potatoes first.

1. Peel and dice the potatoes; boil in salted water, covered, for 5 minutes or until just fork-tender. Let cool.
2. Place all the remaining ingredients in a mixing bowl. Toss the potatoes in the mixture to coat the potatoes evenly with the spices. Serve immediately.

Curried Mixed Nuts
(Masala Nuts)

1 teaspoon cumin seeds
1 teaspoon coriander seeds
¼ teaspoon black peppercorns
2 cloves
1 dried red chili, roughly pounded

3 tablespoons vegetable oil
¼ teaspoon ground ginger
3 cups raw mixed nuts
1 teaspoon table salt

1. Heat a small skillet on medium. Add the cumin seeds, coriander seeds, black peppercorns, cloves, and dried red chili. Toast the spices, stirring constantly, for about 3 to 5 minutes. They will darken and release a wonderful aroma. Remove from heat and transfer them to a bowl to cool. Using a spice grinder or a coffee grinder, grind the spices.
2. In a large skillet, heat the oil on low. Add the ground spice mixture, the ground ginger, and the nuts. Cook gently, stirring constantly for about 3 minutes. Cover and cook for an additional 5 minutes, shaking the pan occasionally.
3. Remove from heat, uncover, and sprinkle with salt. Cool to room temperature, then serve.

❋ Scorching Spices

Sometimes adding powdered spices to an already hot pan can scorch them. If this is a problem for you, try adding 1 tablespoon of water to the spices before you sauté them. The water will quickly evaporate and the spices will sauté without burning.

CHAPTER 4
Drinks, Teas, and Soups
(Sharbats, Chai, Aur Shorbas)

Rose-Flavored Yogurt Drink
(Gulabi Lassi)

Serves 4
Prep Time: 5 minutes
Cook Time: None

If you cannot find rose water, substitute your favorite syrup. Lassi has a short shelf life and is best served fresh.

3 cups Hung Yogurt (see recipe on page 14)
2 tablespoons sugar
1½ tablespoons rose water
½ cup water
5–6 ice cubes
Rose petals, for garnish

In a blender, combine the yogurt, sugar, rose water, water, and ice cubes; blend well. Add more water if you like a thinner consistency. Serve garnished with rose petals.

✲ Rose Water

Rose water is made, as the name suggests, from roses. Cotton balls doused in chilled rose water make wonderful facial cleansers.

Fizzy Rose Drink
(Gulabi Ka Sharbat)

Serves 4
Prep Time: 2 minutes
Cook Time: None

Rooh afza, a fragrant syrup used in desserts, milkshakes, and sherbets, is readily available in most Indian grocery stores or at www.namaste.com.

4 tablespoons rose syrup or rooh afza
4 cans lemon soda, chilled
1 sprig mint, stemmed

1. Put 1 tablespoon of rose syrup into a tall glass.
2. Pour in 1 can of lemon soda as slowly as you can. The rose syrup will stay at the bottom, and the lemon soda will form another layer on top. Repeat the same process for the remaining 3 glasses.
3. Garnish with mint and serve.

Fresh Lime Soda
(Nimbu Ka Sharbat)

2 tablespoons ginger juice
4 teaspoons sugar
¼ teaspoon black salt
1 tablespoon fresh lime juice

4 cans lime soda
Ice cubes
Thin lemon slices, for garnish

Add all the ingredients *except* the lemon slices to a blender; blend well. Serve immediately, garnished with thin lemon slices.

Serves 4
Prep Time: 5 minutes
Cook Time: None

This is one of the most popular drinks in India. To get ginger juice, place grated ginger in a garlic press and squeeze out the juice.

Mint-Ginger Cooler
(Jal Jeera)

1 tablespoon minced cilantro
1 tablespoon minced mint
2 teaspoons tamarind pulp
4 cups water
½ teaspoon black salt
1 teaspoon cumin seeds,
  roasted

1½ tablespoons sugar
1 teaspoon fresh lemon juice
¼ teaspoon ginger powder
Dried mint, for garnish

1. In a blender, blend the cilantro and mint with a bit of water to form a paste; transfer to a large jug.
2. Add the tamarind pulp, water, black salt, cumin seeds, sugar, lemon juice, and ginger; mix well. Chill and serve garnished with mint.

Serves 4
Prep Time: 10 minutes, plus time to chill
Cook Time: None

A digestive drink, Jal Jeera is often served with little chickpea fritters called boondi. Boondi look like small pearls and are available in most Indian stores.

THE EVERYTHING INDIAN COOKBOOK

Mango Yogurt Drink
(Aam Ki Lassi)

Serves 4
Prep Time: 5 minutes
Cook Time: None

You can use fresh ripe mangoes for this recipe—add a few teaspoons of sugar to the lassi if you do.

3 cups Hung Yogurt (see recipe on page 14)
1 cup canned mango pulp

½ cup water
5–6 ice cubes

Combine all the ingredients in a blender; blend well. Add more water if you like a thinner consistency. Serve immediately.

❊ **More on Mangoes**
Many varieties of mangoes have been cultivated in India for thousands of years. One very popular Indian favorite is the alphonso mango.

Nutty Milk
(Masala Doodh)

Serves 4
Prep Time: 5 minutes
Cook Time: 10 minutes

This refreshing drink can be served either hot or cold.

4 cups 2% milk
¼ teaspoon Roasted Saffron (see recipe on page 16)
4 tablespoons ground almonds
2 tablespoons ground unsalted pistachios

¼ teaspoon cardamom seeds, roughly pounded
4 teaspoons sugar

1. In a deep pan, bring the milk to a boil.
2. Add the saffron, almonds, pistachios, and cardamom. Lower the heat and simmer for 5 minutes.
3. Add the sugar and mix well. Remove from heat. Let cool and refrigerate if serving cold.

Cold Coffee
(Thandi Coffee)

4 cups 2% milk
4 tablespoons low-fat sweet-
    ened condensed milk
8 ice cubes

4 teaspoons instant coffee
    (such as Nescafé)
Powdered cinnamon, for garnish

Combine all the ingredients *except* the cinnamon in a blender; blend well. Serve immediately, garnished with powdered cinnamon.

> **Serves 4**
> **Prep Time:** 5 minutes
> **Cook Time:** None
>
> A simple, charming drink that is very refreshing.

Saffron Lemonade
(Kesari Shikanji)

4 cups cold water
Juice of 1 large lemon
4 tablespoons sugar
¼ teaspoon crushed saffron
    threads

Fresh mint and lemon slices,
    for garnish

In a blender, blend together all the ingredients *except* the garnishes until the sugar is dissolved. Serve garnished with mint leaves and lemon slices.

> **Serves 4**
> **Prep Time:** 5 minutes
> **Cook Time:** None
>
> Saffron seems to lend a certain sense of royalty to this refreshing cooler. You can also use orange juice instead of lemon juice.

☀ Juicing Lemons

Lemons that are at room temperature are easier to juice than cold ones. You can microwave lemons that have been in the refrigerator for a few seconds to make juicing easier.

Maharastrian Buttermilk
(Maharastrian Mattha)

Serves 4
Prep Time: 10 minutes
Cook Time: None

This is a spicier version of the North Indian lassi, or yogurt drink. It helps with digestion and is great served after a heavy meal.

2 cups plain yogurt
1 cup water
½ serrano green chili, seeded (optional)
1 tablespoon minced cilantro
¼ teaspoon cumin seeds, roasted
Table salt, to taste

Combine all the ingredients in a blender; blend well. Chill and serve.

Mixed Fruit Juice
(Ganga Jamuma Saraswati)

Serves 4
Prep Time: 5 minutes
Cook Time: Time to chill

Street vendors have been selling this drink in India for ages. Traditionally in India this juice is made with sweet limes and oranges.

2 cups sweetened tangerine juice
2 cups sweetened naval orange juice
¼ cup pineapple juice
2 tablespoons lemon juice
½ teaspoon black salt
Thin orange slices, for garnish

In a blender, blend together all the ingredients *except* the orange slices. Chill and serve garnished with orange slices.

❋ Selecting Pineapples

Trust your nose for this. Turn the pineapple upside down and smell the bottom. A ripe pineapple should smell sweet. Remember, pineapples do not ripen after they have been picked, so make your selection carefully.

Minty Yogurt Drink
(Pudine Ki Lassi)

½-inch piece ginger, grated
¼ teaspoon cumin seeds,
    roasted and roughly
    pounded
2 teaspoons minced fresh mint

¼ teaspoon black salt
2 teaspoons sugar
3 cups plain yogurt
1 cup water
6–8 ice cubes

Combine all the ingredients in a blender; blend well. Add more water if you like a thinner consistency. Serve immediately.

Serves 4
Prep Time: 10 minutes
Cook Time: None

If you use low-fat or nonfat yogurt, you might need less water than what's called for here.

Watermelon Cooler
(Kalingar Ka Sharbat)

3 cups chopped watermelon,
    seeded
8–12 ice cubes
¼ teaspoon black salt (optional)

1 tablespoon honey
¼ teaspoon fresh lemon juice
Fresh mint, for garnish

Combine all the ingredients *except* the garnish in a blender; blend well. If you like, you can strain the juice. Serve garnished with mint.

Serves 4
Prep Time: 5 minutes
Cook Time: None

In the summertime when watermelons are plentiful, serve this for breakfast. It makes a nice change from the standard orange juice.

Ginger Tea
(Adrak Ki Chai)

Serves 2
Prep Time: 5 minutes
Cook Time: 10 minutes

Ginger tea aids in digestion and is commonly served after a meal. It is one of the most popular beverages in India.

1½ cups water
1-inch piece fresh ginger, peeled and grated
1 (1-inch) cinnamon stick
3 cardamom pods, bruised
2 cloves
½ cup milk
1 tablespoon loose Indian tea leaves
Sugar, to taste

1. In a saucepan, heat the water. Add the ginger, cinnamon, cardamom, and cloves; bring to a boil.
2. Add the milk and continue to boil for 1 minute. Add the tea leaves and continue to boil for another 1 to 2 minutes.
3. Remove from heat and strain. Add sugar to taste and serve.

Grandma's Chai
(Dadi Ma Ki Masala Chai)

Serves 2
Prep Time: None
Cook Time: 5 minutes

Your local Indian grocer will have many blends and types of tea—try several to see which one suits your taste buds.

2 cardamom pods, bruised
1 clove
1½ cups water
½ cup milk
2 tea bags or 1 tablespoon loose tea
Sugar, to taste

Place the cardamom, clove, water, and milk in a pan over high heat; bring to a boil. Add the tea bags, cover, and turn off the heat. Let the tea steep for 2 minutes; then strain, add sugar to taste, and serve.

☀ Saffron Tea

If you are not a fan of caffeine, try this. Heat 1 cup of water. Add a pinch of saffron, a bruised cardamom, and tiny piece of cinnamon. Simmer for about 1 minute. Strain. Add honey for some sweetness, and serve.

Chilled Soup
(Thanda Shorba)

1 large cucumber, peeled and
   grated
1 small garlic clove, crushed
2 cups plain yogurt
2 cups water
Table salt, to taste

1 tablespoon vegetable oil
¼ teaspoon cumin seeds
1 teaspoon finely chopped
   fresh mint for garnish

> **Serves 6**
> **Prep Time:** 10 minutes,
> plus 2½ hours to chill
> **Cook Time:** 5 minutes
>
> In the sweltering heat
> of summer, this soup
> has a wonderful
> cooling effect.

1. Place the cucumber in a bowl and chill for about 30 minutes. Pour off the cucumber juice that collects in the bowl. Press down on the cucumber to get out as much juice as possible.
2. Combine the cucumber and garlic, then stir in the yogurt and water. Combine thoroughly. Add salt to taste. Set aside.
3. Heat the oil in a small skillet on medium. Add the cumin seeds and sauté for about 1 minute or until the seeds start to crackle and you can smell the aroma. Remove from heat.
4. Stir the cumin into the yogurt soup. Cover and refrigerate for 2 hours.
5. When ready to serve, pour equal portions into 6 shallow bowls and garnish with the mint.

❈ Watermelon Skins

In the princely Indian state of Rajasthan, the watermelon skins are cooked to make a delightful side dish. After removing all the red flesh, you are left with the white flesh on the inside of the watermelon skin. Cut out this white flesh and set it aside. In a skillet, heat some oil, then add mustard seeds and cumin seeds. Add the white watermelon flesh, salt, and a pinch of garam masala. Cook for about 7 minutes or until tender. Serve hot.

Tangy Ginger Soup
(Adrak Ka Shorba)

Serves 4
Prep Time: 5 minutes
Cook Time: 30 minutes

You can omit the milk and add ½ cup of cream instead for a richer-tasting soup.

2-inch piece fresh gingerroot, peeled
2 tablespoons butter
1 teaspoon vegetable oil
1 teaspoon cumin seeds, roasted
¼ teaspoon turmeric powder
1 small tomato, chopped

2 dried red chilies, roughly pounded
1 serrano green chili, minced
2 cups milk
1 cup plain yogurt, whipped
Table salt, to taste
½ teaspoon dried mint

1. In a blender or with a hand grater, grind the ginger to a fine paste. If using a blender, you may add up to 1 tablespoon of water.
2. In a deep pan, heat the butter and the oil on medium. Add the ginger and sauté until well browned. Add the cumin and turmeric; sauté for about 20 seconds, then add the tomatoes. Cook for another 7 to 8 minutes or until the tomatoes are soft. Add the red and green chilies, then add the milk. Bring to a boil.
3. Reduce heat and add the yogurt. Simmer for about 20 minutes, stirring occasionally. Remove from heat. Add the salt. You can serve the soup as is or strained. Garnish with dried mint.

☀ Yellow Countertops?

Turmeric powder can stain your countertops. If you have yellow turmeric stains, use a cleaner with bleach—it usually gets rid of the stains. Baking soda or a few drops of lemon juice work well for this, too.

Mild Buttermilk Soup
(Chaas Ka Shorba)

1 tablespoon vegetable oil
6–8 curry leaves
1/4 teaspoon black mustard
   seeds
1 dried red chili, roughly
   pounded

4 peppercorns, roughly pounded
1/4 teaspoon cumin seeds,
   roughly pounded
2 garlic cloves, crushed
4 cups buttermilk
Table salt, to taste

> **Serves 4**
> **Prep Time:** 5 minutes
> **Cook Time:** 20 minutes
>
> Use curry leaves for this; curry powder is not a substitute. A lovely variation is to add 1 tablespoon of lightly roasted, thinly sliced coconut.

1. In a deep pan, heat the oil on medium. Add the curry leaves and mustard seeds. When the seeds pop, in quick succession add the red chili, peppercorns, cumin seeds, and garlic.
2. Reduce the heat to low. Add the buttermilk and mix well. Simmer on low heat for about 15 minutes. Add salt to taste. Serve immediately.

Goan Shrimp Soup
(Sopa De Camarao)

2 tablespoons butter
1 teaspoon vegetable oil
1 small onion, peeled and
   chopped
1/2 cup canned crushed
   tomatoes

1/2 teaspoon garlic paste
2 cups chicken stock
2 cups water
1 cup cooked medium-sized
   shrimp
Table salt, to taste

> **Serves 6**
> **Prep Time:** 15 minutes
> **Cook Time:** 30 minutes
>
> This simple soup can be cooked unattended for the most part. Serve this soup garnished with slit green chilies or even shredded cheese.

1. In a deep stockpot, heat the butter on medium. Add the vegetable oil. Add the onions and sauté for about 7 to 8 minutes, until soft. Add the tomatoes and garlic paste; sauté for another 2 to 4 minutes.
2. Add the chicken stock and water. Cook, covered, for about 15 minutes.
3. Add the cooked shrimp and salt. Simmer uncovered on low heat for about 5 minutes. Serve hot.

Special Goan Soup
(Sopa Grossa)

Serves 6
Prep Time: 15 minutes
Cook Time: 30 minutes

This traditional mild soup is made with Goan red rice; I use the more readily available basmati rice.

2 tablespoons butter
1 teaspoon vegetable oil
1 small onion, peeled and
    chopped
1 small tomato, chopped
2 small potatoes, peeled and
    chopped
1 cup cauliflower florets
½ cup green peas (fresh or
    frozen)

¼ cup green beans (fresh or
    frozen)
4 cups chicken stock
2 tablespoons cooked rice
½ cup diced cooked chicken
    (your choice of cut)
Table salt, to taste

1. In a deep stockpot, heat the butter on medium. Add the vegetable oil. Add the onions and sauté for about 7 minutes, until soft. Add the tomatoes and sauté for another 7 minutes.
2. Add all the vegetables and the chicken stock. Cover, and cook until the vegetables are soft.
3. Add the rice, chicken, and salt. Simmer, uncovered, on low heat for about 10 minutes. Serve hot.

☀ Keeping Butter from Burning
When you are heating butter, always add a little bit of oil to the pan; this will keep the butter from burning. Before you add any spices, ensure that your oil is hot. Heated oil retains the flavors of spices.

Coconut and Tomato Soup
(Tamatar Ka Shorba)

4 large tomatoes, peeled
½ teaspoon cumin seeds,
  roasted
Table salt, to taste
1 cup water
1 (14-ounce) can light coconut
  milk

1 tablespoon vegetable oil
2 sprigs curry leaves, stemmed
½ teaspoon black mustard
  seeds
1 dried red chili, roughly
  pounded

Serves 4
Prep Time: 10 minutes
Cook Time: 30 minutes

Use vine grown tomatoes to get the divine red color that is characteristic of this soup.

1. Combine the tomatoes, cumin seeds, and salt in a blender; blend well.
2. In a deep stockpot, combine the blended tomatoes and the water. Heat on medium heat for about 20 minutes, stirring occasionally. Add the coconut milk and simmer for another 5 minutes.
3. While the soup is cooking, heat the oil in a skillet on medium. Add the curry leaves, mustard seeds, and the red chili. When the mustard seeds pop, remove the skillet from the heat and add the mixture to the soup; mix well.
4. Serve hot or cold, or poured over a mound of steaming rice.

❋ Peeling Tomatoes

Drop the tomatoes into a pot of boiling water for about 1 minute. Use a pair of tongs to transfer the tomatoes from the boiling water directly into a bowl of cold water. The skins will peel off easily. Your tomatoes are ready to use.

Spicy Kokum Drink
(Sol Kadhi)

Serves 4
Prep Time: 5 minutes,
plus 1 hour to soak
Cook Time: 5 minutes,
plus time to chill

You can find kokum,
which is becoming
increasingly popular in
North America, at
Indian grocers.

8 pieces kokum
1 cup hot water
2 cloves garlic, peeled and
    crushed
1½ (14-ounce) cans light
    coconut milk

Pinch of table salt
Pinch of sugar

1. Soak the *kokum* in the hot water for about 1 hour. Strain and reserve the pink liquid. Discard the *kokum*.
2. In a deep stockpot, combine the pink liquid with all the remaining ingredients; mix well. This beautiful pink soup should be served chilled in bowls that allow you to show off its color.

Spinach Soup
(Palak Ka Shorba)

Serves 4
Prep Time: 10 minutes
Cook Time: 45 minutes

This soup comes to
you straight from my
great-grandmother's
kitchen. This nutritious
soup can be pre-
pared up to 2 days in
advance.

1 tablespoon Clarified Butter
    (see recipe on page 15)
¼ teaspoon cumin seeds
1 small red onion, chopped
1½ teaspoons grated gingerroot
1 medium turnip, peeled and
    chopped

¼ teaspoon turmeric powder
¼ teaspoon red chili powder
Table salt, to taste
2 cups vegetable stock
1 pound frozen chopped
    spinach, thawed

1. In a stockpot, heat the Clarified Butter. Add the cumin seeds and stir-fry about 1 minute. Add the onion, ginger, and turnip; sauté for about 5 minutes on medium heat. Add the turmeric, red chili powder, and salt; sauté for about 1 more minute. Add the vegetable stock and cook, covered, on medium heat for about 20 minutes or until the turnips are soft.
2. Add the spinach and cook for another 5 to 8 minutes. Remove from heat and let cool.
3. Purée the spinach soup in a blender, then reheat it. Serve immediately.

CHAPTER 5

Salads (Salaads)

Sprouted Mung Bean Salad
(Moong Dal Ka Salaad)

Serves 4
Prep Time: 15 minutes,
plus 20 minutes to chill
Cook Time: None

If you don't like eating raw beans, you can either sauté them lightly or boil them in lightly salted water for about 2 minutes.

1 clove garlic, crushed
½ English cucumber, finely diced
1 teaspoon grated fresh gingerroot
2 serrano green chilies, finely chopped (optional)

Table salt, to taste
2 teaspoons fresh lemon juice
¼ teaspoon sugar
1 cup sprouted mung beans (bean sprouts)
Finely chopped cilantro, for garnish

In a salad bowl, combine all the ingredients *except* the garnish. Chill for 20 minutes. Garnish with cilantro.

Indian-Style Coleslaw
(Kachumbars)

Serves 4
Prep Time: 10 minutes,
plus 20 minutes to chill
Cook Time: None

Prepare this fresh; if left too long in the refrigerator, the cucumbers will release too much water.

1½ tablespoons fresh lemon juice
1½ tablespoons finely ground peanuts
¼ teaspoon red chili powder
Table salt, to taste
1 small red onion, peeled and diced

1 small tomato, diced
1 medium cucumber, peeled and diced
1 tablespoon finely chopped cilantro

In a bowl, combine the lemon juice, peanuts, red chili powder, and salt; mix well. Add the red onion, tomato, and cucumber; toss well. Chill for about 20 minutes. Serve chilled, topped with the cilantro.

Maharastrian Mung Salad
(Moong Dal Misal)

2 tablespoons vegetable oil
1 teaspoon Ginger-Garlic Paste (see recipe on page 13)
Pinch of asafetida (optional)
¼ teaspoon red chili powder
¼ teaspoon turmeric powder
2 small potatoes, peeled and diced
1 cup sprouted mung beans (bean sprouts)
3 cups water

Table salt, to taste
½ cup peeled and chopped red onion
¼ cup peeled and chopped tomato
1 tablespoon Dry Garlic Chutney (see recipe on page 226)
1 tablespoon fresh lemon juice
Fresh cilantro, for garnish

Serves 4
Prep Time: 10 minutes
Cook Time: 20 minutes

You can make this salad with different types of beans.

1. In a deep pan, heat the oil on medium. Add the Ginger-Garlic Paste, asafetida, red chili powder, and turmeric powder; sauté for about 30 seconds.
2. Add the potatoes and mung beans; sauté for 2 to 3 minutes. Add the water. Cover and cook over medium heat until the potatoes are soft, about 10 to 12 minutes. Remove from heat. (There may still be a little bit of water remaining—this is okay.) Add salt to taste.
3. Transfer the cooked mixture to a platter. Spread the onions and tomatoes on top. Sprinkle with the chutney and the lemon juice. Garnish with cilantro and serve at room temperature.

❋ Delicious Toppings

Many folks like to top their salads with bhel puri. Bhel puri is a crunchy snack commonly sold on the streets of India. It is comprised of puffed rice and tiny fried noodles made of chickpea flour and spices. This mix is readily available at your Indian grocers.

Spicy Papaya Salad
(Papete Ka Salaad)

Serves 4
Prep Time: 10 minutes, plus 30 minutes to chill
Cook Time: None

This salad looks magnificent as a centerpiece on the table during summertime. Use seasonal fruit of your choice to make variations.

2 tablespoons fresh lemon juice
½ teaspoon black salt
1 tablespoon finely chopped cilantro

½ teaspoon sugar
½ cup diced papaya
½ cup diced mango
½ cup diced kiwi
¼ cup chopped strawberries

In a bowl, combine the lemon juice, black salt, cilantro, and sugar; mix well. Add the papaya, mango, kiwi, and strawberries; gently toss. Chill for about 30 minutes, then serve.

Creamy Walnut Salad
(Akhrot Ka Raita)

Serves 4
Prep Time: 10 minutes, plus 20 minutes to chill
Cook Time: None

Raitas are made with fresh vegetables, cooked vegetables, or with spices or nuts. Serve this alongside Ground Meat–Stuffed Bread (page 208).

2 cups plain yogurt, whipped
1 teaspoon cumin seeds, toasted
¼ teaspoon red chili powder

½ teaspoon sugar
Table salt, to taste
¾ cup coarsely chopped walnuts

In a bowl, combine the yogurt, cumin seeds, red chili powder, sugar, and salt; mix well. Add the walnuts and mix well. (Add more walnuts if you prefer a nuttier taste.) Chill, covered, for about 20 minutes before serving.

Smoked Eggplant in Yogurt
(Baigan Ka Raita)

1 small eggplant
1 tablespoon vegetable oil
2 cups plain yogurt
1 small red onion, peeled and
   chopped
½-inch piece fresh gingerroot,
   grated
1 serrano green chili, seeded
   and minced

1 tablespoon minced cilantro
Table salt, to taste
½ teaspoon Warm Spice Mix
   (see recipe on page 12)
Ground red pepper (i.e.,
   cayenne pepper), for garnish

Serves 4
Prep Time: 10 minutes,
plus 20 minutes to chill
Cook Time: 50 minutes

You can add some
grated fresh coconut
to this for a flavorful
variation.

1. Heat the broiler. Brush the eggplant with vegetable oil. Place the eggplant under the broiler and cook until the eggplant is soft and the skin is charred—almost black. Remove from the broiler. Let cool, then peel off and discard the skin. Mash the eggplant into a smooth pulp. Set aside.
2. In a bowl, whip the yogurt. Add the onion, ginger, chili, cilantro, salt, and spice mix; mix well.
3. Add the eggplant pulp to the yogurt mixture and mix well. Chill, covered, for about 20 minutes. Serve garnished with the ground red pepper.

❈ Quick Eggplant Snack
This is a very common snack in eastern India. Thinly slice the eggplant. Season with salt and pepper. Add a pinch of turmeric powder. Set aside for about 15 minutes. Pan-fry in hot oil and serve immediately.

Fried Okra in Yogurt Sauce
(Bhindi Ka Raita)

Serves 4
Prep Time: 15 minutes
Cook Time: 20 minutes

Do not let this dish sit for a long time, or the okra will loose its crunchiness.

Vegetable oil for deep-frying
½ pound okra, chopped
2 cups plain yogurt
1 tablespoon minced cilantro
½ teaspoon cumin powder

¼ teaspoon red chili powder
Table salt, to taste
1 tablespoon cumin seeds, toasted

1. Heat about 1 inch of oil in a deep pan to 350° on a deep-fry thermometer.
2. Add a few pieces of okra and deep-fry until crisp. Remove from the oil using a slotted spoon and transfer to a paper towel to drain. Continue until all the okra is fried. Set aside.
3. In a bowl, whip the yogurt. Add the cilantro, cumin powder, red chili powder, and salt; mix well.
4. Add the okra to the yogurt mixture. Sprinkle with cumin seeds, and serve.

✳ Toasting Cumin Seeds
To toast cumin seeds, heat a skillet on medium. Add the cumin seeds. Roast until the seeds release their aroma and begin to darken. Remove from heat and store in an airtight jar.

Potato and Yogurt Salad
(Aloo Ka Raita)

3 small potatoes
2 cups plain yogurt, whipped
½ cup cold water
1 teaspoon cumin seeds,
    toasted and roughly pounded

¼ teaspoon red chili powder
Table salt, to taste
Slit serrano green chilies, for
    garnish

Serves 4
Prep Time: 10 minutes,
plus 20 minutes to chill
Cook Time: 10 minutes

This raita is so versatile it can be served alongside almost any dish. And it is easy to whip up even when you are rushed.

1. Peel and cut the potatoes into ½-inch dice; boil in salted water to cover for 5 to 8 minutes or until just fork-tender. Drain.
2. In a bowl, combine the yogurt, water, cumin seeds, red chili powder, and salt; mix well. (Omit the water if you prefer a thicker consistency.) Add the potatoes and mix gently.
3. Chill, covered, for 20 minutes. Serve garnished with slit green chilies.

Red Onion Salad
(Rani Pyaz)

1 cup frozen pearl onions,
    thawed
½ cup white vinegar
½ cup water
½ teaspoon ground black mustard seeds

1 serrano green chili, seeded
    and chopped
½ teaspoon table salt
A few drops red food coloring
    (optional)

Yields 1 cup
Prep Time: 10 minutes
Cook Time: 20 minutes,
plus 48 hours to set

These pickles have a short shelf life, so use them up quickly.

1. Boil the pearl onions in about 2 cups of water for about 5 to 7 minutes. Drain and set aside.
2. In a deep pan, bring the vinegar and water to a boil. Remove from heat and set aside.
3. In a bowl, combine the pearl onions, mustard seeds, green chili, salt, and food coloring; mix well. Pour the vinegar-water liquid over the onion mixture.
4. Cool and transfer to an airtight container. Refrigerate for 48 hours.

South Indian Cucumber Salad
(Kheera Pachadi)

Serves 4
Prep Time: 15 minutes,
plus at least
30 minutes to chill
Cook Time: 5 minutes

Do not add the
cucumbers until 30
minutes before you
are ready to serve, or
the salad will become
too watery.

2 cups plain yogurt, whipped
½ teaspoon table salt
1 serrano green chili, minced
2 teaspoons chopped cilantro
1 teaspoon sugar
1 large seedless cucumber
1 tablespoon unsweetened desiccated coconut
1 tablespoon vegetable oil
½ teaspoon black mustard seeds
4 fresh curry leaves
1 dried red chili, roughly pounded
Pinch of asafetida (optional)

1. In a bowl, combine the yogurt, salt, green chili, cilantro, and sugar; mix well. Refrigerate, covered, for at least 30 minutes.
2. Peel and cut the cucumber into ½-inch dice, then refrigerate.
3. About 30 minutes before serving, drain the cucumber and add it to the yogurt mixture along with the coconut. Set aside.
4. In a small skillet, heat the vegetable oil. When the oil is close to smoking (after about 1 minute), quickly add the mustard seeds, curry leaves, red chili, and asafetida. As soon as the mustard seeds start to sputter, remove from heat.
5. Pour over the cucumber-yogurt mix and serve immediately.

※ Curry Leaves
Curry powder has no relation to and is not a substitute for curry leaves. If you buy the leaves in bulk, you can freeze them for use at a later date.

Chicken Tikka Salad
(Murgh Tikke Ka Salaad)

1 small head lettuce
8 cherry tomatoes
1 small seedless cucumber
1 small red onion, peeled
2 tablespoons fresh lemon juice

4 cups Chicken Tikka (see
*   recipe on page 24)*
1 tablespoon Chaat Spice Mix
*   (see recipe on page 14)*

Serves 4
Prep Time: 10 minutes
Cook Time: None

Generally, in India, salads are not the main dish, but are served on the side. This dish, however, can definitely be an entire meal.

1. Wash the lettuce thoroughly. Drain well. Tear the lettuce leaves into bite-sized pieces and place in a bowl; set aside.
2. Cut the tomatoes, cucumber, and red onion into ½-inch dice. Place in a bowl, add the lemon juice, and toss well.
3. Add the Chicken Tikka to the cucumber mixture; mix well. Divide the mixture into 4 equal portions.
4. Place a few lettuce leaves in 4 salad bowls. Add 1 portion of the Chicken Tikka mixture to each. Sprinkle each salad bowl with ¼ teaspoon of Chaat Spice Mix, and serve.

Red Radish Salad
(Mooli Ka Salaad)

10 small red radishes
1 small seedless cucumber
1 tablespoon finely chopped
*   cilantro*

2 tablespoons fresh lemon juice
1 garlic clove, peeled and
*   crushed*
Table salt, to taste

Serves 4
Prep Time: 20 minutes
Cook Time: None

Serve this with Lamb Curry with Turnips (page 115) and Simple Naan Bread (page 205).

1. Cut off the tops of the radishes and julienne the radishes as finely as you can. Peel the cucumber, cut it into small pieces, and julienne.
2. In a bowl, combine all the ingredients; toss to mix well. Serve immediately.

Sesame Potato Salad
(Til Aur Aloo Ka Salaad)

Serves 4
Prep Time: 10 minutes
Cook Time: 10 minutes

Serve this alongside Spinach Bread (page 209) or Carom-Flavored Fried Bread (page 218). The complex flavors harmonize.

4 medium potatoes
1 serrano green chili, minced
1 tablespoon sesame seeds, roasted
2 tablespoons fresh lemon juice
Table salt, to taste
A few tablespoons warm water

1 dried red chili, roughly pounded
½ teaspoon freshly ground black pepper
Finely chopped cilantro, for garnish

1. Peel and cut the potatoes into ½-inch dice; boil in salted water, covered, for 5 to 8 minutes or until just fork-tender. Drain.
2. In a large mixing bowl, combine the potatoes, green chili, sesame seeds, lemon juice, and salt; mix well. Add the warm water and toss well.
3. When you are ready to serve, sprinkle with the dried red chili, ground black pepper, and the chopped cilantro. Serve immediately.

Carrot and Tomato Salad
(Gajar Aur Tamatar Ka Salaad)

Serves 4
Prep Time: 10 minutes, plus time to chill
Cook Time: None

This mild salad can be prepared ahead of time and chilled until you are ready to serve. Serve this with Spicy Shrimp Rice (page 180).

2 ripe small tomatoes
2 small carrots, peeled
1 tablespoon minced fresh mint leaves
2 tablespoons fresh lemon juice

1 teaspoon cumin seeds, roasted and roughly pounded
1 teaspoon sugar
Table salt, to taste
A few dates, finely chopped (optional)

1. Cut the tomatoes and carrots into ½-inch dice and place them in a bowl; set aside.
2. In a separate bowl, combine the mint leaves, lemon juice, cumin seeds, sugar, and salt; mix well.
3. Pour the mint-lemon mixture on the tomatoes and the carrots; toss well. Cover, and chill in the refrigerator. Serve topped with a few dates, if desired.

South Indian Mango Salad
(Amba Pachadi)

2 cups plain yogurt, whipped
½ teaspoon table salt
1 serrano green chili, minced
*2 teaspoons finely chopped
  cilantro*
1 teaspoon sugar
*2 small green mangoes, peeled
  and diced*
*2 tablespoons unsweetened des-
  iccated coconut*

*¼ cup mung beans, cooked
  (optional)*
1 tablespoon vegetable oil
*½ teaspoon black mustard
  seeds*
4 fresh curry leaves
*1 dried red chili, roughly
  pounded*
Pinch of asafetida (optional)

Serves 4
Prep Time: 20 minutes,
plus at least
30 minutes to chill
Cook Time: 5 minutes

Try making this salad
without the yogurt.
You could also use
grated mangoes rather
than diced ones.

1. In a bowl, combine the yogurt, salt, green chili, cilantro, and sugar;
   mix well. Add the mangoes and coconut; mix well. If you are using
   mung beans, add them now. Refrigerate, covered, for at least
   30 minutes.

2. In a small skillet, heat the vegetable oil. When the oil is close to
   smoking (after about 1 minute), quickly add the mustard seeds,
   curry leaves, red chili, and asafetida. As soon as the mustard seeds
   start to sputter, remove from heat; pour over the yogurt mixture.
   Serve immediately.

☀ Raw Mangoes

*Watch any old Indian movie, and the minute the leading lady reaches
for a green mango, the audience gasps, "She's pregnant!" In India, it
is believed that because of its sour taste, pregnant women crave this
crisp raw fruit. For an easy snack, slice the mango (with skin),
sprinkle with Chaat Spice Mix (page 14) or black salt, and enjoy!*

Minty Potato in Yogurt Sauce
(Aloo Pudine Ka Raita)

Serves 4
Prep Time: 10 minutes
Cook Time: 10 minutes,
plus 20 minutes to chill

Serve this dish along-
side White Chicken
Rice (page 173). You
can also make this
salad with minced
cooked spinach
instead of the mint.

3 small potatoes
2 cups plain yogurt, whipped
1 teaspoon cumin seeds,
    roasted and roughly pounded
¼ teaspoon red chili powder
¼ teaspoon black salt
2 tablespoons chopped fresh
    mint leaves
Chopped fresh red chilies, for
    garnish

1. Peel and cut the potatoes into ½-inch dice; boil in salted water, covered, for 5 to 8 minutes or until just fork-tender. Drain.
2. In a bowl, combine the yogurt, cumin seeds, red chili powder, and
   salt; mix well. Add the potatoes and mint leaves, mixing gently.
3. Chill, covered, for 20 minutes. Garnish with red chilies and serve.

Maharastrian Cabbage Salad
(Bundh Gobi Ka Salaad)

Serves 4
Prep Time: 20 minutes,
plus at least
1 hour to chill
Cook Time: None

Serve with Coconut
and Tomato Soup
(page 51) and
Green Peas Stuffing
(page 213).

2 cups finely shredded cabbage
¼ cup finely shredded red bell
    pepper
¼ cup shredded baby spinach
½ cup unsweetened desiccated
    coconut
¼ cup salted, roasted peanuts,
    roughly pounded
2 tablespoons fresh lemon
    juice
Table salt, to taste
Finely chopped cilantro, for
    garnish
Crushed black pepper, to taste,
    for garnish

In a bowl, combine the cabbage, red bell peppers, spinach leaves,
coconut, peanuts, lemon juice, and salt; mix well. Cover and chill in
the refrigerator for at least 1 hour. Sprinkle with cilantro and black
pepper to garnish before serving.

Maharastrian Bread and Corn Salad
(Sanja)

2 slices white bread
2 tablespoons vegetable oil
½ teaspoon black mustard
   seeds
1-inch piece fresh gingerroot,
   peeled and chopped
1 small red onion, peeled and
   minced
1 serrano green chili, seeded
   and minced

Table salt, to taste
¼ teaspoon turmeric powder
1 dried red chili, roughly
   pounded
2 cups corn kernels, cooked
¼ cup unsweetened desiccated
   coconut
1 tablespoon fresh lemon juice
2 tablespoons minced cilantro

Serves 4
Prep Time: 15 minutes
Cook Time: 5–10 minutes

You can serve this dish for breakfast along-side Saffron Lemonade (page 43) or Maharastrian Buttermilk (page 44).

1. Cut the bread into small pieces; set aside.
2. In a medium skillet, heat the oil. Add the mustard seeds and ginger. When the mustard seeds crackle, add the onions, green chili, salt, turmeric powder, and red chili. Sauté until the onions are transparent, about 2 to 3 minutes.
3. Add the bread and the corn kernels to the skillet. Mix well, and cook for another 2 to 3 minutes.
4. Remove from heat and transfer to a serving platter. Sprinkle with coconut, lemon juice, and cilantro. Serve warm.

✸ Corn for Breakfast

Yes, you can have corn for breakfast. Heat a medium skillet, add some sweet corn (creamed), tiny cubes of bell pepper, a little bit of butter, grated cheese, and a few tablespoons of milk; mix well. Season with salt and pepper to taste. Serve atop lightly buttered bread of your choice.

Punjabi Onion Salad
(Punjabi Laccha)

Serves 4
Prep Time: 5 minutes
Cook Time: None

Add Chaat Spice Mix (page 14) to this dish instead of salt for a unique tangy flavor.

1 red onion, peeled
2 serrano green chilies, sliced
1 tablespoon fresh lemon juice
Table salt, to taste
½ teaspoon minced cilantro

Slice the onion into rings and arrange on a platter. Top with the green chilies, then sprinkle with lemon juice and salt. Garnish with cilantro and serve.

Coconut Milk Salad
(Nariel Ka Raita)

Serves 4
Prep Time: 10 minutes, plus 20 minutes to chill
Cook Time: None

The Indian name for this dish is misleading, since the term raita generally refers to a dish that has yogurt. This dish uses coconut milk instead.

1 small red onion, peeled
1 small tomato
1-inch piece fresh ginger, grated
1 serrano green chili, seeded and minced
2 tablespoons minced cilantro
2 tablespoons dried coconut flakes or fresh shredded coconut
4–6 tablespoons light coconut milk
Table salt, to taste

Chop the onion and the tomato and place in a large bowl. Add the ginger, green chili, cilantro, coconut, and salt; mix well. Pour the coconut milk onto the salad. Cover and refrigerate for at least 20 minutes. Serve cold.

Pineapple Salad
(Ananas Ka Raita)

2 cups plain yogurt, whipped
1 teaspoon red chili powder
1 teaspoon cumin seeds,
roasted and roughly pounded
1 cup pineapple chunks (fresh,
or canned and drained)

Table salt, to taste
1 tablespoon vegetable oil
½ teaspoon black mustard
seeds
4 fresh curry leaves

Serves 4
Prep Time: 10 minutes
Cook Time: 5 minutes

This dish is very popular in South India. Serve this alongside Ginger-Flavored Lamb Chops (page 127) for a unique combination of flavors.

1. In a bowl, combine the yogurt, red chili powder, and cumin seeds; mix well.
2. Add the pineapple chunks and salt to the yogurt mixture, and mix well. Set aside.
3. In a medium skillet, heat the oil. Add the mustard seeds and curry leaves. When the mustard seeds crackle, remove from heat and pour over the yogurt salad. Serve immediately.

Grape Salad
(Angoor Ka Raita)

1 cup seedless green grapes
1 cup seedless black grapes
¼ cup red raspberries
¼ cup blackberries
2 tablespoons dried coconut
flakes or fresh shredded
coconut

1 teaspoon sugar
Table salt, to taste
¼ teaspoon black pepper
½ cup light coconut milk

Serves 4
Prep Time: 5 minutes, plus at least 1 hour to chill
Cook Time: None

Try using jaggery instead of regular sugar for a special sweet taste. Eat this as a side dish with Spicy Minced Lamb Kebabs (page 126).

1. In a large bowl, combine the grapes, berries, and coconut. Add the sugar, salt, and black pepper; mix well.
2. Pour the coconut milk onto the salad. Cover and chill for at least 1 hour. Serve cold.

Spiced Taro Salad
(Chatpata Arvi Ka Salaad)

Serves 4
Prep Time: 10 minutes
Cook Time: 20 minutes

You can spike up this mild salad with a pinch of red chili powder. If you cannot find taro, try yams or sweet potatoes.

2 taro roots (also called dasheen), peeled
2 potatoes, peeled
2 tablespoons fresh lemon juice

½ teaspoon black salt
2 tablespoons minced cilantro, plus extra for garnish

1. Place the taro roots and potatoes in a pot with enough water to cover; boil until just fork-tender. Drain and let cool.
2. Cut the taro and potatoes into cubes and place them in a large bowl. Add the lemon juice, black salt, and cilantro to the bowl and mix well.
3. Serve immediately, garnished with cilantro.

Shredded Carrot Salad
(Gajar Ka Salaad)

Serves 4
Prep Time: 10 minutes
Cook Time: 5 minutes

This brightly colored salad is a perfect side dish for Malabari Chili Fish (page 149).

2 cups shredded carrots
2 tablespoons roasted peanuts, roughly pounded
1 serrano green chili, minced
2 tablespoons fresh lemon juice

1 tablespoon vegetable oil
½ teaspoon black mustard seeds
Table salt, to taste

1. In a bowl, combine the carrots, peanuts, green chili, and lemon juice; mix well. Set aside.
2. In a small skillet, heat the oil. Add the mustard seeds. When the seeds begin to crackle, remove from heat and pour over the carrots.
3. Add salt to taste and mix well. Serve immediately.

CHAPTER 6
From the Vegetable Market (Subzi Mandi Se)

Baby Potatoes in a Creamy Sauce
(Dum Aloo)

Serves 4
Prep Time: 5 minutes
Cook Time: 55 minutes

Serve with Fried
Indian Bread (page
204) or Puffed Bread
(page 216).

12–14 small new potatoes,
  unpeeled
4 cups, plus 2 tablespoons
  vegetable oil
1 teaspoon cumin seeds
1 teaspoon grated gingerroot
1 medium-sized red onion, minced
1/2 teaspoon red chili powder
1/4 teaspoon turmeric powder
1/4 teaspoon Warm Spice Mix
  (see recipe on page 12)

1/2 teaspoon coriander powder
2 cloves
1/2 teaspoon fennel seeds or
  anise seeds
1 (1-inch) cinnamon stick
1 cup puréed tomatoes (fresh
  or canned)
1 cup plain yogurt, whipped
1 cup warm water
Salt, to taste

1. Thoroughly wash the potatoes and boil in water for 10 to 12 minutes, until fork-tender. Drain and let cool.
2. Heat the 4 cups of oil in a deep pan at 370° on a deep-fry thermometer. Prick the potatoes all over with a fork (this will allow the spices to seep in). Add a few potatoes to the oil and deep-fry until brown. Remove the potatoes with a slotted spoon and place on paper towels to drain off excess oil. Continue until all of the potatoes are fried, letting the oil return to 370° between batches. Set aside.
3. In a large skillet, heat the remaining 2 tablespoons of oil on high. Heat until just below the smoking point (about 45 seconds), then add the cumin seeds. When they begin to pop, add the ginger and onions; sauté until the onions are golden brown.
4. In quick succession, add the red chili powder, turmeric powder, spice mix, coriander powder, cloves, fennel seeds, and cinnamon stick. Stirring continuously, fry for about 30 seconds. Add the tomatoes and continue to stir for another 2 to 3 minutes. Add the yogurt and cook for another 5 minutes. Add the potatoes and fry for 1 more minute, stirring constantly. Add the water and return to a boil.
5. Reduce the heat, cover, and cook for about 20 minutes. Add salt to taste. Remove from heat and stir well. Serve hot.

Cheese and Spinach Curry
(Paalak Paneer)

2 tablespoons vegetable oil

1 medium-sized red onion, peeled and minced

2½ teaspoons Ginger-Garlic Paste (page 13)

¼ cup tomato purée (fresh or canned)

2 serrano green chilies, seeded and minced (optional)

¼ teaspoon turmeric powder

½ teaspoon Warm Spice Mix (page 12)

½ teaspoon cumin powder

½ teaspoon coriander powder

¼ teaspoon red chili powder

Table salt, to taste

1 (10-ounce) package chopped frozen spinach, thawed

½ cup water, at room temperature

1 cup Indian Cheese, fried (see below)

1 tablespoon heavy cream, for garnish

Serves 4
Prep Time: 10 minutes
Cook Time: 45 minutes

You can purée the spinach before you begin if you like your sauce really creamy. Serve this with hot Simple Naan Bread (page 205).

1. In a medium-sized pan, heat the vegetable oil on medium. Add the onion and fry, stirring continuously until the onions are golden brown in color, about 5 minutes.
2. Add the Ginger-Garlic Paste and sauté for 1 minute. Add the tomato purée and cook for 2 minutes.
3. Quickly add the green chilies, turmeric powder, spice mix, cumin powder, coriander powder, red chili powder, and salt; sauté for 30 seconds.
4. Add the spinach and fry for about 3 minutes, stirring constantly. Add the water and cook, uncovered, on low heat for about 20 minutes. If the mixture starts to dry out, add more water. Cook until the spinach is soft.
5. Add the Indian Cheese to the spinach mixture; sauté, uncovered, for 5 minutes. Garnish with the heavy cream and serve hot.

✲ Where Can I Find Fried Indian Cheese?

You can buy prefried Indian cheese (paneer) at your local Indian grocer. If you want to fry it at home, prepare the paneer as described on page 12. In a deep skillet, heat oil on medium. Pan-fry a few pieces of paneer until golden brown on all sides. Remove and place on a paper towel to absorb excess oil.

Punjabi Mustard Greens
(Sarson Da Saag)

Serves 4
Prep Time: 5 minutes
Cook Time: 45 minutes

This is a delicious dish from the Indian state of Punjab. Serve along with Indian Corn Flatbread (page 221).

1 pound frozen mustard leaves, thawed
¼ pound frozen spinach leaves, thawed
1 small turnip, peeled and diced
3 cups water (or more, as needed)
2 tablespoons Clarified Butter (see recipe on page 15)
1 teaspoon Ginger-Garlic Paste (see recipe on page 13)
2 tablespoons cornmeal
Table salt, to taste
Butter, cut into cubes, for garnish

1. In a deep pan, combine the mustard leaves, spinach leaves, and turnip. Add about 2 cups of the water and bring to a boil. Cook until the turnips become tender, about 12 minutes. Remove from heat and drain any water. Let the vegetables cool to room temperature.
2. Use a food processor to purée the vegetable mixture into a thick paste. Set aside.
3. In a large pan, heat the Clarified Butter, add the Ginger-Garlic Paste, and sauté for 30 seconds. Add the vegetable purée; sauté for 2 minutes. Add the cornmeal to the skillet and mix well. To ensure that the cornmeal does not form lumps, use the back of your cooking spoon to blend it in. Add salt to taste.
4. Add 1 cup of water to the skillet. Simmer for 25 minutes on low heat. Add more water if the vegetables start to become dry. Serve hot, garnished with a few butter cubes.

☀ Cornmeal Does Come from Corn

Cornmeal comes from maize, or corn, as the name suggests. This coarse yellow flour is used to provide texture to dishes. Don't mistake it for cornstarch, which is white and powdery and generally used as a thickening agent.

Potato Sticks
(Bengali Aloo Charchari)

4 medium potatoes, peeled
1 small red onion, peeled
2 tablespoons vegetable oil
¼ teaspoon turmeric powder

½ teaspoon red chili powder
Table salt, to taste
Approximately ¼ cup water,
 at room temperature

> **Serves 4**
> **Prep Time:** 10 minutes
> **Cook Time:** 20 minutes
>
> Bengal, a state in eastern India where this dish originates, is often called Sonar Bangla (Golden Bengal) because of the fields of mustard that cover the countryside.

1. Cut the potatoes and the onions lengthwise, as you would for fries. Set aside.
2. In a medium-sized skillet, heat the vegetable oil on medium. Add the onions and sauté until transparent, about 3 to 4 minutes.
3. Add the potatoes to the skillet; sauté for another 3 to 5 minutes.
4. Add the turmeric, red chili powder, and salt to the skillet; sauté, stirring constantly, for 1 minute.
5. Add the water, cover, and cook until the potatoes are soft.

❋ Bengali Panch Phoron

Panch phoron, or five-spice mix, is a trademark of Bengali cuisine. Not to be confused with the Chinese five-spice powder, this mixture contains fennel, cumin, mustard, fenugreek, and wild fennel seeds (also called nigella seeds). Unlike some of the other spice mixes discussed in this book, this mix is stored unroasted. The seeds in the mixture are whole and not pounded.

Roasted Eggplant
(Baigan Ka Bhartha)

Serves 4
Prep Time: 10 minutes
Cook Time: 1 hour

To get an authentic smoked flavor, roast the eggplant over hot charcoal.

3 pounds eggplant (about 2 medium-sized eggplants)
4 tablespoons vegetable oil
1 small red onion, peeled and roughly chopped
1 teaspoon Ginger-Garlic Paste (see recipe on page 13)

¼ teaspoon red chili powder
1 teaspoon coriander powder
2 medium tomatoes, finely chopped
Table salt, to taste
Fresh chopped cilantro, for garnish (optional)

1. Preheat oven to 475°.
2. Brush the eggplant with 2 tablespoons of the vegetable oil. Place the eggplant on a foil-lined baking sheet and place it in the oven. Cook until the eggplant is soft and the skin is charred, about 40 minutes. Remove from the oven to cool.
3. Peel the eggplant and discard the skin. Mash the eggplant with a fork into a smooth pulp. Set aside.
4. In a large skillet, heat the remaining 2 tablespoons of vegetable oil over medium heat. Add the onions and sauté until transparent. Add the Ginger-Garlic Paste, red chili powder, and coriander powder; sauté for 30 seconds.
5. Add the tomatoes and sauté for about 5 minutes, stirring constantly. Use the back of your spatula to mash the tomatoes. When the mixture is ready, oil will start to separate from the mixture.
6. Add the eggplant and salt; mix well. Fry for about 7 to 10 minutes, stirring constantly. Remove from heat. Serve hot and garnish with cilantro (optional).

❈ Roasting Eggplants
You can use the burner on your gas stove to roast eggplant. Use tongs to hold the eggplant over the flame. Rotate constantly until all the sides are charred and the eggplant is roasted completely.

Mixed Vegetables
(Makki Ki Subzi)

2 tablespoons vegetable oil
½ teaspoon black mustard
　seeds
4–5 fresh curry leaves
1-inch piece ginger, peeled and
　julienned
2 cups cooked corn kernels or
　canned corn kernels, drained
1 red bell pepper, seeded and
　diced
1 green bell pepper, seeded
　and diced

1 yellow bell pepper, seeded
　and diced
1 dried red chili, crushed
Water, if needed
2 tablespoons unsweetened
　desiccated coconut
¼ teaspoon sugar
Table salt, to taste

Serves 4
Prep Time: 15 minutes
Cook Time: 15 minutes

The colors of the bell
pepper make this dish
very striking in
appearance. Serve
these with Spinach
Bread (page 209) or
Seasoned Bread
(page 210).

1. In a large skillet, heat the vegetable oil on medium. Add the mustard
   seeds. When they begin to crackle, add the curry leaves and ginger.
   Sauté for a few seconds.
2. Add the corn, all the bell peppers, and the dried red chili. Sauté for
   several minutes until the bell peppers are tender. If the mixture starts
   to stick, add a few tablespoons of water at a time.
3. Add the coconut, sugar, and salt; sauté for 1 more minute. Serve hot.

❋ Chilies That Bite

*If you bite into a green chili, don't reach for the water; it will not
help soothe your mouth. Instead, use some sugar or plain yogurt to
get instant relief from the heat.*

Royal Mushrooms with Cashew Nut Sauce
(Nawabi Guchhi)

Serves 4
Prep Time: 10 minutes, plus 20 minutes to soak
Cook Time: 45 minutes

The Nawabs, the Muslim royals of ancient India, introduced nuts into Indian cuisine.

2 tablespoons unsalted cashew nuts
4 tablespoons vegetable oil
2 green cardamom pods
1 black cardamom pod
2 cloves
1 (1-inch) cinnamon stick
1 bay leaf
1 teaspoon minced garlic
½ teaspoon red chili powder
1 teaspoon coriander powder
1 small red onion, minced
Water, as needed
½ cup plain yogurt, whipped
½ cup whole milk
1 pound white button mushrooms, cleaned
Table salt, to taste

1. Soak the cashews in a cup of water for about 20 minutes. Drain and grind to a paste in a food processor. Set aside.
2. In a medium skillet, heat the vegetable oil on medium. Quickly add the green cardamom, black cardamom, cloves, cinnamon stick, bay leaf, and minced garlic; sauté for about 30 seconds.
3. Add the red chili powder, coriander powder, and minced onion; sauté for 2 minutes. If the spice mixture sticks to the pan, add a few tablespoons of water. Continue to sauté until the onions are golden brown, about 7 minutes. Add the cashew nut paste, and stir for 1 more minute.
4. Add the yogurt and milk; mix well. Simmer on low heat until the oil starts to separate from the spice mixture. If you prefer a thinner consistency, add water.
5. Add the mushrooms and salt, and cook for about 5 to 8 minutes or until the mushrooms are cooked completely. Serve hot.

☼ The Value of Fresh

One simple tip, worth its weight in gold, is to use fresh spices. If your spices do not have any aroma, they have lost their potency and should not be used. Fresh spices can completely alter the taste of a dish.

Dill and Potato
(Aloo Soa Ki Subzi)

2 tablespoons vegetable oil
½ teaspoon cumin seeds
2 green chilies, seeded and minced
3 medium potatoes, peeled and diced

½ cup frozen peas, thawed
¼ cup chopped fresh dill
¼ teaspoon turmeric powder
Table salt, to taste
Water, as needed

Serves 4
Prep Time: 10 minutes
Cook Time: 15 minutes

Serve with any salad of your choice and the Baked Fenugreek Bread (page 219).

1. In a medium-sized skillet, heat the oil on medium. Add the cumin seeds. When they begin to crackle, add the green chilies; sauté for 10 seconds.
2. Add the potatoes and sauté for about 2 minutes. Add the peas, dill, turmeric, and salt; sauté for another 2 minutes.
3. Add a few tablespoons of water, cover, and cook on low heat until the potatoes and peas are cooked through, about 10 to 12 minutes. Serve hot.

Whole-Milk Fudge and Peas Curry
(Khoya Wale Matar)

2 tablespoons vegetable oil
1 (1-inch) cinnamon stick
2 cloves
1 teaspoon cumin seeds
½ teaspoon red chili powder
¼ teaspoon turmeric

1 teaspoon coriander powder
½ cup plain yogurt, whipped
2 cups frozen peas, thawed
½ cup Whole-Milk Fudge (see recipe on page 15)
Table salt, to taste

Serves 4
Prep Time: 5 minutes
Cook Time: 20 minutes

This recipe is a classic from the picturesque Indian state of Kashmir.

1. In a medium skillet, heat the oil on medium. Add the cinnamon stick, cloves, and cumin seeds. When the seeds begin to sizzle, add the red chili powder, turmeric powder, and coriander; stir for 10 seconds.
2. Add the yogurt and mix well. Sauté for about 5 minutes, or until the oil starts to separate from the spice mixture.
3. Add the peas, Whole-Milk Fudge, and salt. Simmer for about 10 minutes or until the peas are tender. Serve hot.

Chili Pepper Curry
(Mirchi Ka Salan)

Serves 4
Prep Time: 20 minutes
Cook Time: 30 minutes

This dish is not for the weak of stomach or heart. Serve this with Simple Basmati Rice (page 160) and a large pitcher of cold water!

8 large green chilies, (anaheim or cubanelle)
1 teaspoon tamarind pulp
1 teaspoon cumin seeds
2 teaspoons coriander seeds
¼ teaspoon fenugreek seeds
1 teaspoon white poppy seeds
2 tablespoons sesame seeds
2½ tablespoons unsweetened desiccated coconut

4 tablespoons vegetable oil
1 small red onion, minced
1 tablespoon Ginger-Garlic Paste (see recipe on page 13)
¼ teaspoon red chili powder
¼ teaspoon turmeric powder
Table salt, to taste
1 cup warm water

1. Remove the stems from the green chilies. Cut a slit down the side of each chili to remove the seeds, but don't separate the halves; discard the stems and seeds and set aside the chilies. Add the tamarind pulp to 2 tablespoons of warm water and set aside to soak.

2. In a small skillet, roast the cumin, coriander, fenugreek, poppy, and sesame seeds. As the spices start to darken and release their aroma (less than 1 minute), add the coconut and roast for another 15 seconds. Remove from heat and let cool. Grind to a powder using a pestle and mortar or spice grinder.

3. In a large skillet, heat the oil on medium. Add the green chilies. As soon as the chilies develop brown spots, use a slotted spoon to remove them from the skillet and set aside. In the same oil, sauté the minced onions and the Ginger-Garlic Paste until the onions are golden brown.

4. Add the red chili and turmeric powder, salt, and ground spices. Mix well and sauté for 2 minutes. Return the green chilies to the pan and add the water. Simmer, covered, for 5 to 8 minutes.

5. Strain the tamarind and discard the residue. Add the strained tamarind pulp and mix well. Cook for 1 more minute. Serve hot.

Fried Okra
(Bharwan Bhindi)

1½ pounds okra

1 tablespoon coriander powder

2 teaspoons turmeric powder

1½ teaspoons (or to taste) red chili powder

2 teaspoons Warm Spice Mix (see recipe on page 12)

2 teaspoons cumin powder

1 teaspoon dried mango powder

4 tablespoons vegetable oil

1 medium-sized red onion, peeled and chopped

1 tablespoon Ginger-Garlic Paste (see recipe on page 13)

2 serrano green chilies, slit lengthwise

Table salt, to taste

Water, as needed

Serves 4
Prep Time: 20 minutes
Cook Time: 20 minutes

Serve this with Red Radish Salad (page 61) and Simple Indian Bread (page 202).

1. Wash the okra and dry it well. Cut the stalk off each piece and make a lengthwise slit. Be careful not to cut all the way through.

2. In a bowl, combine the coriander powder, turmeric powder, red chili powder, spice mix, cumin powder, and dried mango powder. Mix well and set aside.

3. Using the pointed end of a knife or a tiny spoon, stuff a little bit of the dry spice mixture into each piece of okra.

4. In a large skillet, heat the oil on medium. Add the onions and the Ginger-Garlic Paste; sauté for about 3 minutes, until the onions are transparent. Add the okra and green chilies, and sauté for about 4 minutes. Add the salt and any remaining dry spice mixture. Reduce the heat to medium-low.

5. Add about 3 tablespoons of water, cover, and cook for about 10 minutes or until the okra is fork-tender. Serve hot.

Cabbage with Black Mustard Seeds
(Muttakos Poriyal)

Serves 4
Prep Time: 10 minutes
Cook Time: 15 minutes

Poriyals, or dried spiced vegetables, originated in southern India. Serve this with Lemon Rice (page 165).

2 tablespoons vegetable oil
1 teaspoon black mustard seeds
2 small dried red chilies, roughly pounded
8 fresh curry leaves
1 pound cabbage, finely shredded
Table salt, to taste
1/2 teaspoon turmeric powder
1/4 teaspoon red chili powder
2 tablespoons coconut flakes

1. Heat the vegetable oil on medium. Add the mustard seeds, red chilies, and curry leaves. When the mustard seeds begin to crackle, add the cabbage.
2. Sauté the cabbage for 2 minutes. Add the salt, turmeric, and red chili powder; mix well and sauté for 1 more minute.
3. Cover, and cook on low heat until the cabbage is tender, about 8 minutes, stirring occasionally. If the cabbage is sticking to the pan, add a few tablespoons of water.
4. Add the coconut and cook for another 2 minutes over medium heat.

Dry-Spiced Carrot and Peas
(Gajar Mattar Ki Subzi)

Serves 4
Prep Time: 5 minutes
Cook Time: 20 minutes

The carrots and peas sautéed in cumin provide a healthy dish with a mild flavor.

2 tablespoons vegetable oil
1 teaspoon cumin seeds
2 medium carrots (fresh or frozen), peeled and diced
2 cups peas (fresh or frozen)
1/2 teaspoon red chili powder
1/4 teaspoon turmeric powder
1 teaspoon coriander powder
Table salt, to taste
Water, as needed

1. In a medium-sized skillet, heat the vegetable oil over high heat. Add the cumin seeds. When the seeds begin to sizzle, add the carrots and peas; sauté for about 2 minutes.
2. Add the dry spices and salt, and mix well; sauté for about 2 minutes (if the dry spices begin to stick, add a few tablespoons of water).
3. Reduce the heat and add 2 to 3 tablespoons of water to the skillet. Cover and cook for about 15 minutes or until the carrots and peas are cooked. Serve hot.

Stir-Fried Cauliflower
(Gobi Ki Subzi)

1½ pounds cauliflower
3 tablespoons vegetable oil
1-inch piece fresh gingerroot,
   julienned
2 teaspoons coriander powder

½ teaspoon red chili powder
¼ teaspoon turmeric powder
Table salt, to taste
Water, as needed

Serves 4
Prep Time: 5 minutes
Cook Time:
15–20 minutes

If you have any left-over, use it in the recipe for Cauliflower Stuffing (page 212) to make some delicious stuffed bread.

1. Break the cauliflower into small florets. Set aside.
2. In a large skillet, heat the vegetable oil on high. Add the ginger and sauté for about 10 seconds. Add the cauliflower florets and sauté for about 3 to 4 minutes. Add the coriander, red chili, and turmeric powder; sauté for 1 minute.
3. Reduce the heat to low. Add the salt and 2 to 3 tablespoons of water. Cover and cook until the cauliflower is done, about 5 to 10 minutes. Serve hot.

Fenugreek-Flavored Potatoes
(Methi Aloo Ki Subzi)

4 medium potatoes
3 tablespoons vegetable oil
2 garlic cloves, crushed
2 tablespoons dried fenugreek
   leaves

¼ teaspoon turmeric powder
½ teaspoon red chili powder
1½ teaspoons coriander powder
Table salt, to taste
Water, as needed

Serves 4
Prep Time: 10 minutes
Cook Time:
15–20 minutes

If you want to use fresh fenugreek leaves in this dish, add about ¼ cup of the fresh leaves, minced.

1. Peel and dice the potatoes. Set aside.
2. In a large skillet, heat the vegetable oil on high. Add the garlic cloves and the potatoes; sauté for about 2 minutes.
3. Add the fenugreek leaves; turmeric, red chili, and coriander powder. Sauté for 1 minute, then add salt.
4. Reduce the heat and add 2 to 3 tablespoons of water. Cover and cook for about 8 to 10 minutes or until the potatoes are soft. Serve hot.

Potato Curry
(Assami Ril Do)

Serves 4
Prep Time: 10 minutes
Cook Time: 40 minutes

Serve this mouthwatering curry with hot Puffed Bread (page 216).

10 small baby potatoes, peeled
3 tablespoons vegetable oil
2 teaspoons Ginger-Garlic Paste (see recipe on page 13)
1 dried red chili, roughly pounded

$1/4$ teaspoon turmeric
1 small tomato, finely chopped
$1/2$ cup plain yogurt, whipped
$1/2$ cup water
Table salt, to taste

1. Boil the potatoes in water to cover until just fork-tender; drain. Lightly prick the potatoes with a fork. Set aside.
2. In a large skillet, heat the oil on high. Add the Ginger-Garlic Paste and sauté for about 10 seconds. Add the dried red chili and turmeric; mix well. Add the tomatoes and sauté for another 2 to 3 minutes.
3. Add the yogurt and cook for about 5 minutes. Add the potatoes. Sauté for 1 minute. Add the water and lower the heat. Cover, and cook for about 20 minutes. Add salt to taste. Serve hot.

❊ Avoid Staining Your Tupperware

Turmeric will turn things yellow—your Tupperware, for instance. To avoid staining any Tupperware in which you store turmeric-flavored dishes, spray the Tupperware with nonstick spray before using it.

Garlic Cauliflower
(Lehsuni Gobi Manchurian)

2 tablespoons corn flour
4 tablespoons all-purpose white
   flour
¼ teaspoon white pepper
   powder
¼ teaspoon table salt
1 tablespoon minced garlic
Vegetable oil for deep-frying,
   plus 1 tablespoon
1 small head cauliflower,
   broken into small florets

1 teaspoon finely minced garlic
2 teaspoons light soya sauce
1 teaspoon vinegar
2 tablespoons tomato ketchup
3 spring onions, finely chopped
1 tablespoon corn flour, dissolved in ¼ cup cold water
Water, as needed

Serves 4
Prep Time: 15 minutes
Cook Time: 20 minutes

Tomato ketchup is very popular in India and is often used in cooking. Serve this dish with steaming hot Vegetable Fried Rice (page 174).

1. In a mixing bowl, mix the 2 tablespoons corn flour, the white flour, pepper, salt, and 1 tablespoon minced garlic. Add enough water to make a thin batter.
2. In a deep pan, heat about 1 inch of vegetable oil to 370° on a deep-fry thermometer. Dip each piece of cauliflower in the batter and add to the hot oil, a few pieces at a time. Deep-fry until golden brown. Remove the cauliflower using a slotted spoon. Place the cauliflower on a paper towel to drain. Let the oil return to temperature and continue until all the cauliflower is fried. Set aside.
3. In a large skillet, heat the 1 tablespoon vegetable oil on medium. Add the finely minced garlic and sauté for 10 seconds. Quickly add the soya sauce, vinegar, tomato ketchup, and spring onions; cook for about 1 minute. Add water to desired consistency. Add more salt to taste, if desired. Simmer for about 5 minutes.
4. Add the corn flour dissolved in water and mix well. Add the cauliflower florets. Serve hot.

South Indian Rice and Vegetable Delight
(Bissi Bela Hulianna)

Serves 4
Prep Time: 15 minutes, plus 1 hour to soak
Cook Time: 60 minutes

Don't let the long list of ingredients worry you; you can buy the spice mix premade. I recommend the MTR's bissi bela hulianna.

½ cup pigeon peas (toor dal)
1½ cups basmati rice
½ cup cauliflower florets (fresh or frozen)
½ cup peas (fresh or frozen)
1 tablespoon vegetable oil
1 tablespoon chana dal or yellow split peas
¾ tablespoon split black gram, or black lentils (safeed urad dal)
1 (1-inch) cinnamon stick
2 cloves
2 teaspoons coriander seeds

½ teaspoon cumin seeds
½ teaspoon black mustard seeds
½ teaspoon fenugreek seeds
2 tablespoons unsweetened desiccated coconut
2 small tomatoes, finely chopped
1 tablespoon tamarind pulp, soaked in ¼ cup water for 10 minutes
½ teaspoon red chili powder
¼ teaspoon turmeric powder
Table salt, to taste

1. Rinse the *toor dal* 3 or 4 times; soak in 3 cups of water for 1 hour. Meanwhile, rinse the rice until the water runs clear; soak for 30 minutes in enough water to cover.
2. Bring the *toor dal* to a boil, using the soaking water, and cook for about 25 minutes. Drain and set aside. In a deep pan, combine the *toor dal*, the drained basmati rice, cauliflower, and peas. Add about 5 cups water and bring to a boil. Cover and simmer until the rice and vegetables are cooked through, about 15 to 20 minutes.
3. In a medium-sized skillet, heat the vegetable oil. Add the *chana dal, safeed urad dal,* cinnamon, cloves, coriander, cumin, mustard, and fenugreek seeds; sauté for about 1 minute or until the spices release their aroma. Remove from heat and let cool, about 6 minutes. Add the coconut. Using a spice grinder, grind this to a powder. Set aside.
4. When the rice is done cooking, add the tomatoes, tamarind pulp, red chili, and turmeric powder, and salt. Add the reserved spice mix. Stir well. Simmer until the tomatoes are soft, about 15 minutes. Add more water, if needed. (The consistency of the dish should be like thick porridge.) Serve hot.

Mixed Vegetables in Coconut Sauce
(Avial)

1 cup unsweetened desiccated
  coconut
1 tablespoon cumin seeds,
  toasted
2 serrano green chilies, seeded
1/2 pounds carrots, peeled
2 small potatoes, peeled
1 green banana or plantain,
  peeled (optional)

1/2 pound frozen cut green
  beans, thawed
1/2 cup plain yogurt, whipped
1/2 teaspoon turmeric powder
Table salt, to taste
1 tablespoon vegetable oil
1 teaspoon black mustard
  seeds
8 curry leaves

> **Serves 4**
> **Prep Time:** 15 minutes
> **Cook Time:** 10–15
> minutes
>
> Use your choice of
> seasonal vegetables
> to make this dish.
> Serve with Simple
> Basmati Rice (page
> 160) and your choice
> of any hot pickle.

1. In a food processor, grind the coconut, cumin seeds, and green chilies along with a few tablespoons of water, to make a thick paste. Set aside.
2. Cut the carrots and potatoes into 1/4-inch sticks. Peel and chop the banana. In a deep pan, combine the carrots, potatoes, banana, and green beans and enough water to just cover the vegetables. Cook over medium heat until the vegetables are soft, about 5 to 7 minutes. Drain off any remaining water.
3. Add the yogurt, the reserved coconut paste, turmeric, and salt to the vegetables. Simmer until the vegetables are completely cooked through, another 3 or 4 minutes. Remove from heat and set aside.
4. In a small skillet, heat the vegetable oil on medium. Add the mustard seeds and curry leaves. When the seeds begin to crackle, remove from heat and pour over the cooked vegetables. Serve hot.

✳ Vegetable Drumsticks
The next time you are at your Indian grocer, ask for a can of vegetable drumsticks, and use it in this dish. Add this along with the other vegetables in Step 2. These delightful vegetables add something special to your dishes. Eat only the jellylike portion inside, discarding the outside skin.

Maharastrian Potatoes
(Batate Che Bhajji)

4 medium potatoes, peeled
½ teaspoon tamarind pulp, soaked in ¼ cup warm water for 10 minutes
2 tablespoons vegetable oil
½ teaspoon black mustard seeds
6–8 fresh curry leaves
¼ teaspoon turmeric powder
½ teaspoon red chili powder
Table salt, to taste

Dice the potatoes and boil in water for 5 to 8 minutes. Roughly mash the potatoes and set aside. Strain the tamarind pulp and discard the residue. Set aside. Heat the vegetable oil on medium. Add the mustard seeds; when they begin to crackle, add the curry leaves. Sauté for about 30 seconds. Add the mashed potatoes, tamarind pulp, turmeric powder, red chili powder, and salt; mix well. Sauté for about 3 minutes, adding a few tablespoons of water if the mixture starts sticking. Serve hot.

Bengali Potatoes
(Aloo Pooshto)

4 medium potatoes, peeled
2 tablespoons white poppy seeds
3 tablespoons vegetable oil
½ teaspoon turmeric powder
½ teaspoon red chili powder
Table salt, to taste

Cut the potatoes into ½-inch dice. Set aside. Heat a small skillet on medium. Dry roast the poppy seeds until they start to change color, stirring constantly. Remove from heat and let the seeds cool. In a spice grinder, grind the seeds into a thick paste using a few tablespoons of water. Set aside. In a large skillet, heat the vegetable oil on medium. Add the potatoes, and sauté for 4 to 5 minutes. Add the poppy seed paste, turmeric powder, red chili powder, and salt; mix well. Sauté for another 2 to 3 minutes. Add about ½ cup water. Cover, and cook until the potatoes are tender, about 10 to 12 minutes. Serve hot.

Cauliflower Takatak
(Gobi Takatak)

*Vegetable oil for deep-frying,
plus 2 tablespoons*
*1 small head cauliflower,
broken into florets*
1 teaspoon cumin seeds
*1 small red onion, finely
chopped*
1 tablespoon grated gingerroot

Table salt, to taste
¼ teaspoon red chili powder
*1 teaspoon dried fenugreek
leaves*
½ cup plain yogurt, whipped
1 small tomato, finely chopped

Serves 4
Prep Time: 15 minutes
Cook Time: 30 minutes

Serve this dish imme-
diately. Letting it sit
for too long will make
the cauliflower lose its
crispiness.

1. Heat the oil in a deep pan or deep fryer to 375° on a deep-fry thermometer. Fry a few cauliflower florets at a time until golden brown.
   Remove from the oil with a slotted spoon and transfer to a paper
   towel to drain. Let oil return to temperature and continue until all the
   florets are fried. Set aside.
2. In a large skillet, heat the 2 tablespoons vegetable oil on medium.
   Add the cumin seeds. When they begin to sizzle, add the onions and
   ginger; sauté for 2 to 3 minutes, until the onions are transparent.
3. Add the salt, red chili powder, dried fenugreek leaves, and yogurt. Mix
   well and sauté for about 1 minute.
4. Add the tomatoes and fried cauliflower. Mix well and sauté for 1 to 2
   minutes or until the cauliflower is heated through. Serve hot.

❈ Ginger Tips
*To make ginger easier to grate, freeze it first. When buying ginger,
choose young ginger that has not dried out.*

Green Beans with Coconut
(Nariel Wale Hare Beans)

Serves 4
Prep Time: 10 minutes
Cook Time: 10–12
minutes

Serve this with the
Malabari Coconut Rice
(page 177).

2 tablespoons butter
1 teaspoon vegetable oil
½ teaspoon black mustard
  seeds
Pinch of asafetida
2 dried red chilies, roughly
  pounded
½ teaspoon turmeric powder

1 pound frozen cut green
  beans, thawed
Table salt, to taste
Water, as needed
2 tablespoons unsweetened
  desiccated coconut
2 tablespoons minced cilantro

1. In a large skillet, heat the butter and oil on medium. Add the mustard seeds and the asafetida. When the seeds begin to crackle, add the red chilies and the turmeric powder; then add the green beans and sauté for about 3 to 4 minutes.
2. Add salt to taste and about ½ cup of water. Cover and cook until the beans are almost cooked through, about 3 to 4 minutes.
3. Add the coconut and cilantro. Simmer for another 3 to 4 minutes. Serve hot.

※ Snipping Herbs
Use kitchen shears to snip herbs like cilantro or mint; it is much easier than trying to cut them with a knife. Snip only as much as you need, since cut herbs do not store well.

CHAPTER 7
Chicken and Egg (Murgh Aur Ande)

Lollipop Chicken
(Lollipop Murgh)

Serves 4
Prep Time: 10 minutes,
plus 3–4 hours
to marinate
Cook Time: 20 minutes

Serve this with the
Vegetable Fried Rice
(page 174) and Chili
Garlic Sauce
(page 236).

2 tablespoons Ginger-Garlic Paste
  (see recipe on page 13)
4 tablespoons all-purpose flour
4 tablespoons corn flour
3 tablespoons soya sauce
1 teaspoon red chili powder
1 teaspoon sugar
½ tablespoon white vinegar
Water, as needed
8–10 small chicken drumsticks
  or chicken wings, skinned
1½ cups vegetable oil

1. In a large bowl, combine the Ginger-Garlic Paste, all-purpose flour, corn flour, soya sauce, red chili powder, sugar, and vinegar. Add enough water to make a thin, smooth consistency. Add the chicken and refrigerate for 3 to 4 hours.
2. In a deep pan, heat 5 to 6 tablespoons of vegetable oil. Add a few pieces of chicken to the oil, and pan-fry until crisp. If the oil begins to splatter, you can cover the pan with a splatter guard or a cover. Continue until all the pieces are cooked. Discard any remaining marinade.
3. Remove the chicken pieces and place on a paper towel to drain off any excess oil. Serve immediately.

☀ Light Spinach Salad
A spinach salad is the perfect side to many meat dishes in this book. Tear up some baby spinach leaves and place them in a bowl. Add 1 cup of green mango and a handful of pecans or walnuts. Add lemon juice and a pinch of Chaat Spice Mix (page 14). Mix well and serve.

Chicken with Pickling Spices
(Murgh Achari)

2 tablespoons mustard oil or
   vegetable oil
½ teaspoon black mustard
   seeds
½ teaspoon wild fennel seeds
   (also called nigella seeds)
2 dried red chilies
¼ teaspoon fenugreek seeds
1 tablespoon Ginger-Garlic Paste
   (see recipe on page 13)

8 skinless chicken thighs
½ teaspoon red chili powder
¼ teaspoon turmeric powder
Table salt, to taste
1 cup plain yogurt
1 cup water
Juice of ½ lemon

Serves 4–5
Prep Time: 10 minutes
Cook Time:
30–35 minutes

You can also substitute Indian Cheese (page 12), lamb, or potatoes for the chicken in this recipe—just adjust the cooking times accordingly.

1. In a large skillet, heat the oil until almost smoking. Reduce the heat to medium. Quickly add the mustard and nigella seeds, red chilies, and fenugreek seeds. Fry for about 30 seconds or until the seeds start to change color and release their aroma.
2. Add the Ginger-Garlic Paste and sauté for another 10 seconds. Add the chicken and sauté for about 2 minutes. Reduce heat to medium.
3. Add the red chili, and turmeric powder, and salt; sauté until the chicken is well browned on all sides.
4. Add the yogurt and mix well. Add about 1 cup of water. Reduce the heat to low, cover the skillet, and cook for 20 to 25 minutes or until the chicken is cooked and the fat begins to surface.
5. Add the lemon juice and cook for 1 more minute. Serve hot.

❊ Cooking with Mustard Oil
Mustard oil is very pungent. When you are using it, make sure it's smoking hot first, then decrease the heat. It's now ready for use. Smoking the oil allows you to enjoy the taste without the pungency.

Ginger-Flavored Chicken Curry
(Murgh Adraki)

Serves 4–5
Prep Time: 10 minutes, plus 3–4 hours to marinate
Cook Time: 20–30 minutes

Use fresh tender ginger for this recipe. Serve with plain Simple Naan Bread (page 205).

2 tablespoons grated gingerroot
1 teaspoon coriander powder
1 teaspoon Warm Spice Mix (see recipe on page 12)
½ teaspoon red chili powder
¾ cup plain yogurt, whipped
4 tablespoons vegetable oil, divided

8 skinless chicken thighs
½ teaspoon cumin seeds
1 black cardamom pod
1 bay leaf
2 medium-sized fresh tomatoes, puréed
Table salt, to taste
Water, as needed

1. In a large bowl or resealable plastic bag, combine the ginger, coriander powder, spice mix, red chili powder, yogurt, and 2 tablespoons of the vegetable oil; mix well. Add the chicken and coat all pieces evenly with the marinade. Cover and refrigerate for 3 to 4 hours.
2. In a large skillet, heat the remaining 2 tablespoons of vegetable oil. Add the cumin seeds, cardamom, and bay leaf. When the seeds begin to sizzle, add the tomato purée.
3. Sauté over medium heat until the tomatoes are cooked and the oil begins to separate from the tomato mixture, about 3 to 4 minutes.
4. Add the chicken and the marinade to the tomato mixture, along with the salt. Mix well and cook for about 4 to 5 minutes. Add about ½ cup of water, cover, and cook for 20 minutes or until the chicken is completely cooked and the juices run clear, stirring occasionally. If you like a thinner gravy, add some more water. Remove the black cardamom pod and bay leaf before serving. Serve hot.

❊ Indian Cooking Oils

Indian cooking uses peanut, vegetable, mustard, sesame, and corn oil for cooking. There are two varieties of ghee that are used, vanaspathi (vegetable) and ghee (clarified butter). Indian cooking does not use any animal fat or lard as a cooking medium.

Sizzling Tandoori Chicken
(Murgh Tandoori)

¾ cup Hung Yogurt (see recipe on page 14)

1 tablespoon Ginger-Garlic Paste (see recipe on page 13)

1 tablespoon Tandoori Spice Mix (see recipe on page 13)

¼ teaspoon carom seeds

Table salt, to taste

2 tablespoons fresh lemon juice

A few drops of red food coloring (optional)

2 tablespoons vegetable oil

8 skinless bone-in chicken thighs

Melted butter for basting

Chaat Spice Mix, for garnish (see recipe on page 14)

Serves 4–5
Prep Time: 15 minutes, plus at least 8 hours to marinate
Cook Time: 25–35 minutes

Serve this with the Punjabi Onion Salad (page 66), Simple Naan Bread (page 205), and Creamy Black Gram Dahl (page 190).

1. In a large bowl, combine the yogurt, Ginger-Garlic Paste, Tandoori Spice Mix, carom seeds, salt, lemon juice, red food coloring, and vegetable oil. Add the chicken and mix well to coat the chicken evenly. Cover and refrigerate for at least 8 hours, overnight.
2. Preheat oven to 400°.
3. Place the chicken in a single layer in a roasting pan. Discard any remaining marinade. Roast for about 20 to 30 minutes or until the chicken is cooked and the juices run clear. Baste as needed with the melted butter. Brown under the broiler for 6 to 7 minutes, turning once.
4. Garnish with a sprinkling of Chaat Spice Mix and serve hot.

❈ Marinating Tip

When marinating chicken with bones, make small cuts in the chicken flesh. This allows the marinade to penetrate the chicken pieces. You can freeze the marinated chicken for use at a later date.

Butter Chicken
(Murgh Makhanwala)

Serves 4
Prep Time: 10 minutes
Cook Time: 20 minutes

The velvety butter
sauce provides an
excellent base for the
Sizzling Tandoori
Chicken. Serve with
Simple Naan Bread
(page 205) or with
Simple Basmati Rice
(page 160).

4 tablespoons butter
½ teaspoon vegetable oil
2 teaspoons Ginger-Garlic Paste
(see recipe on page 13)
2 medium tomatoes, finely
chopped
¼ cup tomato purée (canned
or fresh)

½ teaspoon red chili powder
Table salt, to taste
1 teaspoon dried fenugreek
leaves
1 recipe Sizzling Tandoori
Chicken (page 93)
½ cup heavy cream

1. In a large skillet, heat the butter and oil on medium. Add the Ginger-
   Garlic Paste and sauté for about 30 seconds.
2. Add the tomatoes and the purée. Cook the tomatoes, stirring constantly. Use the back of a spatula to mash the tomatoes as they cook.
   Continue until the tomatoes are completely mashed and soft, about
   10 minutes.
3. Add the red chili powder, salt, fenugreek leaves, and chicken and mix
   well. Simmer, covered, for about 10 minutes.
4. Add the cream and simmer for 1 minute. Serve hot.

❋ Naked Chicken

*Indian marinades need skinless chicken to work their magic, so it's
best to skin your poultry prior to use. Also, make deep incisions to
help the marinade sink into the chicken for a much better tasting dish.*

Chicken Curry
(Murgh Tariwala)

3 tablespoons vegetable oil
1 black cardamom pod
2 green cardamom pods, bruised
2 cloves
1 (1-inch) cinnamon stick
1 bay leaf
1 large red onion, finely
   chopped
1 tablespoon Ginger-Garlic Paste
   (see recipe on page 13)
2 medium tomatoes, finely
   chopped

½ teaspoon red chili powder
1 teaspoon Warm Spice Mix
   (see recipe on page 12),
   plus extra for garnish
¼ teaspoon turmeric powder
2 teaspoons coriander powder
Table salt, to taste
½ cup plain yogurt, whipped
2½ pounds skinless chicken
   pieces, cuts of your choice
Water, as needed
2 tablespoons minced cilantro

Serves 4–5
Prep Time: 15 minutes
Cook Time: 45 minutes

This is an easy-to-make, simple Chicken curry. Serve with Simple Basmati Rice (page 160) or Simple Indian Bread (page 202).

1. In a large skillet, heat the oil on medium. Add the cardamom, cloves, cinnamon stick, and bay leaf. When the spices begin to sizzle, add the onion and the Ginger-Garlic Paste. Sauté for about 5 to 7 minutes or until the onion is well browned.

2. Add the tomatoes and cook for about 8 minutes or until the tomatoes are soft and the oil begins to separate from the sides of the mixture.

3. Add the red chili powder, the spice mix, turmeric powder, coriander powder, and salt; cook for 1 minute. Add the yogurt and mix well. Cook, stirring constantly for 1 more minute.

4. Add the chicken and cook, stirring constantly for 5 to 7 minutes or until brown on all sides. Add 1 cup of water, cover, and simmer for 20 minutes or until the chicken is cooked through. Stir occasionally, and add more water if the sauce dries up or if you want a thinner gravy. Add the minced cilantro and cook for 1 minute. Serve hot, sprinkled with Warm Spice Mix.

Ginger Chicken Bites
(Adraki Murgh Tikka)

Serves 4
Prep Time: 5 minutes,
plus at least 5–6 hours
to marinate
Cook Time: 15 minutes

A fairly mild dish,
serve this with
Spinach Bread
(page 209) and
Carrot and Tomato
Salad (page 62).

1 cup Hung Yogurt (see recipe
    on page 14)
2 tablespoons grated gingerroot
1 teaspoon fresh lemon juice
1 tablespoon vegetable oil
½ teaspoon (or to taste) red
    chili powder

Table salt, to taste
1½ pounds skinless, boneless
    chicken breast, cubed
2 tablespoons melted butter
Lemon wedges, for garnish

1. In a bowl or resealable plastic bag, combine the yogurt, grated ginger, lemon juice, oil, red chili powder, and salt; mix well. Add the chicken cubes. Marinate, covered and refrigerated, for 5 to 6 hours or, preferably, overnight.
2. Preheat oven to 425°.
3. Thread the chicken onto skewers and baste with the melted butter. Place the chicken on a foil-lined baking sheet and bake for about 7 minutes. Turn once and baste with any remaining butter. Bake for another 7 minutes or until golden brown and the juices run clear. Serve hot, garnished with lemon wedges.

※ Tandoors

Tandoors are large clay ovens that are used to roast meats and bake breads. The meats cooked in a tandoor tend to stay moist on the inside and dry on the outside. Tandoors use charcoal for heating. They provide a characteristic taste to the food that is almost impossible to duplicate in a conventional home oven. Small, portable home-use tandoors are now available in the United States. I use a conventional home oven or an outdoor charcoal grill for my tandoori dishes.

Almond-Flavored Chicken
(Badaami Murgh)

¼ cup blanched almonds
Water, as needed
4 tablespoons vegetable oil
1 bay leaf
2 cloves
5 peppercorns
1 green chili, seeded and
    minced
1 tablespoon Ginger-Garlic Paste
    (see recipe on page 13)
8 pieces skinless, bone-in
    chicken thighs

½ teaspoon red chili powder
¼ teaspoon turmeric powder
1 teaspoon coriander powder
½ teaspoon Warm Spice Mix
    (see recipe on page 12)
Table salt, to taste
¼ cup plain yogurt, whipped
¼ cup heavy cream

Serves 4–5
Prep Time: 10 minutes
Cook Time: 35–40
minutes

The nuts add a rich
creamy taste to the
chicken. Serve this
with the Carom-
Flavored Flatbread
(page 214).

1. In a blender or food processor, blend the almonds with a few table-spoons of water to make a thick, smooth paste. Set aside.
2. In a large pan, heat the vegetable oil on medium. Add the bay leaf, cloves, peppercorns, green chili, and Ginger-Garlic Paste; sauté for about 10 seconds. Add the chicken and sauté until well browned on both sides, about 5 to 10 minutes.
3. Add the red chili, turmeric, coriander, the spice mix, and salt; cook for about 5 minutes.
4. Add the yogurt and sauté until the fat begins to separate. Add about ½ cup of water. Cover and simmer until the chicken is tender and cooked through, about 10 to 15 minutes. Stir occasionally, adding a few tablespoons of water if the dish seems too dry.
5. Add the almond paste and the cream. Cook, uncovered, on medium heat for about 8 minutes. Serve hot.

Chicken Tikka Masala
(Murgh Tikka Masala)

Serves 4
Prep Time: 10 minutes
Cook Time: 20 minutes

This is probably one of the most popular Indian dishes on restaurant menus worldwide. This dish is often called the national dish of the United Kingdom!

3 tablespoons vegetable oil
1 medium-sized red onion, finely chopped
1 tablespoon Ginger-Garlic Paste (see recipe on page 13)
2 medium tomatoes, finely chopped
½ teaspoon red chili powder
¼ teaspoon turmeric powder
Table salt, to taste
½ teaspoon Warm Spice Mix (see recipe on page 12)
¾ cup heavy cream.
1 recipe Chicken Tikka (page 24)

1. In a large pan, heat the vegetable oil on medium. Add the onions and sauté until well browned, about 7 to 8 minutes. Add the Ginger-Garlic Paste and sauté for another minute.
2. Add the tomatoes and cook for about 8 minutes or until the tomatoes are cooked and the oil begins to separate from the sides of the mixture.
3. Add the red chili, turmeric, salt, and the spice mix; sauté for 1 minute.
4. Add the cream and cook for about 2 minutes. Add the Chicken Tikka and mix well. Cook for 2 minutes or until the chicken is heated through. Serve hot.

❈ **Chicken Tikka Rolls**

Here's another simple recipe for leftovers. Brush 1 side of a piece of Simple Indian Bread (page 202) or a flour tortilla with egg wash. Place on a hot griddle and cook it on both sides. Place a few pieces of chicken on the side of the bread with the egg, add a few slices of onions, 1 tablespoon of Mint-Cilantro Chutney (page 224), roll up, and serve.

Chicken in a Creamy Sauce
(Murgh Korma)

2 small red onions, peeled and
  chopped
1-inch piece fresh gingerroot,
  peeled and sliced
4 garlic cloves, peeled
4 dried red chilies
2 teaspoons coriander powder
Water, as needed
3 tablespoons unsalted cashew
  nuts, soaked in water for
  10 minutes
2 tablespoons white poppy
  seeds, soaked in water for
  20 minutes
2 tablespoons almonds, blanched

3 tablespoons Clarified Butter
  (see recipe on page 15)
2 (1-inch) cinnamon sticks
2 black cardamom pods, bruised
1 large bay leaf
4 cloves
2 green cardamom pods, bruised
1 teaspoon cumin powder
1 cup plain yogurt, whipped
1½ pounds boneless diced
  chicken
Table salt, to taste
1 teaspoon Warm Spice Mix
  (see recipe on page 12)
Roasted cumin seeds, for garnish

Serves 4–5
Prep Time: 25 minutes,
plus 10 minutes to soak
Cook Time: 45 minutes

The secret to preparing the perfect sauce is to let it simmer slowly until it thickens completely.

1. In a blender or food processor, blend together the onions, ginger, garlic, red chilies, coriander powder, and up to ¼ cup of water to make a paste. Set aside.
2. Process or blend together the cashew nuts, poppy seeds, almonds, and just enough water to make a smooth, thick paste. Set aside.
3. In a deep pan, heat the Clarified Butter over medium heat. Add the cinnamon sticks, black cardamom, bay leaf, cloves, and green cardamom; sauté until fragrant, about 1½ minutes. Add the onion paste and cumin. Sauté over medium-low heat, stirring constantly, until the butter separates from the onion paste. Add the yogurt and continue cooking for about 12 minutes, stirring constantly.
4. Add the chicken pieces. Simmer, covered, for 15 to 20 minutes or until the chicken is tender.
5. Add the nut paste and simmer, uncovered, for about 4 minutes. Stir in the salt and the Warm Spice Mix. Garnish with roasted cumin seeds and serve hot.

Coriander Chicken
(Dhaniye Wala Murgh)

Serves 4–5
Prep Time: 15 minutes
Cook Time: 40 minutes

Serve this with a raita of your choice (see Chapter 5, Salads) and Simple Naan Bread (page 205).

4 tablespoons vegetable oil
2 cloves
2 green cardamom pods
1 (1-inch) cinnamon stick
2 teaspoons Ginger-Garlic Paste (see recipe on page 13)
1½ medium tomatoes, finely chopped
½ teaspoon red chili powder
Table salt, to taste
2 tablespoons coriander powder
½ cup plain yogurt, whipped
8 skinless chicken thighs
Water, as needed
1 cup minced cilantro

1. In a large pan, heat the vegetable oil. Add the cloves, cardamom, and cinnamon. When they begin to sizzle, add the Ginger-Garlic Paste and sauté for about 15 seconds.
2. Add the tomatoes and cook for 6 to 8 minutes or until the tomatoes are cooked and the oil begins to separate from the sides of the mixture.
3. Add the red chili powder, salt, and coriander powder; fry for 1 minute.
4. Add the yogurt and mix well. Cook for about 2 minutes.
5. Add the chicken and fry, stirring constantly, for about 15 minutes. Add about ½ cup of water. Bring back to a boil, cover, and simmer until the chicken is tender and cooked through, about 15 minutes. Stir occasionally, adding a few tablespoons of water if the dish dries up too much.
6. Add the cilantro leaves and mix well. Serve hot.

❋ Handling Poultry

Be careful when handling raw poultry. Clean your preparation area thoroughly with hot, soapy water or a commercial kitchen cleaner. Ensure that you place the chicken in the fridge to marinate. This will prevent the breeding of any harmful bacteria.

Spiced Chicken in Green Curry
(Murgh Hariyali)

3 tablespoons vegetable oil
1 large onion, minced
2 teaspoons Ginger-Garlic Paste
   (see recipe on page 13)
2 green chilies, seeded and
   minced (optional)
4 tablespoons minced cilantro
4 tablespoons minced mint
5 tablespoons minced spinach

1½ pounds skinless, boneless
   chicken chunks (your choice
   of cut)
Table salt, to taste
¼ teaspoon red chili powder
Water, as needed
½ cup heavy cream

Serves 4
Prep Time: 15 minutes
Cook Time: 35–40 minutes

This dish is at its best when fresh herbs are used. Serve this with a Garlic Rice (page 172).

1. In a large pan, heat the vegetable oil on medium. Add the onions and sauté until well browned, about 7 to 8 minutes. Add the Ginger-Garlic Paste and sauté for 1 minute.
2. Add the green chilies, cilantro leaves, mint leaves, and spinach leaves; fry for about 4 to 5 minutes.
3. Add the chicken, salt, and red chili powder; fry for about 5 minutes. Add ½ cup of water, cover, and cook the chicken until done, about 10 to 15 minutes. Stir occasionally to ensure that the chicken is not sticking to the pan. Add more water if needed.
4. Add the cream and cook for 1 minute. Serve hot.

✵ Dried Mint Chicken

My grandmother used to make this: Dry fresh mint (or use dried mint leaves) and crush it. Create a marinade of the mint, red chili powder, salt, pepper, and vegetable oil. Add chicken to the marinade and let it marinate for at least 4 hours. Grill or roast in an oven. Simple yet flavorful.

Cardamom Chicken
(Eliachi Murgh)

Serves 4–5
Prep Time: 10 minutes
Cook Time: 30–40 minutes

The cooking time of the chicken will depend on the cut that you choose. This dish is perfect with Simple Basmati Rice (page 160).

3 tablespoons vegetable oil
6 green cardamom pods, roughly pounded
1 medium-sized red onion, minced
2 teaspoons Ginger-Garlic Paste (see recipe on page 13)
1½ pounds skinless, boneless chicken chunks (your choice of cut)

Table salt, to taste
½ teaspoon red chili powder
¼ teaspoon turmeric powder
1 cup Hung Yogurt (see recipe on page 14)
Water, as needed

1. In a pan, heat the vegetable oil on medium. Add the cardamom pods and sauté for 10 seconds. Add the onions and sauté until well browned, about 7 to 8 minutes. Add the Ginger-Garlic Paste and sauté for 1 minute.
2. Add the chicken cubes and sauté until well browned, about 7 to 8 minutes.
3. Add the salt, red chili powder, and turmeric powder; mix well. Sauté for 1 minute.
4. Add the yogurt and mix well. Fry for another 5 minutes, stirring constantly.
5. Add about ½ cup of water, cover, and cook on low heat until the chicken is cooked through, about 10 to 15 minutes.

☼ Green Cardamoms

Green cardamoms are one of the most expensive spices in the world. In Arab countries, this aromatic spice is most often used for spicing coffee. In India, green cardamom is used as a mouth freshener.

Chicken Chettinad
(Kozi Chettinad)

3 teaspoons black peppercorns, roughly pounded
2 teaspoons Ginger-Garlic Paste (see recipe on page 13)
1 dried red chili, roughly pounded
¾ cup Hung Yogurt (see recipe on page 14)
8 skinless chicken thighs

4 tablespoons vegetable oil
8 fresh curry leaves
1 large red onion, chopped
1½ medium tomatoes, chopped
¼ teaspoon turmeric powder
Table salt, to taste
½ cup water

Serves 4–5
Prep Time: 10 minutes
Cook Time: 40–50 minutes

If you like your food milder, reduce the number of peppercorns in this dish. Serve with Simple Naan Bread (page 205).

1. In a bowl, combine the peppercorns, Ginger-Garlic Paste, red chili, and yogurt; mix well. Add the chicken thighs, making sure that the chicken is well covered in the marinade. Set aside.
2. In a pan, heat the vegetable oil on medium. Add the curry leaves; when they begin to sizzle, add the onions. Sauté until the onions are well browned, about 7 to 8 minutes.
3. Add the tomatoes and cook for about 6 to 8 minutes or until the tomatoes are cooked and the oil begins to separate from the sides of the mixture. Add the turmeric and salt; cook for 1 minute.
4. Add the chicken along with all the marinade; cook for about 6 to 8 minutes. Add the water and bring to a boil. Cover and simmer until the chicken is done, about 15 to 20 minutes. Serve hot.

❋ Prepacked Spice Mixes
If you need a spice mix in a hurry, you can buy most prepacked spice mixes (like the Garam Masala, Tandoori Masala, and Chaat Masala) at your local Indian grocery stores instead of making them yourself. I suggest the MDH brands.

Chicken Manchurian
(Murgh Manchurian)

Serves 4–5
Prep Time: 10 minutes
Cook Time: 30–40 minutes

This recipe is great with Vegetable Fried Rice (page 174). If you want to make a colorful presentation, add bell peppers in a variety of colors.

1 egg
2 tablespoons corn flour
2 tablespoons all-purpose flour
1 teaspoon Ginger-Garlic Paste (see recipe on page 13)
1 teaspoon plus 1 tablespoon red chili sauce (optional)
Water, as needed
1½ pounds skinless, boneless chicken, cubed
Vegetable oil for deep-frying, plus 3 tablespoons

1-inch piece fresh gingerroot, grated
2 green chilies, seeded and minced
2 tablespoons soya sauce
¼ teaspoon white pepper powder
Table salt, to taste
1 small red onion, thinly sliced
1 small green bell pepper, seeded and thinly sliced
1 cup chicken stock or water
3 tablespoons corn flour dissolved in ½ cup cold water

1. In a bowl, combine the egg, 2 tablespoons corn flour, the all-purpose flour, Ginger-Garlic Paste, and 1 teaspoon of the red chili sauce. Add enough water to make a thin batter; mix well. Add the chicken pieces to the batter.
2. In a deep pan, heat the vegetable oil to 350°. Add a few pieces of chicken at a time and deep-fry until the chicken is crisp and golden brown. Using a slotted spoon, remove the chicken from the oil, and drain on paper towels. Let the oil return to temperature. Continue until all the chicken pieces are fried. Set aside. Discard any remaining batter.
3. In a large skillet, heat the 3 tablespoons of vegetable oil. Add the ginger and green chilies, and sauté for about 30 seconds.
4. Add the soya sauce, remaining 1 tablespoon red chili sauce, white pepper powder, and salt; mix well. Add the onion and bell pepper; sauté for 2 to 3 minutes.
5. Add the chicken stock (or water), and corn flour mixture (restir the corn flour mix if you made it ahead). Bring to a boil. Lower the heat and add the chicken pieces. Simmer for 1 to 2 minutes. Serve immediately.

Goan Chicken Curry
(Goan Murgh Xcautti)

2 dried red chilies
1 tablespoon white poppy seeds
1 teaspoon black mustard
   seeds
2 teaspoons cumin seeds
1 tablespoon coriander seeds
¼ teaspoon black peppercorns
1 (1-inch) cinnamon stick
3 cloves
¼ cup unsweetened desiccated
   coconut

3 tablespoons vegetable oil
1 large red onion, minced
1 tablespoon Ginger-Garlic Paste
   (see recipe on page 13)
1½ pounds skinless, boneless
   chicken chunks
Table salt, to taste
Water, as needed
1 tablespoon fresh lemon juice
   (optional)

Serves 4–5
Prep Time: 15 minutes
Cook Time: 30–35
minutes

This delight from
western India takes a
bit of an effort to
make, but the results
are really rewarding.

1. In a small skillet on medium heat, dry roast the red chilies, poppy seeds, mustard seeds, cumin seeds, coriander seeds, black peppercorns, cinnamon stick, and cloves. When the spices release their aroma, remove from heat and let cool. In a spice grinder, grind the spices, along with the coconut, to a coarse powder. Set aside.

2. In a large skillet, heat the vegetable oil. Add the onions and sauté until well browned, about 7 to 8 minutes. Add the Ginger-Garlic Paste and sauté for 1 minute.

3. Add the chicken and sauté until browned, about 5 to 7 minutes. Add the reserved spice powder and the salt; sauté for 2 minutes.

4. Add about ½ cup of water and bring to a boil. Reduce the heat, cover, and simmer until the chicken is cooked through, about 10 to 15 minutes. Add 1 tablespoon of lemon juice to the dish before serving, if desired. Serve hot.

Dill Chicken
(Soa Wali Murgh)

Serves 4
Prep Time: 10 minutes, and marinate overnight
Cook Time: 30–35 minutes

Try this chicken in pocket pitas along with shredded lettuce and tomatoes. Serve the pitas with Sweet and Spicy Fruits (page 22).

2 tablespoons fresh lemon juice
4 tablespoons vegetable oil
1 tablespoon Warm Spice Mix (see recipe on page 12)
Table salt, to taste
A few sprigs of dill
2 garlic cloves, crushed
4 skinless chicken breasts
Butter for basting.

1. In a bowl or resealable plastic bag, combine all the ingredients, *except* the chicken and butter, and mix well. Add the chicken to the marinade. Make sure the breasts are well coated. Cover and refrigerate overnight.
2. Preheat oven to 350°.
3. Place the chicken in a single layer in a roasting pan. Discard any remaining marinade and the sprigs of dill. Bake for about 30 minutes or until the chicken is cooked through and the juices run clear. Baste as needed with the melted butter. Serve hot.

Creamy Chicken Kebab
(Murgh Malai Kebab)

Serves 4–5
Prep Time: 15 minutes, plus at least 2 hours to marinate
Cook Time: 25 minutes

These mild chicken kebabs can be served as appetizers or as an entrée. Serve with Spicy Papaya Salad (page 56).

2 teaspoons Ginger-Garlic Paste (see recipe on page 13)
1 teaspoon white pepper powder
2 serrano green chilies, seeded and minced
3/4 cup heavy cream
2 tablespoons corn flour
Table salt, to taste
1 1/2 pounds boneless, skinless chicken chunks
Butter for basting

1. In a bowl, combine the Ginger-Garlic Paste, white pepper powder, green chilies, cream, corn flour, and salt. Add the chicken to the marinade. Cover and refrigerate for at least 2 hours, or overnight.
2. Preheat oven to 400°. Place the chicken in a single layer in a roasting pan. Discard any remaining marinade. Bake for about 20 minutes or until the chicken is cooked through. Baste as needed with the melted butter. Brown under the broiler for 2 to 3 minutes. Serve hot.

Velvety Chicken Kebab
(Murgh Reshmi Kebab)

2 tablespoons cashews, roughly
  pounded
1 egg, whisked
½ teaspoon cumin seeds,
  roasted and roughly
  pounded
½ teaspoon Warm Spice Mix
  (see recipe on page 12)

1½ pounds minced chicken
2 teaspoons vegetable oil
½ small red onion, minced
1-inch piece fresh gingerroot,
  grated
Table salt, to taste
Butter for basting

Serves 4–5
Prep Time: 20 minutes
Cook Time: 20–25 minutes

Traditionally these are shaped like sausages and skewered lengthwise on long skewers. Serve with the Mint Chutney (page 235).

1. In a bowl, combine all the ingredients, *except* the butter, and mix well, using your hands.
2. Preheat oven to 350°.
3. Divide the chicken mixture into 8 portions and make equal-sized small patties, flattening them between the palms of your hands.
4. Place the chicken patties on a baking sheet and roast for about 10 minutes. Turn once and baste with any remaining butter. Roast for another 10 minutes or until golden brown and the juices run clear. Serve hot.

❈ Ginger-Garlic Paste

I have provided a recipe to make this paste at home; you can also buy this at your local Indian grocer. Many regular grocery stores now sell ginger paste and crushed garlic, which can also be used as a substitute.

Chili Coconut Chicken
(Mangalorian Murgh Gassi)

Serves 4
Prep Time: 15 minutes
Cook Time: 40 minutes

The coconut milk provides a nice balance to the red chilies. Serve this with Simple Basmati Rice (page 160).

½ teaspoon black mustard seeds
½ teaspoon cumin seeds
½ teaspoon coriander seeds
3 tablespoons vegetable oil
8 curry leaves
2 medium-sized red onions, finely chopped
2 teaspoons Ginger-Garlic Paste (see recipe on page 13)
3 dried red chilies, roughly pounded
½ teaspoon turmeric powder
Table salt, to taste
1½ pounds boneless, skinless chicken, cubed
Water, as needed
1 cup light coconut milk

1. In a small skillet on medium heat, dry roast the mustard seeds, cumin seeds, and coriander seeds. When the spices release their aroma, remove from heat and let cool. In a spice grinder, grind to a coarse powder. Set aside.
2. In a large skillet, heat the oil on medium. Add the curry leaves and the onions; sauté for about 1 minute.
3. Add the Ginger-Garlic Paste and red chilies. Sauté on medium heat until the onions are well browned and the oil begins to separate from the sides of the onion mixture, about 8 minutes.
4. Add the ground spices, turmeric powder, and salt; sauté for 1 minute.
5. Add the chicken pieces and sauté for about 10 minutes. Add about ½ cup of water, cover, and simmer for about 15 minutes or until the chicken is cooked through.
6. Add the coconut milk and simmer on low heat for about 5 minutes. Serve hot.

✵ Coconut Milk

Don't confuse coconut water with coconut milk. Coconut water is the liquid inside a coconut. Coconut milk is produced by steeping grated coconut in hot water and straining it. Regular coconut milk is high in saturated fat. I would advise using light coconut milk.

Fenugreek-Flavored Chicken
(Murgh Methiwala)

4 tablespoons vegetable oil
2 cloves
1 green cardamom pod,
    bruised
1 (1-inch) cinnamon stick
1 medium-sized red onion,
    finely chopped
1 tablespoon Ginger-Garlic Paste
    (see recipe on page 13)

2 tablespoons dried fenugreek
    leaves
8 skinless chicken thighs
½ teaspoon red chili powder
Table salt, to taste
½ teaspoon turmeric powder
1 cup plain yogurt, whipped
1 cup water

> **Serves 4–5**
> **Prep Time:** 5 minutes
> **Cook Time:** 30–40 minutes
>
> A very aromatic dish, using either fresh or dried fenugreek leaves. Serve this with the Simple Naan Bread (page 205).

1. In a large skillet, heat the vegetable oil on medium. Add the cloves, cardamom, and cinnamon. When they begin to sizzle, add the onions and sauté for about 2 to 3 minutes.
2. Add the Ginger-Garlic Paste and the dried fenugreek leaves. Sauté on medium heat until the onions are well browned and the oil begins to separate from the onion mixture, about 3 to 4 minutes.
3. Add the chicken thighs and sauté until browned. Add the red chili powder, turmeric powder, and salt; sauté for 2 minutes.
4. Add the yogurt and fry until the fat begins to separate. Add the water, cover, and simmer until the chicken is tender and cooked through, 20 to 25 minutes. Serve hot.

❋ Green Chilies

For the recipes in this book, I use serrano chilies. You can choose another type of chili, but just make sure that you know how much heat they will add! If you like the flavor but not the heat, remove the white seeds from the chili.

Omelet Curry
(Mutta Curry)

Serves 4
Prep Time: 15 minutes
Cook Time: 20 minutes

This unusual curry is common in South India. Serve with freshly baked sliced white bread.

4 eggs
1 serrano green chili, seeded and minced
½ small red onion, minced
3 tablespoons vegetable oil
1 medium-sized red onion, finely chopped

2 teaspoons Ginger-Garlic Paste (see recipe on page 13)
2 small tomatoes, finely chopped
½ teaspoon turmeric powder
½ teaspoon red chili powder
Table salt, to taste
½ cup water

1. In a bowl, whisk the eggs; add the green chilies and minced onion.
2. In a small nonstick skillet, heat about 1 tablespoon of the vegetable oil over medium heat. Pour about ¼ of the egg mixture into the skillet and cook until the base is golden brown. Flip over and cook the other side until the omelet is firm and cooked through. Transfer to a plate. Continue until all the egg mixture is cooked. Cut the omelets into small strips. Set aside.
3. In a large pan, heat the remaining oil on medium. Add the chopped onions and sauté for 2 to 3 minutes.
4. Add the Ginger-Garlic Paste; sauté on medium heat until the onions are well browned, about 7 to 8 minutes. Add the tomatoes and cook for 7 to 8 minutes or until the oil begins to separate from the sides of the onion mixture.
5. Add the turmeric powder, red chili powder, and salt. Mix well, and sauté for 1 minute. Add the water and bring to a boil. Cover and simmer for about 8 minutes.
6. Add the omelet strips to the curry. Serve hot.

❋ Coconuts

Many recipes in the book call for coconut; you can use the unsweetened dry coconut available at your local grocery stores. If you prefer, you can use fresh coconut. A good rule of thumb is that 1 coconut yields about 1½ cups of coconut flesh.

Honey Chili Chicken
(Sahaed Wali Murgh)

3 dried red chilies, roughly
   pounded
½ cup liquid honey
Juice of 1 lemon
1 teaspoon soya sauce

2 teaspoons Ginger-Garlic Paste
   (see recipe on page 13)
1½ pounds skinless, boneless
   chicken chunks
Vegetable oil for basting

Serves 4–5
Prep Time: 5 minutes,
plus 2 hours to marinate
Cook Time: 20 minutes

The contrasting tastes of hot red chili and the sweet honey make this dish very appealing.

1. In a bowl, combine all the ingredients *except* the oil; mix well. Cover and refrigerate for at least 2 hours.
2. Preheat oven to 400°.
3. Place the chicken on a baking sheet and roast for about 10 minutes. Turn once and baste with oil. Roast for another 10 minutes or until cooked through. Serve hot.

Easy Masala Egg
(Anda Masala)

2 tablespoons vegetable oil
½ small red onion, finely
   chopped
1 serrano green chili, seeded
   and minced

1 tablespoon minced cilantro
½ teaspoon red chili powder
¼ teaspoon turmeric powder
Table salt, to taste
4 eggs, whisked

Serves 4
Prep Time: 10 minutes
Cook Time: 10 minutes

A favorite weekend brunch dish, serve atop Spinach Bread (page 209) for a healthy and hearty meal.

1. In a large nonstick skillet, heat the vegetable oil on medium. Add the onions and sauté until transparent.
2. Add the green chili, cilantro, red chili powder, turmeric, and salt. Mix well, and sauté for 2 to 3 minutes.
3. Reduce the heat and add the eggs; cook, stirring constantly, until the eggs are done to your liking. Serve immediately.

Parsi-Style Eggs
(Akoori)

Serves 4
Prep Time: 10 minutes
Cook Time: 10 minutes

These scrambled eggs can be served atop your favorite bread.

2 tablespoons vegetable oil
2 spring onions, finely chopped
2 garlic cloves, crushed
1½-inch piece gingerroot, roughly chopped
2 serrano green chilies, seeded and minced

1 small red tomato, finely chopped
½ teaspoon cumin seeds, roasted
4 eggs, whisked
2 tablespoons cream
Table salt, to taste

1. Heat the oil on medium. Add the onions and sauté until transparent.
2. Add the garlic and ginger; sauté for 30 seconds. Add the green chilies, tomatoes, and cumin seeds; sauté for 3 minutes.
3. Add the eggs and cook, stirring constantly. Add the cream. Continue cooking, stirring constantly, until the eggs are cooked to your liking. Salt to taste. Serve immediately.

Egg Curry
(Anda Curry)

Serves 4–6
Prep Time: 20 minutes
Cook Time: 20 minutes

Adding milk to the recipe gives it a nice creaminess. Serve with Simple Indian Bread (page 202).

3 tablespoons vegetable oil
1 medium-sized red onion, minced
1-inch piece grates gingerroot
2 small tomatoes, chopped
½ teaspoon turmeric powder

½ teaspoon red chili powder
1 teaspoon coriander powder
Table salt, to taste
1 cup whole milk
6 eggs, boiled and peeled

1. In a large skillet, heat the oil on medium. Add the red onions and sauté for about 7 to 8 minutes or until the onions are well browned.
2. Add the ginger and cook for 1 minute. Add the tomatoes, and cook until the tomatoes are soft and the oil begins to separate from the onion-tomato mixture. Then add the turmeric, red chili powder, coriander powder, and salt; mix well. Add the milk and bring to a boil. Lower heat, cover, and simmer for about 3 to 4 minutes.
3. Slice the eggs and gently fold them into the sauce. Serve hot.

CHAPTER 8
Meat Dishes (Gosht)

Meat Belli Ram
(Belli Ram Ka Gosht)

Serves 4
Prep Time: 15 minutes, plus 4 hours to marinate
Cook Time: 1 hour, 30 minutes

Belli Ram was a celebrated Indian chef from northern India. This dish, named for him, is a delicacy served on special occasions.

2 cups plain yogurt, whipped
2 medium-sized red onions, peeled and thinly sliced
3 tablespoons Ginger-Garlic Paste (see recipe on page 13)
2 cloves
2 green cardamom pods, roughly pounded
1 (1-inch) cinnamon stick
1 teaspoon red chili powder

Table salt, to taste
1½ pounds lean boneless lamb, cut in 1-inch cubes
2 tablespoons Clarified Butter (see recipe on page 15) or vegetable oil
1 tablespoon coriander seeds, roughly pounded
1 cup water

1. In a bowl or resealable plastic bag, combine the yogurt, onions, Ginger-Garlic Paste, cloves, cardamom pods, cinnamon, red chili powder, and salt; mix well. Add the lamb and coat evenly with the marinade. Refrigerate, covered, for at least 4 hours, or overnight.
2. In a deep pan, heat the butter. Add the coriander seeds. When they begin to sizzle, add the lamb and any remaining marinade.
3. Cook for about 15 minutes. Add the water and bring to a boil. Reduce heat and simmer, covered, for 1 hour or until the lamb is tender.
4. Uncover and increase heat to high. Cook until the fat begins to leave the sides of the lamb. This will take about 5 to 8 minutes, depending on the leanness of your meat. Remove from heat. Serve hot.

❊ Indian Lamb Curries
Most of the curries taste even more awesome if you allow the spices to do their magic overnight. Cook the dish according to directions. Cool to room temperature. Cover and refrigerate overnight. The next day, heat the dish on high and serve.

Lamb Curry with Turnips
(Shalgam Wala Gosht)

3 tablespoons vegetable oil

2 cloves

1 bay leaf

2 medium-sized red onions, peeled and finely chopped

1 tablespoon Ginger-Garlic Paste (see recipe on page 13)

1½ pounds boneless lean lamb chunks

2 dried red chilies, roughly pounded

½ teaspoon turmeric powder

1½ teaspoons coriander powder

Table salt, to taste

½ teaspoon Warm Spice Mix (see recipe on page 12)

1 cup plain yogurt, whipped

Water, as needed

2 small turnips, peeled and diced

Serves 4
Prep Time: 10 minutes
Cook Time: 1 hour, 10 minutes

Turnips are a mild vegetable, but this dish provides them with a delicious taste. Serve with Simple Basmati Rice (page 160).

1. In a deep pan, heat the vegetable oil. Add the cloves and bay leaf. When the spices begin to sizzle, add the onion and Ginger-Garlic Paste. Sauté for about 5 to 7 minutes or until the onion is well browned.

2. Add the lamb and fry for about 20 minutes, stirring constantly. If the mixture starts to stick to the sides of the pan, add 1 tablespoon of water.

3. In quick succession, add the red chilies, turmeric, coriander, salt, and spice mix; sauté for 2 minutes.

4. Add the yogurt and cook for 10 minutes. Add 1 cup of water and bring to a boil. Lower the heat, cover, and simmer for about 15 minutes. Stir occasionally.

5. Add the turnips and cook covered for another 15 minutes or until the lamb has cooked through and the turnips are soft. Serve hot.

☀ Pressure-Cooking Meats

To drastically reduce the cooking time for meats, invest in a good pressure cooker. Most Indian homes have pressure cookers. They are a boon not only for meats but for lentils as well.

Fiery Lamb Vindaloo
(Gosht Ka Vindaloo)

Serves 4
Prep Time: 10 minutes, plus 1 hour to marinate
Cook Time: 60 minutes

You can prepare this with pork or beef; adjust seasonings to taste (cooking times stay the same).

¾ cup rice vinegar
¼ cup water
1 teaspoon black peppercorns, roughly pounded
1 tablespoon minced garlic
2 teaspoons red chili powder
2 serrano green chilies, minced
1½ pounds boneless lean lamb, cubed

3 tablespoons vegetable oil
1 tablespoon grated gingerroot
1 large red onion, peeled and finely chopped
6 whole dried red chilies, roughly pounded
1 (1-inch) cinnamon stick
½ teaspoon turmeric powder
Table salt, to taste

1. In a nonreactive bowl, combine the rice vinegar, water, black pepper, garlic, red chili powder, and green chilies. Add the lamb and coat evenly with the marinade. Refrigerate, covered, for 1 hour.
2. In a deep pan, heat the oil. Add the gingerroot and sauté for about 10 seconds. Add the onion and sauté for about 7 to 8 minutes or until golden brown.
3. Add the red chilies, cinnamon stick, and turmeric powder; sauté for 20 seconds.
4. Remove the lamb pieces from the marinade and set the marinade aside. Add the lamb and sauté on high heat for about 10 minutes or until the lamb is browned and the oil starts to separate from the mixture. Add the marinade and bring to a boil. Reduce heat and simmer, covered, for about 30 to 45 minutes or until the lamb is tender.
5. Add salt to taste. Serve hot.

❋ Selecting Lamb

Color can be a great help when buying lamb. Younger lamb is pinkish red with a velvety texture. It should have a thin layer of white fat surrounding it. If the meat is much darker in color, it means that the lamb is older and flavored more strongly.

Hot Shredded Meat
(Tala Gosht)

2 teaspoons Ginger-Garlic Paste
   (see recipe on page 13)
½ teaspoon Warm Spice Mix
   (see recipe on page 12)
¼ teaspoon turmeric powder
1 dry red chili, roughly
   pounded
1 pound boneless lean lamb
   (steak cut), shredded

3 tablespoons vegetable oil,
   plus more for deep-frying
½ cup water
Table salt, to taste
2 serrano green chilies, seeded
   and minced
Fried Onions (see recipe on
   page 16)

Serves 4
Prep Time: 10 minutes,
plus 3 hours to marinate
Cook Time: 40 minutes

Don't let this dish sit
for too long before
serving or it will lose
its texture. Serve with
Minty Potato in Yogurt
Sauce (page 64).

1. In a bowl, combine the Ginger-Garlic Paste, Warm Spice Mix, turmeric, and red chili. Add the lamb and mix well. Refrigerate, covered, for 3 hours.

2. In a medium skillet, heat the 3 tablespoons of vegetable oil. Add the lamb and fry for about 10 minutes, stirring constantly. Add the water, cover, and cook until the lamb is tender, about 15 minutes. Uncover and cook on high heat until most of the liquid dries up. Remove from heat and cool to room temperature.

3. Heat about 1 inch of vegetable oil in a deep pan to 350°. Using tongs, dip a few pieces of the lamb into the hot oil and deep-fry just until crispy. Drain on a paper towel. Continue until all the lamb is fried. Salt to taste and serve hot topped with green chilies and Fried Onions.

✵ Reruns

Many of the kebab recipes in this book lend themselves well to being used as stuffing for sandwiches. Take a pocket pita and fill with shredded lettuce, sliced tomatoes, 1 tablespoon of Hung Yogurt (page 14), ½ tablespoon of dried mint, and leftover meat from kebabs. Serve with the cooling Mango Yogurt Drink (page 42).

Kebabs from Peshawar
(Gosht Peshawari)

Serves 4
Prep Time: 10 minutes, plus 2 hours to marinate
Cook Time: 15 minutes

Serve these kebabs with Punjabi Onion Salad, Mint-Cilantro Chutney, and Fresh Lime Soda (pages 66, 224, and 41).

1 cup plain yogurt, whipped
1 tablespoon Ginger-Garlic Paste (see recipe on page 13)
1 teaspoon Warm Spice Mix (see recipe on page 12)

½ teaspoon red chili powder
Juice of ½ lemon
1½ pounds boneless lamb chunks
Table salt, to taste
Vegetable oil for basting

In a bowl or resealable plastic bag, combine the yogurt, Ginger-Garlic Paste, spice mix, red chili powder, and lemon juice; mix well. Add the lamb and mix well. Refrigerate, covered, for about 2 hours. Preheat oven to 350°. Place the lamb in a single layer on a foil-lined baking sheet. Discard the remaining marinade. Roast in the oven for 15 minutes or until the lamb is cooked through. Baste and turn at least once. Salt to taste.

Lamb Chops with Mint Chutney
(Chutney Wali Chaampe)

Serves 4
Prep Time: 5 minutes, plus 4 hours to marinate
Cook Time: 30 minutes

These minty lamb chops are easy to prepare and can be served with the Red Radish Salad (page 61).

1 teaspoon cumin, roasted and roughly pounded
2 teaspoons Ginger-Garlic Paste (see recipe on page 13)
2 teaspoons Warm Spice Mix (see recipe on page 12)
1 cup Mint-Cilantro Chutney (see recipe on page 224)

Juice of ½ a lemon
1 cup Hung Yogurt (see recipe on page 14)
Table salt, to taste
8 lamb chops (rib or loin), all visible fat removed
Vegetable oil for basting

In a bowl or resealable plastic bag, combine the cumin, ginger paste, spice mix, chutney, lemon juice, yogurt, and salt; mix well. Add the lamb chops and coat evenly with the marinade. Refrigerate, covered, for 4 hours. Preheat oven to 350°. Place the lamb chops in a single layer on a foil-lined baking sheet. Bake for 10 to 15 minutes. Baste with oil. Bake for another 10 to 15 minutes or until the lamb is cooked through.

Spinach Lamb Curry
(Saag Gosht)

½ pound frozen chopped spinach
4 tablespoons vegetable oil
2 bay leaves
1 (1-inch) cinnamon stick
4 cloves
4 black peppercorns
2 black cardamom pods
2 medium-sized red onions, peeled and finely chopped
2 teaspoons Ginger-Garlic Paste (see recipe on page 13)

1¼ pounds boneless lean lamb, cut into chunks
2 small tomatoes, finely chopped
1 teaspoon Warm Spice Mix (see recipe on page 12)
½ teaspoon red chili powder
¼ teaspoon turmeric powder
Table salt, to taste
½ cup plain yogurt, whipped
½ cup water

Serves 4
Prep Time: 15 minutes
Cook Time: 1 hour, 35 minutes

This dish graces menus at innumerable Indian restaurants. Serve with Simple Naan Bread (page 205), brushed with spiced garlic butter.

1. Cook the spinach in boiling water until just wilted; drain. Purée in a food processor. Set aside.
2. In a large skillet, heat the vegetable oil. Add the bay leaves, cinnamon stick, cloves, black peppercorns, and cardamom pods. When the spices begin to sizzle, add the onions. Stirring constantly, fry until the onions are golden brown, about 7 to 8 minutes. Add the Ginger-Garlic Paste and sauté for 1 minute.
3. Add the lamb and fry for about 10 to 15 minutes, stirring constantly. Add the tomatoes and fry, stirring constantly, for 10 minutes or until the oil starts to separate from the mixture.
4. Add the spice mix, red chili powder, turmeric powder, and salt; mix well. Add the yogurt and cook for about 4 minutes.
5. Add the water and bring to a boil. Reduce heat to low, cover, and simmer for about 45 minutes or until the lamb is cooked through.
6. Add the spinach and cook for another 5 minutes. Serve hot.

Meatball Curry
(Kofta Curry)

4 tablespoons vegetable oil
2 bay leaves
1 (1-inch) cinnamon stick
4 cloves
4 black peppercorns
2 black cardamom pods
2 medium-sized red onions,
    peeled and finely chopped
2 teaspoons Ginger-Garlic Paste
    (see recipe on page 13)

2 small tomatoes, finely chopped
1 teaspoon Warm Spice Mix
    (see recipe on page 12)
½ teaspoon red chili powder
¼ teaspoon turmeric powder
Table salt, to taste
½ cup plain yogurt, whipped
2 recipes Fenugreek-Flavored
    Meatballs (page 20)
½ cup water

1. In a large skillet, heat the vegetable oil. Add the bay leaves, cinnamon stick, cloves, black peppercorns, and cardamom pods. When the spices being to sizzle, add the onions. Stirring constantly, fry until the onions are golden brown, about 7 to 8 minutes. Add the Ginger-Garlic Paste and sauté for 1 minute.
2. Add the tomatoes and fry, stirring constantly, for 10 minutes or until the oil starts to separate from the mixture.
3. Add the Warm Spice Mix, red chili powder, turmeric powder, and salt; mix well. Add the yogurt and cook for about 4 minutes.
4. Add the water and bring to a boil. Reduce heat to low, cover, and simmer for about 10 minutes.
5. Add the meatballs and cook for 5 to 8 minutes. Serve hot.

❋ Using Bay Leaves

When using bay leaves, tear them and roughly crush them. They should be quite aromatic, sweet, and pungent. Don't use more than 1 or 2 leaves or the food will get an acrid and unpleasant taste. Always remove the bay leaves before serving—the leaf is inedible.

Peas and Minced-Meat Curry
(Kheema Mattar)

4 tablespoons vegetable oil
2 bay leaves
1 (1-inch) cinnamon stick
4 cloves
4 black peppercorns
2 black cardamom pods
2 medium-sized red onions,
   peeled and finely chopped
2 teaspoons Ginger-Garlic Paste
   (see recipe on page 13)

1¼ pounds minced lamb
2 small tomatoes, puréed
1 teaspoon Warm Spice Mix
   (see recipe on page 12)
½ teaspoon red chili powder
¼ teaspoon turmeric powder
Table salt, to taste
1 cup frozen peas, thawed

> **Serves 4**
> **Prep Time:** 10 minutes
> **Cook Time:** 50–55 minutes
>
> Make an extra batch and freeze it to make Ground Lamb, Peas, and Rice Casserole (page 170) at a later date.

1. In a large skillet, heat the vegetable oil. Add the bay leaves, cinnamon stick, cloves, black peppercorns, and cardamom pods. When the spices begin to sizzle, add the onions. Stirring constantly, fry until the onions are golden brown, about 7 to 8 minutes. Add the Ginger-Garlic Paste and sauté for 1 minute.

2. Add the lamb and sauté for about 10 to 12 minutes. Break up any lumps with the back of your spoon. Add the tomatoes and fry, stirring constantly, for 15 minutes or until the oil starts to separate from the sides of the mixture.

3. Add the spice mix, red chili powder, turmeric powder, and salt; mix well. Cook for about 2 minutes.

4. Add the peas and cook, covered, for another 15 minutes or until the peas and lamb are cooked through. Remove the cinnamon and black cardamoms. Serve hot.

Stone-Cooked Kebabs
(Pathar Pe Bane Kebab)

Serves 4
Prep Time: 20 minutes, plus 3 hours to marinate
Cook Time: 30 minutes

Originally, this recipe required cooking the lamb on heated slabs of stone. This version can be cooked in the oven, a skillet, or on the grill.

4 tablespoons vegetable oil, divided
1 medium-sized red onion, minced
½ cup plain yogurt, whipped
½ teaspoon Warm Spice Mix (see recipe on page 12)
2 teaspoons Ginger-Garlic Paste (see recipe on page 13)
Table salt, to taste
½ tablespoon dried mint
Juice of ½ lemon
1 pound boneless lean lamb

1. In a small skillet, heat 1 tablespoon of the vegetable oil. Add the minced onion and fry until well browned. Remove from heat and place in a bowl.
2. Add the yogurt, spice mix, ginger paste, salt, mint, and lemon juice to the onion mixture. Mix well and set aside.
3. Using a mallet, flatten the lamb. Cut into slices, about 2½ inches long and 1½ inches wide. The slices should be less than ¾ inch thick.
4. Add the lamb slices to the marinade and mix well. Cover, and marinate in the refrigerator for at least 3 hours.
5. In a medium-sized skillet, heat 1 tablespoon of the oil. Shake off excess marinade from lamb slices, and place 1 or 2 slices at a time in the skillet; cook until golden brown on each side, about 6 minutes. Ensure that the lamb is cooked through. Continue until all the lamb slices are cooked. Add more oil as needed.
6. Discard remaining marinade. Keep the lamb slices warm in a 200° oven, until ready to serve.

※ Lamb or Mutton?
In India, generally, meat means goat meat (which is also called "mutton" in India). It is much stronger in taste and flavor than lamb.

Hot Spiced Lamb
(Andhra Gosht Pittu)

1¼ pounds lean minced lamb
1 teaspoon grated fresh
   gingerroot
½ teaspoon red chili powder
1 teaspoon minced garlic
2 tablespoons plain yogurt,
   whipped
¼ teaspoon turmeric powder
1 serrano green chili, seeded
   and minced

½ cup water
3 tablespoons vegetable oil
1 large red onion, minced
¼ cup unsweetened desiccated
   coconut
Table salt, to taste
½ teaspoon Warm Spice Mix
   (see recipe on page 12)

Serves 4
Prep Time: 10 minutes
Cook Time: 1 hour

Andhra Pradesh, a state in southern India, is famous for its highly spiced meats. The Warm Spice Mix adds a nice zing to the dish.

1. In a deep pan, combine the lamb, ginger, red chili powder, garlic, yogurt, turmeric, and green chili. Add the water and bring to a boil. Cover and simmer over low heat for about 45 minutes or until the lamb is cooked through. Set aside.
2. In a large skillet, heat the vegetable oil. Add the onion and fry, stirring constantly, until well browned, about 8 minutes. Add the lamb and fry for another 4 to 5 minutes. Add the coconut and salt; sauté for another 5 minutes.
3. Serve hot, garnished with Warm Spice Mix.

※ Green Chili Lamb Chops

Here is a really easy recipe for instant lamb chops: In a bowl, combine equal portions of Green Chili Chutney (page 236) and Mint Chutney (page 235); add lamb chops and coat evenly with the marinade. Marinate for about 2 hours, and then cook according to your preference.

Royal Lamb
(Nawabi Gosht)

Serves 4
Prep Time: 20 minutes, plus 2 hours to marinate
Cook Time: 1 hour, 20 minutes

This typically difficult recipe is simplified here into easy, manageable steps. Serve hot with Simple Indian Bread (page 202).

1 large red onion, peeled
8 dried red chilies
1½ teaspoons fennel seeds
Water, as needed
2 teaspoons Ginger-Garlic Paste
(see recipe on page 13)
½ cup yogurt, whipped
1¼ pounds lean, bone-in lamb, cut into 1–1½-inch chunks
Vegetable oil for deep-frying

4 hard-boiled eggs, peeled and quartered
3 tablespoons Clarified Butter (see recipe on page 15)
Table salt, to taste
¼ teaspoon Roasted Saffron (see recipe on page 16)
Unsalted cashews, roasted

1. In a food processor, purée the onion, red chilies, and fennel seeds along with 1 or 2 tablespoons of water to make a paste. Set aside.
2. In a bowl, combine the Ginger-Garlic Paste, yogurt, and lamb; mix well. Refrigerate, covered, for 2 hours.
3. Heat the vegetable oil in a deep pan to about 300°. Deep-fry the eggs until crispy on the outside. Remove with a slotted spoon and place on a paper towel. Set aside.
4. In a large skillet, heat the butter. Add the paste made in step 1. Fry the paste until the oil separates from the onion mixture.
5. Add the lamb, along with the marinade, to the onion mixture. Fry, stirring constantly, for about 15 minutes. If the lamb sticks, add 1 tablespoon of water.
6. Add 1½ cups water and bring to a boil. Cover, and simmer for about 50 minutes or until the lamb is tender. Add the salt, saffron, and eggs. Cook, uncovered, for another 5 minutes. Serve garnished with unsalted roasted cashews.

Kakori Kebab
(Kakori Kebab)

1 pound minced lamb
2 tablespoons vegetable oil
* (if needed)*
5 tablespoons chickpea flour
2 tablespoons Fried Onions
* (see recipe on page 16),*
* roughly pounded*
1 teaspoon Warm Spice Mix
* (see recipe on page 12)*

¼ teaspoon baking soda
½ teaspoon red chili powder
Table salt, to taste
1 tablespoon ground cashews
Butter for basting

Serves 4
Prep Time: 15 minutes,
plus 3 hours to marinate
Cook Time: 20 minutes

These kebabs are
served on special
occasions and are tra-
ditionally made in the
shape of a sausage;
I like to shape mine
into small patties.

1. In a food processor, purée the minced lamb to a smooth paste, adding up to 2 tablespoons of oil to help with the puréeing if needed. Set aside.
2. In a small skillet on medium heat, dry roast the chickpea flour until fragrant. Set aside.
3. In a bowl, combine the lamb, chickpea flour, Fried Onions, spice mix, baking soda, red chili powder, salt, and ground cashews; mix well. Refrigerate, covered, for about 3 hours.
4. Preheat oven to 350°.
5. Using your hands, create equal-sized small patties with the lamb mix-ture, flattening them between the palms of your hands. You should get about 8 patties. Place the lamb patties on a foil-lined baking sheet and bake for about 10 minutes. Turn once and baste with butter. Roast for another 10 minutes or until golden brown and the juices run clear. Serve hot.

Spicy Minced Lamb Kebabs
(Shammi Kebab)

Serves 4
Prep Time: 20 minutes, plus 30 minutes to soak
Cook Time: 40 minutes

You can also freeze these just prior to the frying step. Let them thaw to room temperature just before you are ready to fry.

½ cup chana dal or yellow split peas
1 pound minced lamb
3 tablespoons Ginger-Garlic Paste (see recipe on page 13)
1 medium-sized red onion, sliced
1 teaspoon cumin seeds
2 cloves
2 green cardamom pods
Table salt, to taste
1 teaspoon red chili powder
2 tablespoons chickpea flour
Vegetable oil for frying
Chaat Spice Mix (see recipe on page 14)

1. Soak the *chana dal* in hot water for about 30 minutes. Drain.
2. In a deep pan, combine the *chana dal*, lamb, Ginger-Garlic Paste, onions, cumin, cloves, cardamom, red chili powder, chickpea flour, and salt. Add enough water to cover the mixture and bring to a full boil. Cover, lower heat, and cook until the lamb is cooked through, about 30 minutes. Remove the cover and cook on high heat until all the liquid dries out.
3. Remove from heat and cool to room temperature.
4. In a food processor, grind the lamb mixture to a fine paste. Divide the mixture into 8 small patties, flattening them between the palms of your hands.
5. In a medium-sized skillet, heat about 5 tablespoons of oil. Add the patties and pan-fry until golden brown on all sides. Remove with a slotted spatula and drain on paper towels. Serve hot, sprinkled with Chaat Spice Mix.

❋ Cardamom Pods

There are two primary types of cardamom used in India—one is a smaller green one and the other is larger and black. The smaller variety is used to flavor savory and sweet dishes. The black variety is used primarily in savory dishes. Buy the pods whole and remove the seeds as needed to get the freshest flavor. Occasionally, at your grocer you will see "white cardamom"—this is nothing but the green cardamom that has been bleached.

Ginger-Flavored Lamb Chops
(Adraki Chaampe)

1 teaspoon cumin, roasted and
   roughly pounded
1½ tablespoons grated fresh
   gingerroot
2 teaspoons Warm Spice Mix
   (see recipe on page 12)

1 cup heavy cream
Table salt, to taste
8 lamb chops, no visible fat
Oil for basting

Serves 4
Prep Time: 5 minutes,
plus 4 hours to marinate
Cook Time: 30 minutes

If you like ginger, you
will love these chops.
Serve with Shredded
Carrot Salad (page 68).

1. In a bowl or resealable plastic bag, combine the cumin, ginger, spice mix, cream, and salt; mix well. Add the lamb chops and mix to coat evenly with the marinade. Cover, and refrigerate for 4 hours.
2. Preheat oven to 350°. Place the lamb chops in a single layer in a roasting pan. Bake for 10 to 15 minutes. Baste with oil. Bake for another 10 to 15 minutes or until the lamb is cooked through.

Macaroni Lamb
(Macroni Gosht Wali)

4 tablespoons vegetable oil
2 teaspoons Ginger-Garlic Paste
   (see recipe on page 13)
1¼ pounds minced lamb
2 small tomatoes, puréed

1 teaspoon Warm Spice Mix
   (see recipe on page 12)
½ teaspoon red chili powder
¼ teaspoon turmeric powder
Table salt, to taste
1 cup cooked elbow macaroni

Serves 4
Prep Time: 20 minutes
Cook Time: 50 minutes

Try serving this with
fresh French bread
and a light spinach
salad.

1. In a large skillet, heat the vegetable oil. Add the Ginger-Garlic Paste and sauté for 10 seconds. Add the lamb and sauté for about 10 to 12 minutes. Add the tomatoes and fry, stirring frequently, for 25 minutes or until the oil starts to separate from the sides of the mixture.
2. Add the spice mix, red chili powder, turmeric powder, and salt. Mix well. Cook for about 2 minutes. Add the macaroni and cook, covered, for another 10 minutes or until the lamb is cooked through.

Cardamom-Flavored Lamb
(Eliachi Gosht)

Serves 4
Prep Time: 10 minutes
Cook Time: 1 hour,
30 minutes

Fragrant cardamom pods and powder perfume this dish. Adjust the amount of cardamom to your taste. Serve with warm Simple Indian Bread (page 202).

¼ cup blanched almonds
3 tablespoons vegetable oil
1 large red onion, minced
2 serrano green chilies, seeded and minced
4 green cardamom pods, bruised
1 pound lean lamb chunks

½ cup plain yogurt
1 cup water
2 tablespoons cream
Table salt, to taste
1 teaspoon cardamom powder

1. In a food processor, combine the almonds with a few tablespoons of water to make a thick, coarse paste. Set aside.
2. In a large pan, heat the vegetable oil. Add the onion and sauté until golden brown, about 7 to 8 minutes. Add the green chilies, cardamom pods, and lamb; sauté for about 25 minutes. If the lamb starts to stick to the pan, add about 1 tablespoon of water.
3. Add the yogurt and fry for 5 minutes. Add the almond paste, then add the water and bring to a full boil. Cover, lower heat, and cook for about 50 minutes or until the lamb is tender and cooked through.
4. Add the cream and mix well. Simmer for about 5 minutes. Add salt to taste. Sprinkle with the cardamom powder and serve hot.

☀ Cardamom Powder
Most stores sell this fragrant powder. Use a little at a time—it goes a long way. If you want to make your own, here is a simple recipe: Open the cardamom pods. Remove the seeds and discard the shells. In a spice grinder, grind the seeds to a fine powder. Store in an airtight jar.

Fiery Pork
(Pork Balchao)

½ teaspoon black peppercorns
5 cloves
½ teaspoon cumin seeds
6 dried red chilies
1 tablespoon Ginger-Garlic Paste (see recipe on page 13)
½ cup malt vinegar

4 tablespoons vegetable oil
1 pound lean pork, cut into chunks
1 large red onion, finely chopped
2 small tomatoes, finely chopped
1 tablespoon sugar
Table salt, to taste

Serves 4
Prep Time: 15 minutes
Cook Time: 40 minutes

This tangy pork dish will taste better a couple of days after it is prepared, once the spices are allowed to work their magic.

1. In a spice grinder, grind the black peppercorns, cloves, cumin, and red chilies. Put the spice mixture into a food processor or blender and add the Ginger-Garlic Paste and malt vinegar; process until smooth. Set aside.
2. Heat the oil in a large skillet, add the pork, and sear it until brown on all sides. Remove the pork with a slotted spoon and place on paper towels to drain. Do not discard the oil from the skillet.
3. Reheat the oil and add the onions. Sauté for about 7 to 8 minutes or until the onions are well browned. Add the tomatoes and fry, stirring constantly, until the oil starts to separate from the mixture.
4. Add the pork and mix well; stirring constantly, fry for about 6 minutes.
5. Add the sugar and salt; mix well. Fry for about 5 minutes, stirring constantly. Serve hot.

✳ The Mutiny

Pork is forbidden by many religious sects in India. During the British rule in India, there was a mutiny around the 1850s, when Indian soldiers refused to use the pork grease that was used for oiling rifles. The Christians of Goa, in western India, eat pork regularly.

Pork Bafat
(Pork Bafat)

Serves 4
Prep Time: 5 minutes
Cook Time: 30–40 minutes

Another Goan-inspired dish, this is fiery hot. Add more chilies if you like your dishes really hot!

1 tablespoon Ginger-Garlic Paste (see recipe on page 13)
4 black peppercorns
4 cloves
1 teaspoon cumin seeds
1/4 teaspoon black mustard seeds
8 dried red chilies
1/4 cup malt vinegar
4 tablespoons vegetable oil
1 pound pork, cubed
1 tablespoon tamarind pulp, soaked in 1/4 cup hot water for 10 minutes
1 cup frozen pearl onions
Table salt, to taste
Water, as needed

1. In a food processor, grind together the Ginger-Garlic Paste, black peppercorns, cloves, cumin seeds, mustard seeds, red chilies, and malt vinegar. Set aside.
2. In a large skillet, heat the vegetable oil; add the pork and brown on all sides, about 8 to 10 minutes. Add the ground paste and sauté for 10 more minutes.
3. Strain the tamarind and discard the residue. Add the strained liquid to the pork and mix well. Add the frozen onions and salt; cook, uncovered, for about 5 minutes.
4. Add ½ cup of water. Lower the heat and simmer, uncovered, until the pork is cooked, about 10 to 15 minutes. Stir occasionally. Add more water if the dish becomes too dry or starts to stick. Serve hot.

❈ Need a Quick, Healthy Pick-Me-Up?

Try dates. The kind you eat! A single serving of dates (5 to 6 pieces) contains over 30 grams of carbohydrates, making them a powerhouse of energy.

CHAPTER 9
From the Fisherman's Net (Machwari Ke Jal Se)

Fish in a Velvety Sauce
(Bengali Doi Maach)

Serves 4
Prep Time: 20 minutes
Cook Time: 30 minutes

For this recipe, you can use tilapia or catfish. Serve this with Simple Basmati Rice (page 160).

4–5 catfish filets
3/4 teaspoon turmeric powder
8 tablespoons vegetable oil, divided
1 bay leaf
1/2 teaspoon cumin seeds
2 teaspoons Ginger-Garlic Paste (see recipe on page 13)

1 large red onion, minced
1 teaspoon red chili powder
2 serrano green chilies, seeded and minced
1/2 cup plain yogurt, whipped
Table salt, to taste
Water, as needed

1. Place the catfish filets in a bowl. Rub the filets well with the turmeric and set aside for about 10 minutes. Rinse the filets and pat dry.
2. In a medium-sized skillet, heat 6 tablespoons of the vegetable oil. Add 1 filet at a time and fry until brown on both sides. Remove from heat with a slotted spoon and drain on a paper towel. Continue until all the filets are fried. Set aside.
3. In a large skillet, heat the remaining 2 tablespoons of vegetable oil. Add the bay leaf and cumin seeds. When the spices begin to sizzle, add the Ginger-Garlic Paste and onions; sauté for about 7 to 8 minutes or until the onions are well browned.
4. Add the red chili powder and green chilies; mix well. Add the yogurt and salt, and mix well. Add about 1/2 cup of water. Simmer, uncovered, on low heat for about 10 minutes, stirring constantly.
5. Add the fish filets and simmer for another 5 minutes. Be careful not to break the filets when you stir. Serve hot.

❋ Green Chilies

Wear gloves when handling fresh chilies. They can be quite unforgiving if they get on your hands. I often use kitchen scissors instead of a knife to snip the chilies.

Shrimp in Coconut Milk
(Chingri Maacher Malai Curry)

1 bay leaf
1 teaspoon cumin seeds
1 (1-inch) cinnamon stick
2 cloves
4 black peppercorns
1-inch piece fresh gingerroot,
    peeled and sliced
4 garlic cloves
Water, as needed

3 tablespoons vegetable oil
1 large red onion, minced
½ teaspoon turmeric powder
1 pound shrimp, peeled and
    deveined
1 (14-ounce) can light coconut
    milk
Table salt, to taste

Serves 4
Prep Time: 10 minutes
Cook Time: 20 minutes

A nice variation is to fry the shrimp first. It adds a nice crispness. Serve with steamed white rice.

1. In a spice grinder, roughly grind the bay leaf, cumin seeds, cinnamon stick, cloves, peppercorns, ginger, and garlic. Add 1 tablespoon of water if needed.
2. In a medium-sized skillet, heat the vegetable oil. Add the ground spice mixture and sauté for about 1 minute. Add the onions and sauté for 7 to 8 minutes or until the onions are well browned.
3. Add the turmeric and mix well. Add the shrimp and sauté for about 2 to 3 minutes, until no longer pink.
4. Add the coconut milk and salt. Simmer for 10 minutes or until the gravy starts to thicken. Remove from heat and serve hot.

❄ Defrosting Frozen Shrimp

If you are using frozen shrimp, thaw them in the refrigerator or under running cold water. It is not advisable to defrost shrimp in the microwave or at room temperature—doing so will cause the shrimp to lose a lot of flavor and texture.

Fish Fry
(Mom's Tali Macchi)

Serves 4
Prep Time: 10 minutes
Cook Time: 15 minutes

Serve this with Mint-Cilantro Chutney, Spicy Papaya Salad, and Mixed Fruit Juice (pages 224, 56, and 44) for a complete, light summertime meal.

2 teaspoons turmeric powder
2 dried red chilies, crushed
2 teaspoons coriander seeds, roughly pounded
2 garlic cloves, minced
1 teaspoon Warm Spice Mix (see recipe on page 12)
Table salt, to taste

3 heaping tablespoons all-purpose flour
4 whitefish filets (such as tilapia, catfish, cod)
4 tablespoons oil
1 tablespoon fresh lemon juice

1. In a shallow dish, combine the turmeric, red chilies, coriander, garlic, and spice mix; mix well.
2. In a second dish, combine the salt and flour; mix well.
3. Coat each filet lightly, first with the spice mix and then with the flour. Discard any remaining spice mix and flour.
4. Heat the vegetable oil in a medium skillet. Fry each filet, 1 at a time, for about 3 to 4 minutes or until golden brown on each side. Drain on a paper towel. Serve immediately, sprinkled with lemon juice.

❊ Getting Rid of Fishy Smells

Soak fish for 1 hour in milk or let frozen fish thaw in milk. This will not only freshen the fish and enhance the taste but will also remove any smell.

Tandoori Fish
(Tandoori Macchi)

3 teaspoons Ginger-Garlic Paste
    (see recipe on page 13)
4 tablespoons heavy cream
1 teaspoon cumin seeds
1 teaspoon red chili powder
½ teaspoon turmeric powder
½ teaspoon Tandoori Spice Mix
    (see recipe on page 13)
½ teaspoon carom seeds
1 egg
Table salt, to taste
4 whitefish filets (such as
    tilapia, catfish, cod)
Oil for basting
Fresh lemon juice

Serves 4
Prep Time: 5 minutes,
plus 1 hour to marinate
Cook Time: 15 minutes

Serve with the Punjabi
Onion Salad, Green
Chili Chutney, and an
ice-cold Watermelon
Cooler (pages 66,
236, and 45).

1. In a bowl, combine the ginger paste, cream, cumin seeds, red chili powder, turmeric, spice mix, carom seeds, egg, and salt; mix well.
2. Pour the marinade over the fish filets, turning them to ensure that they are well coated. Refrigerate, covered, for about 1 hour.
3. Preheat oven to 350°.
4. Bake for about 7 minutes on each side, basting once with oil. Serve hot, sprinkled with lemon juice.

☀ Chutney Reruns
Use leftover chutneys as a topping for grilled fish. A grilled trout topped with a Mint-Cilantro Chutney is a mouthwatering combination.

Creamy Shrimp
(Malai Jhinga)

Serves 4
Prep Time: 15 minutes
Cook Time: 20 minutes

Start cooking the tomatoes while the shrimp is marinating. Serve with warmed store-bought pita or steamed white rice.

1 pound shrimp, peeled and deveined
1 teaspoon turmeric powder, divided
3 tablespoons vegetable oil
2 teaspoons Ginger-Garlic Paste (see recipe on page 13)
2 medium tomatoes, chopped

Water, as needed
1 teaspoon red chili powder
2 teaspoons coriander powder
Table salt, to taste
4 tablespoons light cream

1. Place the shrimp in a bowl. Rub about ¾ teaspoon of the turmeric on the shrimp and set aside for about 10 minutes. Rinse them well and pat dry.
2. In a large skillet, heat the vegetable oil. Add the Ginger-Garlic Paste and sauté for about 30 seconds. Add the tomatoes and sauté for 7 to 8 minutes or until the oil begins to separate from the tomatoes. Add 1 tablespoon of water if the mixture appears to be sticking.
3. Add the remaining turmeric, the red chili powder, coriander powder, and salt; mix well. Sauté for 1 minute.
4. Add 1 cup of water and bring to a boil. Reduce the heat and simmer, covered, for about 5 minutes. Add the shrimp. Cook for about 5 to 6 minutes or until the shrimp are cooked through.
5. Remove from heat and add the light cream; mix well. Serve hot.

✴ Cilantro or Coriander?

People often confuse these two spices, but they are not the same. Cilantro is the plant, and coriander is the seeds. I store my cilantro wrapped in newspaper in the refrigerator. The newspaper helps absorb any excess moisture, keeping the cilantro fresh for a longer period of time.

Shrimp Koliwada
(Jhinga Koliwada)

*1 pound medium shrimp,
   peeled and deveined*
¾ teaspoon turmeric powder
*1 teaspoon grated fresh
   gingerroot*
1 teaspoon minced fresh garlic
1 teaspoon red chili powder
*1 teaspoon Warm Spice Mix
   (see recipe on page 12)*

*½ teaspoon dried mango
   powder*
½ teaspoon carom seeds
4 tablespoons corn flour
Water, as needed
Vegetable oil for deep-frying

Serves 4
Prep Time: 15 minutes
and 20 minutes
to marinate
Cook Time: 15 minutes

Named for a suburb
of Mumbai, Koliwada-
style dishes are a
delight to the palate.
Serve with your
choice of chutney.

1. Place the shrimp in a bowl. Rub the turmeric on the shrimp and set aside for about 10 minutes. Rinse them well and pat dry.
2. In a bowl, combine the ginger, garlic, red chili powder, spice mix, mango powder, carom seeds, and corn flour. Add enough water to make a batter of coating consistency. Add the shrimp to the batter and marinate for about 20 minutes.
3. Heat the vegetable oil in a deep fryer or a deep pan to 300° on a deep-fry thermometer. Add a few shrimp and deep-fry until golden brown and crisp on all sides. Remove from the oil with a slotted spoon and drain on a paper towel. Let the oil return to temperature. Continue until all the shrimp are fried. Discard any remaining marinade. Serve immediately.

❖ Spices as Medicine

Indian cuisine rests on the shoulders of ancient medicine. Each spice or herb that is used is deemed to have value in the world of medicine. For example, turmeric is an antiseptic, and cumin and carom seeds aid in digestion.

Shrimp Jalfrezi Style
(Jhinga Jalfrezi)

Serves 4
Prep Time: 10 minutes
Cook Time: 10 minutes

Don't let the unusual name of the dish scare you away. You can also make this with chicken or Indian Cheese (page 12).

3 tablespoons vegetable oil
½ teaspoon cumin seeds
3 dried red chilies, broken
3 serrano green chilies, slit down the sides and seeded
1 large red onion, peeled and diced
1 large tomato, deseeded and diced
2 medium bell peppers, deseeded and diced
2-inch piece fresh gingerroot, julienned
½ cup tomato purée
1 pound medium shrimp, peeled and deveined
½ teaspoon turmeric powder
Table salt, to taste

1. In a medium-sized skillet, heat the vegetable oil. Add the cumin seeds; when they begin to sizzle, add the red and green chilies, onion, diced tomato, ginger, and bell peppers in quick succession. Sauté on high heat for about 2 minutes.
2. Add the tomato purée and cook for 3 to 4 minutes.
3. Add the shrimp, turmeric, and salt; sauté for 3 to 4 minutes or until the shrimp are cooked through. The vegetables will still have a slight crunch to them. Serve hot.

❊ Monday Night Grilled Shrimp

Marinate shrimp in yogurt along with grated ginger, Warm Spice Mix (page 12), fresh minced mint, lemon juice, salt, and red chili powder. Grill and serve hot.

Kerala Fish Curry
(Meen Moilee)

4–5 whitefish filets (such as tilapia, catfish, or cod)
1 teaspoon turmeric powder
6 tablespoons vegetable oil
½ teaspoon black mustard seeds
2 green cardamom pods, bruised
2 cloves
8 fresh curry leaves

1 large red onion, finely chopped
1 teaspoon grated fresh gingerroot
Table salt, to taste
1 teaspoon red chili powder
¼ teaspoon turmeric powder
1 teaspoon coriander powder
1 (14-ounce) can light coconut milk

> **Serves 4**
> **Prep Time:** 15 minutes
> **Cook Time:** 35–40 minutes
>
> This popular dish comes to you from the gorgeous state of Kerala on the west coast of India. Serve with Simple Basmati Rice (page 160).

1. Place the fish filets in a bowl. Rub the filets well with the turmeric and set aside for about 10 minutes. Rinse the filets and pat dry.

2. In a medium-sized nonstick skillet, heat 4 tablespoons of the vegetable oil. Add 1 filet at a time and shallow-fry until brown on both sides. Remove from the skillet with a slotted spoon and drain on a paper towel. Continue until all the filets are fried. Set aside.

3. In a large skillet, heat the remaining vegetable oil. Add the mustard seeds, cardamom, and cloves. As soon as they begin to sputter, add the curry leaves, onions, and ginger; sauté for 7 to 8 minutes or until the onions are well browned.

4. Reduce heat. Add the salt; red chili, turmeric, and coriander powder; sauté for 1 minute. Add the coconut milk and simmer for about 10 minutes. Don't let the coconut milk boil.

5. Add the fried fish to the coconut curry and spoon the sauce over the fish. Simmer for 5 to 7 minutes or until the fish is completely heated through. Serve hot.

Shrimp Patio
(Kolmino Patio)

Serves 4
Prep Time: 10 minutes
Cook Time: 15 minutes

Serve with Simple Basmati Rice (page 160). You can substitute brown sugar for jaggery if you like.

3 dried red chilies
2 teaspoons coriander seeds
1 teaspoon cumin seeds
1 teaspoon mustard seeds
4 fresh garlic cloves
1/4 teaspoon black peppercorns
1 (1-inch) cinnamon stick
1/2 teaspoon turmeric powder
1/2 teaspoon red chili powder

1/4 cup white vinegar
Water, as needed
3 tablespoons vegetable oil
1 large red onion, minced
1 1/2 pounds shrimp, peeled and deveined
1 tablespoon jaggery or brown sugar
Table salt, to taste

1. In a spice grinder, grind together the red chilies, coriander seeds, cumin seeds, mustard seeds, cloves, black peppercorns, and cinnamon, as finely as possible. Place in a glass bowl and add the turmeric, red chili powder, and vinegar; mix well. If you need more liquid, add a little water. Set aside.
2. In a large skillet, heat the vegetable oil. Add the onions and sauté for about 7 to 8 minutes or until the onions are well browned. Add the spice paste from step 1 and cook for 1 minute. Add the shrimp and cook for 2 to 3 minutes.
3. Add the jaggery and salt. Add about 1 cup of water. Bring to a boil. Reduce heat and simmer for 2 minutes. Serve hot.

❊ Deveining Shrimp
To devein shrimp, run the tip of a small knife down the back of the shrimp. Use the tip of the knife or your finger to pull out the vein. Make sure you rinse all the shrimp after deveining.

Fried Fish
(Amritsari Tali Macchi)

1 cup chickpea flour
1 teaspoon carom seeds
1 teaspoon red chili powder
2 tablespoons Ginger-Garlic Paste
(see recipe on page 13)
1½ tablespoons lemon juice
Table salt, to taste

Water, as needed
2 pounds whitefish chunks
(such as tilapia, catfish, cod)
Vegetable oil for deep-frying
Chaat Spice Mix (see recipe
on page 14)

Serves 4
Prep Time: 5 minutes,
plus 25 minutes
to marinate
Cook Time: 20 minutes

This crispy fish is a North Indian favorite. Named for the holy city of Amritsar, it is served garnished with cilantro leaves and sliced onions.

1. In a large bowl, combine the chickpea flour, carom seeds, red chili powder, Ginger-Garlic Paste, lemon juice, and salt. Add water as needed to make a thick batter. Mix well and make sure there are no lumps.
2. Add the fish pieces to the batter. Combine to ensure that the fish is well coated. Let stand for about 25 minutes.
3. In a deep pan, heat the vegetable oil to 300°. Deep-fry a few pieces at a time until crisp and golden brown. Remove with a slotted spoon (tongs also work well here) and drain on a paper towel. Continue until all the pieces are fried. Discard any remaining batter.
4. Serve immediately, sprinkled with Chaat Spice Mix.

☼ Ugadi—The Day of Creation

Raw or green mangoes hold a special significance during the Indian festival of Ugadi. Ugadi pachchadi, a dish made with jaggery, raw mango pieces, bitter neem leaves, and tangy tamarind, is said to be reflective of one's real life—a combination of sweet, sour, and bitter tastes.

Kashmiri Fish Curry
(Kashmiri Macchi)

Serves 4
Prep Time: 15 minutes
Cook Time: 20 minutes

Traditional Kashmiri cooking uses dried ginger powder, but I like the taste of fresh ginger.

4–5 whitefish filets (such as tilapia, catfish, or cod)
¾ teaspoon turmeric powder
1 teaspoon ginger, finely ground
1 teaspoon anise seeds, roughly pounded

4 tablespoons vegetable oil
1 teaspoon red chili powder
2 teaspoons coriander powder
Table salt, to taste
1 cup plain yogurt, whipped

1. Place the fish filets in a bowl. Rub the filets well with the turmeric, ginger, and anise seeds; set aside for about 10 minutes.
2. In a medium-sized skillet, heat the vegetable oil. Add 1 filet at a time and shallow-fry until brown on both sides. Remove from the skillet with a slotted spoon and drain on paper towels. Continue until all the filets are fried. Set aside. Keep the oil.
3. In the same skillet (with the oil) on low heat, add the red chili powder, coriander, and salt; mix well. Add the yogurt (it will appear to curdle a bit, but continue to cook it).
4. Simmer on low heat for about 10 minutes. The oil will begin to separate from the yogurt. Add the fried fish.
5. Cover and simmer on low heat until the fish is completely heated through. Serve hot.

❋ Tips on Buying Whole Fish
When buying whole fish, look for fish with bright eyes. The flesh should be shiny and bounce back to the touch.

Grilled Yogurt-Flavored Fish
(Dahi Macchi Tikka)

1 pound whitefish, cut in chunks
¾ teaspoon turmeric powder
¾ cup Hung Yogurt (see recipe on page 14)
¼ cup heavy cream
2 teaspoons Ginger-Garlic Paste (see recipe on page 13)

1 teaspoon Warm Spice Mix (see recipe on page 12)
Table salt, to taste
Oil for basting
1 teaspoon Chaat Spice Mix (see recipe on page 14), for garnish

> **Serves 4**
> **Prep Time:** 15 minutes, plus 2 hours to marinate
> **Cook Time:** 15 minutes
>
> This delicately flavored grilled fish can be served as an appetizer or an entrée. Serve with spicy Green Chili Chutney (page 236).

1. Place the fish chunks in a bowl. Rub them well with the turmeric and set aside for about 10 minutes. Rinse and pat dry
2. In a bowl, combine the yogurt, cream, Ginger-Garlic Paste, Warm Spice Mix, salt, fish, and mix well. Refrigerate, covered, for 2 hours.
3. Preheat oven to 350°.
4. Place the fish in a single layer on a roasting pan. Bake in the oven, basting once, for 10 to 15 minutes or until the fish is cooked through. (Alternatively, you can skewer the fish and grill it.) Serve hot, sprinkled with Chaat Spice Mix.

❋ Garlic Flavor

To get the true strong flavor of garlic cloves, crush them with the flat of your knife blade or use a garlic press. Chopping or mincing them with a knife will not release the depth of flavor that you will get from crushing them.

Parsi Fish
(Patrani Macchi)

Serves 4
Prep Time: 10 minutes
Cook Time: 20–30 minutes

A perfect recipe when you have lots of leftover chutney and very little time. Serve with plain white rice.

4 (1-inch-thick) fish steaks (your choice of type)
¾ teaspoon turmeric powder

8 tablespoons Green Chili and Coconut Chutney (see recipe on page 225)

1. Place the fish steaks in a bowl. Rub the steaks well with the turmeric and set aside for about 10 minutes. Rinse and pat dry.
2. Cut 4 squares of aluminum foil large enough to accommodate the steaks. Place a steak in the center of each piece of foil. Cover the fish with 2 generous tablespoons of the chutney. Fold the foil over it as if you were wrapping a present. Leave a little room for the steam to expand.
3. Preheat the oven to 400°.
4. Place the foil packages on a baking sheet. Bake until the fish is completely cooked through (20 to 25 minutes for 1-inch-thick steaks). The timing will depend on the thickness of your steak. Serve hot.

✵ Crunchy Bread Fritters Stuffed with Tuna
Using the recipe for Crunchy Bread Fritters (page 32), stuff the fritters with tuna prior to frying. You can season the tuna with red chili powder and roasted cumin seeds prior to stuffing.

Fish Kebabs
(Kebab Macchi Ke)

2 teaspoons turmeric powder
2 dried red chilies, crushed
2 serrano green chilies, seeded
* and minced*
2 eggs, beaten
Table salt, to taste

4 heaping tablespoons semolina
4 small whitefish filets
4 tablespoons oil
1 tablespoon fresh lemon juice

Serves 4
Prep Time: 10 minutes
Cook Time: 15 minutes

Refrigerating the filets for a few minutes before you fry will make the coating stay on better. Serve with Mint-Cilantro Chutney (page 224).

1. In a shallow dish, combine the turmeric, red chilies, green chilies, eggs, and salt; mix well. Place the semolina in a second shallow dish.
2. Coat each filet lightly, first with the spice mix and then with the semolina. Discard any remaining spice mix and semolina.
3. Heat the vegetable oil in a medium-sized skillet. Fry each filet, 1 at a time, for about 3 to 4 minutes or until golden brown on each side. Drain on a paper towel. Serve immediately, sprinkled with lemon juice.

❋ Semolina

Semolina, called rava or sooji in India, is used for preparing sweet and savory dishes. Buy the coarse variety. You can also substitute cream of wheat in a pinch for all the recipes indicated in this book (unless otherwise specified).

Shrimp Fritters
(Jhinge Ke Pakore)

Serves 4
Prep Time: 15 minutes
Cook Time: 10 minutes

These butterflied shrimp are perfect with cocktails or as an entrée for a light summer lunch.

1 pound shrimp, tail on and deveined
1 teaspoon turmeric powder
1 teaspoon red chili powder
1 serrano green chili, seeded and minced
1 tablespoon grated fresh gingerroot
1 tablespoon minced fresh garlic cloves
1 tablespoon fresh lemon juice
Table salt, to taste
2 eggs, beaten
3 heaping tablespoons all-purpose flour
Vegetable oil for deep-frying

1. Butterfly the shrimp and set aside.
2. In a shallow bowl, combine the turmeric, red chili powder, green chili, ginger, garlic, lemon juice, and salt; mix well.
3. Place the eggs in a second dish. Place the flour in a shallow dish.
4. Coat each shrimp with the spice mixture, then dip in the egg, and then coat with the flour. Continue until all the shrimp are coated. Discard any remaining eggs and flour.
5. Heat the vegetable oil in a deep fryer or a deep pan to 350°. Deep-fry the shrimp, a few at a time, until golden brown. Remove with a slotted spoon and drain on paper towels. Serve hot.

❊ Butterfly Shrimp

To butterfly the shrimp: Devein the shrimp, but leave the tail on. Using the flat blade of a knife, press down gently along the cut you made to remove the vein until the shrimp halves are opened flat, but still connected. Don't press too hard or you will split the shrimp in two!

CHAPTER 9: FROM THE FISHERMAN'S NET

Tamarind Fish Curry
(Imli Wale Macchi)

1½ pounds, whitefish, cut into chunks

¾ teaspoon and ½ teaspoon turmeric powder

2 teaspoons tamarind pulp, soaked in ¼ cup hot water for 10 minutes

3 tablespoons vegetable oil

½ teaspoon black mustard seeds

¼ teaspoon fenugreek seeds

8 fresh curry leaves

1 large onion, minced

2 serrano green chilies, seeded and minced

2 small tomatoes, chopped

2 dried red chilies, roughly pounded

1 teaspoon coriander seeds, roughly pounded

½ cup unsweetened desiccated coconut

Table salt, to taste

1 cup water

Serves 4
Prep Time: 15 minutes
Cook Time: 35 minutes

If you do not have tamarind, add a bit of lemon juice for a flavor that is similar. Serve with Simple Basmati Rice (page 160).

1. Place the fish in a bowl. Rub well with the ¾ teaspoon turmeric and set aside for about 10 minutes. Rinse and pat dry.
2. Strain the tamarind and set the liquid aside. Discard the residue.
3. In a large skillet, heat the vegetable oil. Add the mustard seeds and fenugreek seeds. When they begin to sputter, add the curry leaves, onions, and green chilies. Sauté for 7 to 8 minutes or until the onions are well browned.
4. Add the tomatoes and cook for another 8 minutes or until the oil begins to separate from the sides of the mixture. Add the remaining ½ teaspoon turmeric, the red chilies, coriander seeds, coconut, and salt; mix well, and cook for another 30 seconds.
5. Add the water and the strained tamarind; bring to a boil. Lower the heat and add the fish. Cook on low heat for 10 to 15 minutes or until the fish is completely cooked. Serve hot.

Chili Scallops
(Mirchi Wale Scallops)

Serves 4
Prep Time: 10 minutes
Cook Time: 25 minutes

Red chili sambal brings a fiery flavor to the scallops. If you do not have sambal, grind a few dried red chilies along with some water.

1 pound sea scallops (or cubed
   whitefish of your choice)
1 tablespoon red chili sambal
3 tablespoons vegetable oil
½ teaspoon mustard seeds
8 fresh curry leaves
2 teaspoons Ginger-Garlic Paste
   (see recipe on page 13)

2 small tomatoes, chopped
½ teaspoon turmeric powder
Table salt, to taste
Water, as needed
Coconut milk, for garnish

1. In a bowl, combine the scallops and the sambal. (If you are using dried red chilies instead, add 2 teaspoons of oil as well.) Set aside for 15 minutes.
2. While the scallops are marinating, heat the vegetable oil in a medium-sized skillet. Add the mustard seeds; when they begin to sputter, add the curry leaves, ginger paste, and tomatoes. Sauté for about 8 minutes or until the oil begins to separate from the sides of the mixture.
3. Add the turmeric and salt and stir well.
4. Add about 1 cup of water and cook, uncovered, for 10 minutes. Add the scallops (along with all the red chili sambal) and cook on medium heat until the scallops are cooked through, about 5 minutes.
5. Garnish with the coconut milk and serve hot.

❈ Homemade Coconut Milk
A quick way to make coconut milk is to blend coconut cream with hot water. You can also blend unsweetened desiccated coconut or fresh coconut with hot water, but just be sure to strain before use.

Malabari Chili Fish
(Malabari Mirchi Wali Macchi)

*1 pound whitefish, cut into
 1- to 1½-inch chunks
¾ teaspoon turmeric powder
Juice of ½ lemon
1 teaspoon coriander powder
1 teaspoon cumin powder
¼ teaspoon black peppercorns,
 roughly pounded*

*4 dried red chilies, roughly
 pounded
Table salt, to taste
Vegetable oil for deep-frying
Chaat Spice Mix (see recipe
 on page 14), optional*

Serves 4
Prep Time: 15 minutes
plus 2 hours to marinate
Cook Time: 20 minutes

For an extra zing,
serve this dish with
Green Chili Chutney
(page 236).

1. Place the fish cubes in a bowl. Rub them well with the turmeric and set aside for about 10 minutes. Rinse the fish and pat dry.
2. In a bowl, combine the lemon juice, coriander powder, cumin powder, black pepper, red chilies, and salt; mix well. Add the fish and mix to ensure that all the pieces are well coated. Refrigerate, covered, for 2 hours.
3. Heat the vegetable oil in a deep fryer or a deep pan to 350°. Deep-fry a few pieces of fish at a time. Remove from the oil with a slotted spoon and drain on a paper towel. Continue until all the fish is fried. Discard any remaining marinade. Serve immediately. Sprinkle Chaat Spice Mix on the fish just prior to serving, if desired.

❈ How Hot Is This Chili Pepper?

Generally, the smaller they are, the hotter they are. The color of the peppers is not indicative of the heat of the pepper. You can deseed the peppers before using to remove the heat and retain the flavor.

Green Chili Fish
(Hari Mirch Ki Macchi)

Serves 4
Prep Time: 10 minutes
Cook Time: 20 minutes

If you are not a fan of cilantro, you can use fresh mint. Be sure to seed the chilies if you like your fish mild.

1½ pounds whitefish (such as tilapia, catfish, or cod), cut into 1- to 1½-inch chunks
¾ teaspoon turmeric powder
6 serrano green chilies
1 packed cup cilantro
2 tablespoons unsweetened desiccated coconut
Table salt, to taste
Juice of 1 lemon
¼ teaspoon red chili powder
2 teaspoons Ginger-Garlic Paste (see recipe on page 13)
4 tablespoons Hung Yogurt (see recipe on page 14)
Vegetable oil for deep-frying
1 teaspoon Chaat Spice Mix (see recipe on page 14), for garnish

1. Place the fish in a bowl. Rub well with the turmeric and set aside for about 10 minutes. Rinse and pat dry.
2. In a blender or food processor, purée the green chilies, cilantro, coconut, salt, lemon juice, red chili powder, ginger paste, and yogurt to form a paste.
3. In a bowl, combine the green chili paste with the fish. Mix well to ensure that the fish is well coated with the paste.
4. Heat the vegetable oil in a deep fryer or a deep pan to 350°. Fry the fish, a few pieces at a time, until it is crispy on all sides and cooked through. Using a slotted spoon, remove the fish from the oil and drain on paper towels. Let the oil return to temperature between batches. Continue until all the fish is fried.
5. Serve immediately, sprinkled with the Chaat Spice Mix.

❋ Hard-to-Find Spices

If you're having trouble finding some of the ingredients you are looking for, go to ✑www.namaste.com for a wonderful online selection of Indian spices, herbs, and breads. They ship all over the United States.

Portuguese Indian Shrimp Rolls
(Fofos)

2 small potatoes
1 pound shrimp, peeled and
   deveined
½ teaspoon turmeric powder
Table salt, to taste
½ cup water

2 serrano green chilies, seeded
   and minced
1 teaspoon minced garlic
2 eggs, whisked
1 cup fresh bread crumbs
Vegetable oil for deep-frying

Serves 4
Prep Time: 20 minutes
Cook Time: 15 minutes

Use fresh bread crumbs for the best results. You can also use packaged mashed potatoes as a shortcut to make this dish.

1. Peel and cut the potatoes into 1½-inch dice. Boil in water for about 8 minutes or until tender. Set aside.
2. In a deep pan, combine the shrimp, turmeric powder, salt, and water. Simmer until the shrimp just turn opaque. Drain any water and set the shrimp aside.
3. Coarsely chop the shrimp and mash the potatoes. In a bowl, combine the shrimp, potatoes, green chilies, and garlic; mix well and form into balls. You should get about 12 balls.
4. Place the eggs in a bowl and place the bread crumbs in another shallow bowl.
5. In a deep fryer or a deep pan, heat the vegetable oil to 350°. Take each shrimp roll, dip it into the eggs, and then lightly roll it in the bread crumbs. Deep-fry, 2 at a time, until golden brown. Remove from the oil with a slotted spoon and drain on paper towels. Serve hot.

✳ Fresh Bread Crumbs

To make fresh bread crumbs, remove and discard the crusts of bread slices. Cut or tear the bread into 1-inch pieces and pulse a few times in a food processor. Store in an airtight container.

Lobster in Creamy Sauce
(Lobster Ka Korma)

Serves 4
Prep Time: 15 minutes
Cook Time: 20 minutes

Keep the lobster shell and spoon the dish into the shell for a lovely presentation.

3 tablespoons unsalted cashew nuts, soaked in water for 10 minutes
2 tablespoons white poppy seeds, soaked in water for 20 minutes
Water, as needed
2 tablespoons blanched almonds
2 teaspoons white sesame seeds
3 tablespoons Clarified Butter (see recipe on page 15)
1 (1-inch) cinnamon stick
1 black cardamom pod, bruised
1 small bay leaf

2 cloves
1 green cardamom pod, bruised
1 teaspoon Ginger-Garlic Paste (see recipe on page 13)
2 serrano green chilies, seeded and minced
½ teaspoon red chili powder
¼ teaspoon turmeric powder
1 cup yogurt, whipped
1½ pounds cooked lobster meat
Table salt, to taste
1 teaspoon Warm Spice Mix (see recipe on page 12)

1. Drain the cashews and poppy seeds and process or blend together with the almonds and sesame seeds using just enough water to make a thick paste. Set aside.
2. In a large skillet, heat the butter. Add the cinnamon stick, black cardamom pod, bay leaf, cloves, and green cardamom pod. When the spices begin to sizzle, add the Ginger-Garlic Paste, green chilies, and the nut paste. It will splatter a little; add 1 tablespoon of water to stop the splattering. Fry, stirring constantly, until the oil begins to separate from the mixture.
3. Add the red chili powder, turmeric, yogurt, lobster, salt, and spice mix. Fry, stirring constantly, until the lobster is heated through. Serve hot.

Red Chili Fish Fry
(Lal Mirchi Ki Macchi)

4 whitefish filets (such as
    tilapia, catfish, or cod)
¾ teaspoon turmeric powder
3 tablespoons vegetable oil
½ teaspoon black mustard
    seeds
8 fresh curry leaves
4 dried red chilies, roughly
    pounded

1 large onion, minced
2 teaspoons Ginger-Garlic Paste
    (see recipe on page 13)
½ teaspoon red chili powder
¼ teaspoon turmeric powder
Table salt, to taste
½ cup water

Serves 4
Prep Time: 15 minutes
Cook Time: 20 minutes

Serve with Simple Basmati Rice (page 160). For a milder version, add ½ cup of light coconut milk instead of water in step 4.

1. Place the fish filets in a bowl. Rub them well with the turmeric and set aside for about 10 minutes. Rinse the filets and pat dry.
2. In a large skillet, heat the vegetable oil. Add the mustard seeds and when they begin to sputter, add the curry leaves, red chilies, and onions. Sauté for about 6–7 minutes or until well browned. Add the Ginger-Garlic Paste, red chili powder, turmeric powder, and salt; mix well.
3. Add the fish and fry for 3 minutes. Turn and fry for another 3 minutes.
4. Add ½ cup of water and bring to a boil. Cover, lower heat, and simmer for about 6 to 8 minutes or until the fish is completely cooked through. Serve hot.

✳ Tamarind Lime Sauce

This delicious full-bodied dipping sauce takes its inspiration from a Vietnamese sauce. I love to use this sauce on grilled seafood as well as grilled chicken. The honey in this sauce balances out the tanginess of the tamarind, ginger, and lime juice. In a bowl, combine 1 tablespoon of tamarind concentrate, ¼ cup ice water, 2 teaspoons lime juice, 2 teaspoons fresh grated ginger, 2 tablespoons honey, and ½ teaspoon salt. Mix well and refrigerate until ready to use.

Salmon in Saffron-Flavored Curry
(Zaffrani Macchi)

Serves 4
Prep Time: 10 minutes
Cook Time: 10 minutes

"The king of the sea marries the queen of spices" is the best way to describe this dish. Serve with Simple Naan Bread (page 205).

4 tablespoons vegetable oil
1 large onion, finely chopped
1 teaspoon Ginger-Garlic Paste
 (see recipe on page 13)
½ teaspoon red chili powder
¼ teaspoon turmeric powder
2 teaspoons coriander powder

Table salt, to taste
1 pound salmon, boned and
 cubed
½ cup plain yogurt, whipped
1 teaspoon Roasted Saffron
 (see recipe on page 16)

1. In a large, nonstick skillet, heat the vegetable oil. Add the onions and sauté for 3 to 4 minutes or until transparent. Add the Ginger-Garlic Paste and sauté for 1 minute.
2. Add the red chili powder, turmeric, coriander, and salt; mix well. Add the salmon and sauté for 3 to 4 minutes. Add the yogurt and lower the heat. Simmer until the salmon has cooked through.
3. Add the saffron and mix well. Cook for 1 minute. Serve hot.

❈ Saffron

Saffron is one of the most affordable luxury spices, but consider this: It takes 225,000 stigmas, picked from 75,000 violet crocuses during the 2-week fall flowering period, to produce 1 pound of saffron, which costs about $4,500 per pound.

Garlic Fish Tikka
(Lasuni Macchi)

½ cup heavy cream
1 teaspoon Warm Spice Mix
  (see recipe on page 12)
½ teaspoon red chili powder
¼ teaspoon turmeric powder

Table salt, to taste
2 teaspoons minced garlic
1 pound whitefish, cut into
  chunks
Butter for basting

1. In a bowl or resealable plastic bag, combine the cream, spice mix, red chili powder, turmeric, salt, and garlic; mix well. Add the fish and coat well. Refrigerate, covered, for 2 hours.
2. Preheat oven to 350°.
3. Skewer the fish and bake for 3 to 4 minutes. Baste with butter and bake for 5 to 6 minutes or until the fish is cooked through. Serve hot.

Serves 4
Prep Time: 5 minutes, plus 2 hours to marinate
Cook Time: 10 minutes

Flaky and mild, this grilled fish is a summer favorite. Sometimes I use caramelized garlic in this recipe for a unique taste.

Dried Fenugreek Fish
(Sukhi Methi Wale Macchi)

5 tablespoons fenugreek leaves
1 teaspoon red chili powder
¼ teaspoon turmeric powder
1 teaspoon Ginger-Garlic Paste
  (see recipe on page 13)
Table salt, to taste

½ cup Hung Yogurt (see recipe
  on page 14)
4 tablespoons heavy cream
1 pound whitefish, cut into
  chunks
Butter for basting

1. In a bowl, mix the fenugreek leaves, red chili powder, turmeric powder, ginger paste, salt, yogurt, and cream. Add the fish and coat well. Refrigerate, covered, for 2 hours.
2. Preheat oven to 350°. Skewer the fish cubes; discard any remaining marinade. Place the fish skewers in the oven and roast for about 4 to 5 minutes. Baste with butter. Roast for another 3 to 4 minutes or until the fish is completely cooked through. Serve hot.

Serves 4
Prep Time: 5 minutes, plus 2 hours to marinate
Cook Time: 10 minutes

This aromatic dish is a perfect entrée with a light salad.

Chili Shrimp
(Mirchi Jhinga)

Serves 4
Prep Time: 15 minutes
Cook Time: 20 minutes

This Indian Chinese recipe is best served immediately before the shrimp soften. Serve these with the Vegetable Fried Rice (page 174).

1 egg, whisked
2 tablespoons corn flour
2 tablespoons all-purpose flour (maida)
1 teaspoon Ginger-Garlic Paste (see recipe on page 13)
1 teaspoon plus 1 tablespoon red chili sauce (optional)
Water, as needed
1½ pounds shrimp, peeled and deveined

Vegetable oil for deep-frying, plus 3 tablespoons
1-inch piece fresh gingerroot, peeled and grated
2 serrano green chilies, seeded and minced
2 tablespoons soya sauce
4 tablespoons tomato ketchup
Table salt, to taste
3 tablespoons corn flour, dissolved in ½ cup cold water

1. In a bowl, combine the egg, corn flour, all-purpose flour, Ginger-Garlic Paste, and 1 teaspoon of the red chili sauce. Add enough water to make a thin batter; mix well. Add the shrimp to the batter.
2. Pour the vegetable oil into a deep pan to about 1 inch deep, and heat to 350°. Add a few shrimp at a time and deep-fry until they are crisp and golden brown. Using a slotted spoon, remove the shrimp from the oil and drain on paper towels. Let the oil return to temperature. Continue until all the shrimp are fried. Set aside. Discard any remaining batter.
3. In a large skillet, heat the 3 tablespoons of vegetable oil. Add the ginger and green chilies, and sauté for about 30 seconds.
4. Add the soya sauce, tomato ketchup, the remaining 1 tablespoon red chili sauce, and salt; mix well.
5. Add 1 cup of water and the corn flour mixture (restir the corn flour mix if you made it ahead). Bring to a boil. Lower the heat and add the shrimp pieces. Simmer for 1 or 2 minutes to reheat the shrimp. Serve hot.

Tandoori Shrimp
(Tandoori Jhinga)

3 teaspoons grated fresh
   gingerroot
4 tablespoons heavy cream
½ teaspoon red chili powder
½ teaspoon turmeric powder
½ teaspoon Tandoori Spice Mix
   (see recipe on page 13)

½ teaspoon carom seeds
Table salt, to taste
1½ pounds shrimp, peeled and
   deveined
Lemon juice

Serves 4
Prep Time: 5 minutes,
plus 1 hour to marinate
Cook Time: 10 minutes

You can serve this not
only as an entrée but
also in a bowl of
shredded baby
spinach, as an
enchanting spring
salad.

1. In a bowl, combine all the ingredients *except* the shrimp and lemon juice; mix well.
2. Add the shrimp to the marinade. Make sure that the shrimp are well coated. Refrigerate, covered, for about 1 hour.
3. Preheat oven to 350°.
4. Place the shrimp in a single layer on a foil-lined baking sheet and bake for 8 to 9 minutes or until the shrimp are cooked. Serve hot, sprinkled with lemon juice.

※ Carom Seeds

Carom seeds are said to be very powerful digestive aids. Very similar to thyme in flavor, they are quite often used when cooking seafood.

Saffron-Flavored Grilled Salmon
(Kesari Salmon)

Serves 4
Prep Time: 5 minutes
Cook Time: 10 minutes

The Saffron
Mayonnaise used here
is so flavorful, you
need just a tiny bit to
dress the salmon.

4 salmon steaks
4 tablespoons vegetable oil
1 teaspoon dried red pepper,
   crushed

Table salt, to taste
½ recipe Saffron Mayonnaise
   (page 226)

1. In a bowl, combine the salmon, vegetable oil, red pepper, and salt.
   Coat the salmon with the mixture.
2. Preheat oven to 400°.
3. Place the salmon steaks, along with any remaining oil, on a foil-lined
   baking sheet, in a single layer. Roast for 10 minutes or until the
   salmon is cooked through.
4. Place each piece of salmon on a plate and top with 1 or 2 heaping
   tablespoons (to taste) of the Saffron Mayonnaise. Serve immediately.

※ Mango Chutney Mayonnaise

*Another wonderful topping for grilled fish is mango chutney
mayonnaise. Add 2 tablespoons of ready-made mango chutney
(from your local grocers) to 1 cup mayonnaise. Blend together
until smooth. Refrigerate until ready to use.*

CHAPTER 10
Rice Dishes (Chawal)

Simple Basmati Rice
(Chawal)

Serves 4–5
Prep Time: 5 minutes
Cook Time: 25 minutes

Let the wonderful nutty flavor of the Indian basmati rice shine through. Serve this with any entrée of your choice.

2 cups basmati rice
4 cups water

1 teaspoon table salt
1 teaspoon fresh lemon juice

1. Rinse the rice at least 3 or 4 times with water. Drain and set aside.
2. In a deep pan, bring 4 cups of water to a boil.
3. Add the rice and stir for about 30 seconds. Add the salt and lemon juice and return to boiling.
4. Reduce the heat to low. Loosely cover the rice with a lid and cook for about 12 to 15 minutes or until most of the water has evaporated. You will see small craters forming on top of the rice.
5. Cover and reduce the heat to the lowest setting; cook for 5 to 6 minutes.
6. Remove from heat and let stand, covered, for about 5 minutes. Fluff with a fork before serving.

Tamarind Rice
(Pulihora)

Serves 4–5
Prep Time: 5–10 minutes
Cook Time: 10 minutes

This is a simpler version of a classic of southern India. Serve with South Indian Cucumber Salad (page 60) for a complete meal.

1 recipe Simple Basmati Rice
  (see above)
3 tablespoons vegetable oil
4 fresh curry leaves
½ teaspoon black mustard seeds

2 dried red chilies, broken
¼ cup salted roasted peanuts
1 cup Tamarind Chutney (see
  recipe on page 224)

1. Layer the warm rice on a serving platter. Set aside.
2. In a medium-sized skillet, heat the vegetable oil. Add the curry leaves and mustard seeds. When the mustard seeds begin to sputter, add the red chilies and peanuts; sauté for about 30 seconds.
3. Add the chutney. Lower the heat and simmer for about 5 minutes or until the chutney is completely heated through.
4. Spoon the chutney mixture over the rice. Just before serving, mix together the rice and chutney.

Saffron Rice
(Kesari Chawal)

1 cup basmati rice
2 cups water
2 tablespoons Clarified Butter
   (see recipe on page 15)
3 green cardamom pods,
   bruised
2 cloves
1 cinnamon stick

2 black cardamom seeds,
   bruised
2 tablespoons golden raisins
1/4 cup blanched almonds
1/4 teaspoon salt
3 tablespoons sugar
1/2 teaspoon Roasted Saffron
   (see recipe on page 16)

Serves 4
Prep Time: 5 minutes
Cook Time: 40 minutes

This rice dish can be
served alongside
any spicy chicken or
meat curry.

1. Rinse the rice at least 3 to 4 times with water. Drain and set aside.
2. In a deep pan (with a lid), heat the butter over medium heat. Add the green cardamom pods, cloves, cinnamon stick, and black cardamom seeds. Cook for about 1 to 2 minutes.
3. Add the raisins, almonds, and salt. Stir for another minute. Add the rice and sauté for about 2 minutes. Add the sugar and the saffron; mix well.
4. Add 2 cups of water and cook, uncovered, until the water comes to a boil. Cover tightly and reduce heat to low. Cook the rice for another 8 to 12 minutes or until all the water is absorbed.
5. Remove from heat. Let stand, covered, for about 5 to 6 minutes. Serve hot. Fluff with a fork before serving.

❈ Bruising or Pounding Spices

To bruise whole spices, use a mortar and pestle. You can even add the spices to a plastic bag and pound them lightly with a rolling pin. Lightly bruising a spice is an age-old technique in Indian cooking. It helps to release its aroma and flavor into the dish.

Vegetable Pulao
(Subzi Wale Chawal)

Serves 4
Prep Time: 10 minutes
Cook Time:
30–40 minutes

This is a great way to add your favorite vegetables to your meal. Serve this with a simple Creamy Walnut Salad (page 56).

1 cup basmati rice
3 tablespoons Clarified Butter (see page 15) or vegetable oil
1 small red onion, peeled and thinly sliced
1 bay leaf
2 green cardamom pods, bruised
1 cup cut frozen vegetables of your choice
1 teaspoon fresh lemon juice
2 cups of water
Table salt, to taste
Fried Onions (see page 16), for garnish

1. Rinse the rice at least 3 or 4 times with water. Drain and set aside.
2. In a deep pan, heat the butter. Add the onions, bay leaf, and cardamom pods; sauté for about 3 to 5 minutes or until the onions are soft.
3. Add the vegetables and sauté for about 5 minutes. Add ½ cup of the water and cook for 5 to 8 minutes or until the vegetables are tender.
4. Add the salt, lemon juice, and rice; mix well. Add the remaining 1½ cups of water and bring to a rolling boil. Reduce the heat and loosely cover with the lid partway off the pan so the steam can escape. Cook for about 12 to 15 minutes or until most of the water has evaporated. You will see small craters forming on top of the rice.
5. Cover tightly and reduce the heat to the lowest setting; simmer for another 5 to 6 minutes.
6. Remove from heat and let stand, covered, for about 5 minutes. Fluff with a fork before serving. Serve hot, garnished with the Fried Onions.

✳ Basmati Rice

Known as the "Queen of Fragrance," Basmati rice is a luxury. It is said to be like fine wine, getting better with age. Try Dehraduni basmati rice; it is one of the best-quality rices available in the market today.

Cumin-Scented Rice
(Jeere Wale Chawal)

1 cup basmati rice
2 tablespoons Clarified Butter (see page 15) or vegetable oil
1 small red onion, peeled and thinly sliced

1 teaspoon cumin seeds
2 cloves
1 teaspoon fresh lemon juice
2 cups water
Table salt, to taste

Serves 4
Prep Time: 5 minutes
Cook Time: 25–30 minutes

To reheat the rice, simply sprinkle some water on it, cover loosely, and heat for a few minutes in the microwave.

1. Rinse the rice at least 3 to 4 times with water. Drain and set aside.
2. In a deep pan, heat the butter. Add the onions and sauté for 3 to 4 minutes or until the onions are soft. Add the cumin seeds, cloves, salt, lemon juice, and rice; mix well.
3. Add the water and stir for 1 minute. Bring the water to a boil, then reduce the heat. Loosely cover the rice with a lid and cook for 12 to 15 minutes or until most of the water has evaporated. You will see small craters forming on top of the rice.
4. Cover tightly and reduce the heat to the lowest setting; simmer for another 5 to 6 minutes.
5. Remove from heat and let stand, covered, for about 5 minutes. Fluff with a fork before serving. Serve hot.

✳ Don't Peek!

Curiosity kills the cat! When rice is cooking, covered, resist the urge to open the cover and look inside. The rice needs the steam to cook. Also, allow the rice to rest for a few minutes before you serve it. This will help the grains to separate and will absorb any leftover water, giving you perfect rice each time.

Tomato Rice
(Tamatar Ka Pulao)

1 cup basmati rice
2 medium tomatoes
3 tablespoons vegetable oil
1 small red onion, roughly chopped
1-inch piece gingerroot, peeled and julienned

1½ teaspoons Warm Spice Mix (see recipe on page 12)
2 cups water
Table salt, to taste
Minced cilantro, for garnish

1. Rinse the rice at least 3 to 4 times with water. Drain and set aside.
2. Boil water and plunge the tomatoes into the pot for 30 seconds, then pull them out and run them under cold water. Peel off the tomato skins. In a bowl, roughly mash the blanched tomatoes. Set aside.
3. In a deep pan, heat the vegetable oil. Add the onion and sauté for 5 minutes or until soft. Add the gingerroot and the spice mix; mix well. Add the rice and salt; sauté for 1 minute.
4. Add the water and stir for 1 minute to remove any rice lumps. Bring the water to a boil, then reduce the heat. Loosely cover with a lid and cook for about 12 to 15 minutes or until most of the water has evaporated. You will see small craters forming on top of the rice.
5. Cover tightly and reduce the heat to the lowest setting; simmer for another 5 to 6 minutes.
6. Remove from heat and let stand, covered, for about 5 minutes. Fluff with a fork and garnish with the minced cilantro. Serve hot.

※ Soaking Rice

To reduce the cooking time, soak rice in cold water for about 30 minutes before cooking. Keep in mind that you should use less water to cook soaked rice than you would for dry rice. The water-to-rice ratio for soaked rice is 1½ cups of water to 1 cup of rice. Soaking helps the rice absorb water and expand well during the actual cooking process. Many people like to save the soaking water and use it for cooking later.

Lemon Rice
(Nimbu Wale Chawal)

½ recipe Simple Basmati Rice
(page 160)

3 tablespoons Clarified Butter
(page 15) or vegetable oil

1 teaspoon black mustard
seeds

8 fresh curry leaves

3 dried red chilies, broken

2 tablespoons unsalted peanuts

Table salt, to taste

½ teaspoon turmeric powder

4 tablespoons fresh lemon
juice

Fresh grated coconut, for
garnish

Serves 4
Prep Time: 5–10 minutes
Cook Time: 5 minutes

This is a great way to
perk up leftover rice.
Enjoy a Maharastrian
Buttermilk (page 44)
drink alongside.

---

1. If you are using Simple Basmati Rice that has been prepared earlier
   and refrigerated, warm it for a few minutes before proceeding.
2. In a large skillet, heat the butter. Add the mustard seeds. When they
   begin to sputter, in quick succession add the curry leaves, red chilies,
   and peanuts. Sauté for 1 minute. Add the salt and turmeric; mix well.
3. Add the lemon juice. It will splatter a bit, so do this carefully. Add the
   rice and salt; sauté for 1 minute, mixing well to evenly coat the rice
   with the spice mix. Serve hot garnished with fresh grated coconut.

✳ Rice and the Hindu Religion

*In India, rice has a special religious significance. It is considered a
symbol of fertility and prosperity. Hindu weddings use rice for many
rituals. When a new bride enters her husband's home for the first
time, she gently taps, with her foot, a small urn containing rice,
over the threshold. This signifies that the new bride will bring
wealth and prosperity to the family.*

Chicken Casserole
(Murgh Ki Biryani)

Serves 4–5
Prep Time: 5–10 minutes
Cook Time: 45–55 minutes

These casseroles are meals in themselves and can be served with a raita or small salad of your choice.

1 recipe Chicken Curry
  (page 95)
2 cups basmati rice
4 cups water
2 tablespoons minced cilantro
2 tablespoons minced mint

½ cup mixed, unsalted, roasted
  nuts (slivered almonds,
  cashews, and pistachios)
1 tablespoon raisins (optional)
½ teaspoon Roasted Saffron
  (see recipe on page 16)

1. If you are using Chicken Curry that has been prepared earlier and refrigerated, warm it for a few minutes before proceeding.
2. Rinse the rice at least 3 to 4 times with water. Drain and set aside.
3. In a deep pan, combine the rice with the 4 cups of water. Bring the water to a rolling boil. Cook, uncovered, until the rice is almost cooked but still firm. This should take about 8 minutes. Drain the rice and set aside.
4. Preheat oven to 325°.
5. In a deep, ovenproof pan (with a lid), add a layer of rice (about ½ of the rice). Layer about ¼ of the Chicken Curry over the rice. Add another layer of the rice (about 1 cup), and sprinkle with 1 table-spoon each of the cilantro and mint. Add a layer of the remaining chicken curry. Add a final layer of the rice. Sprinkle with the remaining cilantro and mint. Sprinkle with the mixed nuts, raisins, and saffron.
6. Cover and cook in the oven for 30 to 40 minutes or until the rice is completely cooked and all the liquid has been absorbed. Serve hot.

❈ Raisins

Raisins are used quite often in Indian cooking. They are added to rice dishes, salads, meat dishes, and are even used to prepare chutneys.

Yogurt Rice
(Dahi Bhaat)

1 recipe Simple Basmati Rice
(page 160)
2 cups plain yogurt, whipped
2 tablespoons Clarified Butter
(page 15) or vegetable oil
1 teaspoon black mustard
seeds
2 dried red chilies, roughly
pounded

1 serrano green chili, seeded
and minced
8 curry leaves
1-inch piece fresh gingerroot,
peeled and julienned
1 small red onion, peeled and
finely chopped
Table salt, to taste
Fresh minced cilantro, for garnish

Serves 4–5
Prep Time: 5–10 minutes
Cook Time: 10 minutes

If you use leftover
rice, ensure that the
rice is heated first and
then brought to room
temperature before
proceeding.

1. If you are using Simple Basmati Rice that has been prepared earlier
   and refrigerated, warm it for a few minutes before proceeding.
2. In a bowl, combine the warmed rice with the yogurt. Mix well and
   place in a serving bowl. Set aside.
3. In a small skillet, heat the butter. Add the mustard seeds. When they
   begin to sputter, in quick succession add the red chilies, green chili,
   curry leaves, gingerroot, onions, and salt; mix well. Sauté for about
   3 to 5 minutes or until the onions are just soft.
4. Pour this spice mixture over the rice. Garnish with the fresh cilantro,
   and serve at room temperature.

✳ Onions and Religion
Considered an aphrodisiac, onions are avoided by many Indian
Hindus for religious reasons. Some even avoid ginger and garlic.
Another sect won't eat anything that grows underground!

Lentil and Rice Kedgee
(Ghar Ki Khichdee)

Serves 3–4
Prep Time: 10 minutes
Cook Time: 45 minutes

In India, there is nothing that ails you, apparently, that cannot be cured by eating khichdee.

4 tablespoons Clarified Butter (page 15) or vegetable oil
Pinch of asafetida (optional)
1 teaspoon whole cumin seeds
1 small red onion, peeled and thinly sliced
1-inch piece fresh gingerroot, peeled and julienned
2 black cardamom pods
2 cloves

Pinch of Warm Spice Mix (see recipe on page 12)
¼ teaspoon turmeric powder
¾ cup yellow mung beans, washed and drained
½ cup basmati rice, washed and drained
Salt, to taste
5 cups water

1. Heat the butter in a heavy-bottomed casserole on medium. (Make sure your casserole dish is large enough to hold the rice and mung beans, as the quantity will almost double when it is cooked.) Add the asafetida and cumin seeds. As soon as the seeds sizzle, add the onion and ginger; sauté until the onion begins to turn brown, about 5 to 6 minutes.
2. Add the cardamom pods, cloves, spice mix, and turmeric; sauté for 1 minute.
3. Add the mung beans and rice; sauté for about 1 to 2 minutes. Add the salt. Add the water and bring to a boil. Cover, turn heat to low, and cook gently for 30 minutes, stirring now and then to prevent sticking. Uncover and check to ensure that the rice and lentils have cooked completely. They should be soft to the touch and mash easily. The finished dish should have the consistency of a thick porridge. Serve hot.

❊ White Rice

Adding lemon juice when cooking rice helps the grains stay shining white. Just add a few drops during the cooking process. You can use bottled or fresh lemon juice.

Stir-Fried Peas with Rice
(Mattar Wale Chawal)

1 cup basmati rice
3 tablespoons vegetable oil
1 teaspoon cumin seeds
4 cloves
1 (1-inch) cinnamon stick
1 small bay leaf

1 cup frozen peas, thawed
Table salt, to taste
2 cups water
2 tablespoons Fried Onions
 (see recipe on page 16),
 optional

Serves 4
Prep Time: 10 minutes
Cook Time: 30–35 minutes

This makes a perfect side to any curry. For a more colorful presentation, add a few finely diced carrots along with the peas.

1. Rinse the rice at least 3 to 4 times with water. Drain and set aside.
2. In a deep pan, heat the vegetable oil. Add the cumin seeds, cloves, cinnamon, and bay leaf. When the spices begin to sizzle, add the peas; sauté for 1 minute. Add the salt and rice; mix well.
3. Add the water and stir for 1 minute to get rid of any lumps of rice. Bring the water to a boil, then reduce the heat. Loosely cover with a lid and cook for about 12 to 15 minutes or until most of the water has evaporated. You will see small craters forming on top of the rice.
4. Cover tightly and reduce the heat to the lowest setting; simmer for another 5 to 6 minutes.
5. Remove from heat and let stand, covered, for about 5 minutes. Fluff with a fork before serving and garnish with Fried Onions.

※ Nuke It

A very easy way to make rice when you are in a rush is to microwave it. Wash, soak (for 30 minutes), and drain 1 cup basmati rice. Combine with 2 cups of water and salt to taste in a microwave-safe dish. Cook, uncovered, at full power for 12 to 13 minutes. Carefully stir. Cover loosely, and microwave for another 5 to 6 minutes. Let the rice stand, covered, for a few minutes. Fluff and serve. Note that microwave times may vary slightly depending on the power of the microwave.

Ground Lamb, Peas, and Rice Casserole
(Kheeme Wale Chawal)

Serves 4
Prep Time: 5–10 minutes
Cook Time: 45–55 minutes

Make extra Peas and Minced-Meat Curry (page 121) and freeze it for making this delightful dish. Serve with Fried Okra in Yogurt Sauce (page 58).

1 recipe Peas and Minced-Meat Curry (page 121)
2 cups basmati rice
4 cups water
2 tablespoons minced cilantro
2 tablespoons minced mint

½ cup mixed, unsalted, roasted nuts (slivered almonds, cashews, and pistachios)
½ teaspoon Roasted Saffron (see recipe on page 16)

1. If you are using Peas and Minced-Meat Curry that has been prepared earlier and refrigerated, warm it for a few minutes before proceeding.
2. Rinse the rice at least 3 to 4 times with water. Drain and set aside.
3. In a deep pan, combine the rice and the 4 cups of water. Bring the water to a rolling boil. Cook, uncovered, until the rice is almost cooked but still firm. This should take about 8 minutes. Drain the rice and set aside.
4. Preheat oven to 325°.
5. In a deep, ovenproof pan (with a lid), add a layer of rice (about ½ of the rice). Layer about ¼ of the minced-meat curry over the rice. Add another layer of the rice (about 1 cup), and sprinkle with 1 tablespoon each of the cilantro and mint. Add a layer of the remaining lamb curry. Add a final layer of the remaining rice. Sprinkle with the remaining cilantro and mint. Sprinkle with the mixed nuts and saffron.
6. Cover and cook in the oven for 30 to 40 minutes or until the rice is completely cooked and all the liquid has been absorbed.

❋ Mushy Rice?

Cooking rice is an art, and much depends on the age of the rice and its quality. If the rice turns out too mushy, reduce the amount of water used the next time you prepare it. Also, if you soak the rice prior to cooking it, you will need to reduce the quantity of water used.

Rice with Chutney
(Chutney Wale Chawal)

1 cup basmati rice
2 tablespoons vegetable oil
1 teaspoon sesame seeds
2 serrano green chilies, seeded
    and minced
1 small red onion, peeled and
    finely chopped

Table salt, to taste
¼ cup Mint-Cilantro Chutney
    (see recipe on page 224)
½ cup plain yogurt, whipped
1¾ cups water

Serves 4
Prep Time: 10 minutes
Cook Time: 30 minutes

You can substitute
Green Chili and
Coconut Chutney
(page 225) for the
Mint-Cilantro Chutney
in this dish if you like.

1. Rinse the rice at least 3 to 4 times with water. Drain and set aside.
2. In a deep pan, heat the vegetable oil. Add the sesame seeds, green chilies, and onions; sauté for 3 to 5 minutes or until the onions are soft.
3. Add the salt and the chutney; sauté for 1 minute. Add the yogurt, mix well, and cook for about 2 minutes.
4. Add the rice and mix well. Sauté for about 2 minutes.
5. Add the water and stir for 1 minute. Bring the water to a boil. Reduce the heat. Loosely cover the rice with a lid and cook for about 12 to 15 minutes or until most of the water has evaporated. You will see small craters forming on top of the rice.
6. Cover tightly and reduce the heat to the lowest setting; simmer for 5 to 6 minutes.
7. Remove from heat and let stand, covered, for about 5 minutes. Fluff with a fork before serving.

❋ Texmati Rice

Texmati is a basmati hybrid cultivated in the United States; you can substitute it if you like. Follow the instructions on the box for the amount of water needed, as it varies from brand to brand.

Garlic Rice
(Lasuni Pulao)

Serves 4–5
Prep Time: 10 minutes
Cook Time: 30 minutes

This dish is a garlic lover's delight. It is best if served immediately. Garnish with Fried Onions (page 16).

1 cup basmati rice
3 tablespoons vegetable oil
6 fresh garlic cloves, peeled and crushed
1 serrano green chili, seeded and minced
1/4 cup plain yogurt, whipped

Table salt, to taste
1/2 teaspoon Warm Spice Mix (see recipe on page 12)
1 3/4 cups water
1 tablespoon minced cilantro

1. Rinse the rice at least 3 to 4 times with water. Drain and set aside.
2. In a deep pan, heat the vegetable oil. Add the garlic and green chili; sauté for about 20 seconds or until the garlic turns light brown.
3. Add the yogurt, salt, and spice mix; sauté for 1 minute. Add the rice and mix well.
4. Add the water and stir for 1 minute. Bring the water to a boil. Reduce the heat. Loosely cover the rice with a lid and cook for about 12 to 15 minutes or until most of the water has evaporated. You will see small craters forming on top of the rice.
5. Cover tightly and reduce the heat to the lowest setting; simmer for another 5 to 6 minutes.
6. Remove from heat and let stand, covered, for about 5 minutes. Fluff with a fork before serving.

❋ Stronger Garlic Taste

If you want a stronger garlic taste, use a garlic press to crush the garlic. If you don't have a press, use the flat side of a large kitchen knife and press it firmly on top of the garlic. This will give you more flavor from the garlic than you will get from simply chopping it.

White Chicken Rice
(Safeed Murgh Ka Pulao)

2 cups basmati rice

4 cups water

4 tablespoons vegetable oil

1-inch piece fresh gingerroot, peeled and julienned

2 serrano green chilies, minced

1 small red onion, peeled and finely chopped

4 boneless, skinless chicken breasts, cubed

Table salt, to taste

½ teaspoon Warm Spice Mix (see recipe on page 12)

1 teaspoon red chili powder

1 tablespoon minced cilantro

1 tablespoon minced mint

½ cup whole milk

1 teaspoon Roasted Saffron (see recipe on page 16)

> **Serves 4–5**
> **Prep Time:** 10 minutes
> **Cook Time:** 1 hour
>
> Serve piping hot with the Minty Potato in Yogurt Sauce (page 64).

1. Rinse the rice at least 3 to 4 times with water. Drain and set aside.
2. In a deep pan, combine the rice with the 4 cups of water. Bring to a rolling boil. Cook, uncovered, until the rice is almost cooked but still firm. This should take about 8 minutes. Drain the rice and set aside.
3. In a large skillet, heat the vegetable oil. Add the gingerroot, green chilies, and red onions; sauté for 7 to 8 minutes or until the onions are browned.
4. Add the chicken and sauté for 8 to 10 minutes or until the chicken is well browned and completely cooked. Add the salt, spice mix, and red chili powder; mix well. Remove from heat and set aside.
5. Preheat oven to 325°.
6. In a deep ovenproof pan (with a lid), add a layer of rice (about ½ of the rice). Layer about ¼ of the chicken mixture over the rice. Add another layer of the rice (about 1 cup); sprinkle with 1 teaspoon each of the cilantro and mint. Add a layer of the remaining chicken mixture and then a final layer of the remaining rice. Sprinkle with the remaining cilantro and mint. Sprinkle with the milk and saffron.
7. Cover and cook in the oven for about 30 to 40 minutes or until the rice is completely cooked and all the liquid has been absorbed. Serve hot.

Vegetable Fried Rice
(Sabzi Wale Chawal)

Serves 4
Prep Time: 5 minutes
(plus 2 hours for chilling the rice, if necessary)
Cook Time: 15–20 minutes

Serve with any of the Manchurian recipes in this book. I would recommend using a mix of green beans, carrots, broccoli, and sweet bell peppers.

½ recipe Simple Basmati Rice (page 160)
3 tablespoons vegetable oil
2 green onions, finely chopped
1-inch piece fresh gingerroot, peeled and julienned
4 garlic cloves, minced
1 dried red chili, whole
1 cup cut frozen vegetables of your choice, thawed
¼ cup water
2 teaspoons soya sauce
1 teaspoon white vinegar
Table salt, to taste

1. The cooked rice needs to be cold. If you prepare it fresh for this recipe, refrigerate it for at least 2 hours prior to using it here.
2. In a large skillet, heat the vegetable oil on high. Add the green onions, ginger, and garlic; sauté for 1 minute.
3. Add the red chili and the vegetables; sauté for about 5 minutes. Add the water and cook until the vegetables are tender and most of the water has evaporated, about 8 minutes.
4. Add the soya sauce, white vinegar, and salt; mix well. Add the cold rice and mix well; sauté for about 2 to 3 minutes or until the rice has completely heated through. Serve hot.

☀ Indian Vinegar Salad

Make this mild vinegar salad to serve alongside pulaos (sautéed rice dishes, usually prepared with whole spices) and heavy biryanis (rice casseroles made with meat and/or vegetables). In a small bowl, combine ½ cup diced cucumbers, ½ cup diced radish, a pinch of sugar and salt, 1 tablespoon grated ginger, and a few tablespoons of vinegar. Chill and serve.

Pork Fried Rice
(Pork Wale Chawal)

½ recipe Simple Basmati Rice
(page 160)
2 tablespoons soya sauce
1 tablespoon white vinegar
1 teaspoon cornstarch
3 tablespoons vegetable oil
2 green onions (white and
light green part only), finely
chopped

1-inch piece fresh gingerroot,
peeled and julienned
2 garlic cloves, minced
1 dried red chili, whole
¼ pound boneless pork, cut
into ½-inch dice

> **Serves 4–5**
> **Prep Time:** 5 minutes
> (plus 2 hours for chilling
> the rice, if necessary)
> **Cook Time:** 15 minutes
>
> Substitute your choice
> of meat for this fla-
> vorful stir-fry. Serve
> with Chili Garlic Sauce
> (page 236).

1. The cooked rice needs to be cold. If you prepare it fresh for this recipe, refrigerate it for at least 2 hours prior to using it here.
2. Combine the soya sauce, vinegar, and cornstarch; set aside.
3. In a large nonstick skillet, heat the vegetable oil on high. Add the green onions, ginger, and garlic; sauté for 1 minute.
4. Add the red chili and the pork; sauté for 7 to 8 minutes or until the pork is cooked.
5. Give the soya sauce mixture a quick stir to recombine it, and add it to the pan. Add the cold rice and mix well. Sauté for about 2 to 3 minutes or until the rice has completely heated through. Serve hot.

❈ Another Indian Chinese Favorite

Visit any Indian Chinese restaurant in India and you will be served a hot green chili sauce along with your meal. This Green Chili Vinegar Sauce adds a wonderful zing to any Chinese dish; it is generally sprinkled over a dish before it is served. To prepare about ¼ cup of this sauce: In a deep pan, combine 4 minced green chilies, ¼ cup vinegar, a pinch each of salt and sugar. Simmer on low heat for 3 minutes. Chill and serve.

Bengali Butter Rice
(Bengali Ghee Bhaat)

Serves 4
Prep Time: 5 minutes
Cook Time: 30–35 minutes

Whole spices add an amazing flavor to this aromatic and buttery rice dish. Remove the whole spices before serving.

1 cup basmati rice
3 tablespoons Clarified Butter (see recipe on page 15)
1 bay leaf
1 (1-inch) cinnamon stick
2 cloves

2 black peppercorns
2 green cardamom pods, bruised
2 cups water
Table salt, to taste

1. Wash the rice at least 3 to 4 times with water. Drain and set aside.
2. In a deep pan, heat the butter. Add the bay leaf, cinnamon, cloves, peppercorns, and cardamoms. When the whole spices begin to sizzle (about 1 minute), add the rice and mix well.
3. Add the water and salt; stir for 1 minute. Bring the water to a boil. Reduce the heat. Loosely cover the rice with a lid and cook for about 12 to 15 minutes or until most of the water has evaporated. You will see small craters forming on top of the rice.
4. Cover tightly and reduce the heat to the lowest setting; simmer for another 5 to 6 minutes.
5. Remove from heat and let stand, covered, for about 5 minutes. Fluff with a fork before serving.

❋ Spiced Butter

Brush your favorite Indian breads with spiced butter for an added oomph. Take a stick of butter at room temperature; add 1 teaspoon of crushed garlic and ¼ teaspoon roasted cumin; mix well. Refrigerate and use as needed.

Malabari Coconut Rice
(Thenga Choru)

1 cup basmati rice
3 tablespoons vegetable oil
1 teaspoon black mustard seeds
2 dried red chilies, broken
1-inch piece fresh gingerroot, julienned
4 garlic cloves, minced

½ teaspoon turmeric powder
Table salt, to taste
½ cup unsweetened desiccated coconut
½ cup light coconut milk
1½ cups water

Serves 4
Prep Time: 5 minutes
Cook Time:
30–35 minutes

This recipe comes to you from the shores of southwestern India. Traditionally it is served with hot, spicy curries.

1. Rinse the rice at least 3 to 4 times with water. Drain and set aside.
2. In a deep pan, heat the vegetable oil. Add the mustard seeds. When they begin to sputter, add the red chilies, ginger, and garlic; sauté for about 30 seconds.
3. Add the turmeric, salt, and coconut. Mix well and sauté for 1 minute. Add the rice and mix well; sauté for 1 minute.
4. Add the coconut milk and the water; stir for 1 minute. Bring to a boil.
5. Reduce the heat. Loosely cover the rice with a lid and cook for about 12 to 15 minutes or until most of the water has evaporated. You will see small craters forming on top of the rice.
6. Cover tightly and reduce the heat to the lowest setting; simmer for another 5 to 6 minutes.
7. Remove from heat and let stand, covered, for about 5 minutes. Fluff with a fork before serving.

✳ Using Coconut Milk
Before you open a can of coconut milk, shake it vigorously to ensure that the coconut cream and the coconut water mix well together.

Eggplant and Rice
(Vangi Bhaat)

Serves 4
Prep Time: 5 minutes
Cook Time:
30–35 minutes

A simplified version of an Indian classic. Substitute cauliflower or potatoes for the eggplant if you like. Serve with Potato and Yogurt Salad (page 59).

1 cup basmati rice
4 tablespoons vegetable oil
1 teaspoon black mustard seeds
4 dried red chilies, broken
1-inch piece fresh gingerroot, julienned
4 garlic cloves, minced

½ teaspoon turmeric powder
Table salt, to taste
1 small red onion, peeled and thinly sliced
1 (1-pound) eggplant, diced
2 cups water

1. Rinse the rice at least 3 to 4 times with water. Drain and set aside.
2. In a deep pan, heat the vegetable oil. Add the mustard seeds. When they begin to sputter, add the red chilies, gingerroot, and garlic; sauté for about 30 seconds.
3. Add the turmeric, salt, onion, and eggplant. Mix well and sauté for 7 to 8 minutes or until the eggplant and onion are well browned. Add the rice and mix well; sauté for 1 minute.
4. Add the water and stir for 1 minute. Bring to a boil, then reduce the heat. Cover loosely with a lid and cook for about 12 to 15 minutes or until most of the water has evaporated. You will see small craters forming on top of the rice.
5. Cover tightly and reduce the heat to the lowest setting; simmer for another 5 to 6 minutes.
6. Remove from heat and let stand for about 5 minutes. Serve hot. Fluff with a fork before serving.

✳ An Eggplant by Any Other Name . . .

Also called aubergine or brinjal in India, the eggplant is a native of Asia. When buying eggplant, look for the ones with firm skin. Indian eggplants tend to be less bitter than their Western counterparts.

Minty Rice
(Pudine Wale Chawal)

1 cup basmati rice
2 tablespoons vegetable oil
2 serrano green chilies, seeded
  and minced
1 small red onion, peeled and
  finely chopped

Table salt, to taste
¼ cup minced mint
½ cup plain yogurt, whipped
1¾ cups water

> **Serves 4**
> **Prep Time:** 10 minutes
> **Cook Time:** 40 minutes
>
> A refreshing dish, it is one of the most popular in my classes. You can garnish this dish with fresh grated coconut.

1. Rinse the rice at least 3 to 4 times with water. Drain and set aside.
2. In a deep pan, heat the vegetable oil. Add the green chilies and onions; sauté for 3 to 5 minutes or until the onions are soft.
3. Add the salt and the mint; sauté for 1 minute. Add the yogurt and mix well; cook for about 2 minutes.
4. Add the rice and mix well; sauté for about 2 minutes.
5. Add the water and stir for 1 minute. Bring the water to a boil, then reduce the heat. Loosely cover with a lid and cook for about 12 to 15 minutes or until most of the water has evaporated. You will see small craters forming on top of the rice.
6. Cover tightly and reduce the heat to the lowest setting; simmer for another 5 to 6 minutes.
7. Remove from heat and let stand, covered, for about 5 minutes. Serve hot. Fluff with a fork before serving.

✳ Red Radish

In India, the longer white radish, called daikon, is usually used. Radish flowers are a great garnish for many Indian rice dishes. They are so easy to make. With a small paring knife, cut a zigzag pattern around the circumference of the radish. Make sure your cuts go all the way to the center. Pull the two halves apart.

Spicy Shrimp Rice
(Jhinge Ki Biryani)

Serves 4
Prep Time: 10 minutes
Cook Time: 30–35 minutes

Try this recipe with the seafood of your choice. Garnish with minced cilantro. Serve this along with Shredded Carrot Salad (page 68).

1 cup basmati rice
4 tablespoons vegetable oil
1 teaspoon black mustard seeds
4 fresh curry leaves
1 pound shrimp, peeled and deveined

2 tablespoons unsweetened desiccated coconut
1 teaspoon red chili powder
½ teaspoon turmeric powder
Table salt, to taste
2 cups water

1. Rinse the rice at least 3 to 4 times with water. Drain and set aside.
2. In a deep pan, heat the vegetable oil. Add the black mustard seeds. When they begin to sputter, add the curry leaves and shrimp; sauté for about 2 to 3 minutes.
3. Add the coconut, red chili and turmeric powder, and salt; cook for about 2 minutes.
4. Add the rice and mix well; sauté for 1 minute.
5. Add the water and stir for 1 minute. Bring the water to a boil. Reduce the heat. Loosely cover with a lid and cook for about 12 to 15 minutes or until most of the water has evaporated. You will see small craters forming on top of the rice.
6. Cover tightly and reduce the heat to the lowest setting; simmer for another 5 to 6 minutes.
7. Remove from heat and let stand, covered, for about 5 minutes. Fluff with a fork before serving.

❈ Did You Say Prawns?

Most Indians refer to shrimp as prawns. Indian prawns are much bigger than the shrimp found in the United States; some are as long as the palm of your hand. Use large shrimp for most of the recipes in this book, unless otherwise indicated.

Turmeric Rice
(Peele Chawal)

1 cup basmati rice
2 tablespoons vegetable oil
2 serrano green chilies, seeded
   and minced
1 small red onion, peeled and
   finely chopped

Table salt, to taste
1 teaspoon turmeric powder
2 cups water

Serves 4
Prep Time: 10 minutes
Cook Time: 30 minutes

This simple dish has a spectacular appearance because of its stunning yellow color. Serve with any hot curry of your choice.

1. Rinse the rice at least 3 to 4 times with water. Drain and set aside.
2. In a deep pan, heat the vegetable oil. Add the green chilies and onions; sauté for 3 to 5 minutes or until the onions are soft.
3. Add the salt, turmeric, and rice; sauté for 1 minute.
4. Add the water and stir for 1 minute. Bring to a boil, then reduce the heat. Loosely cover with a lid and cook for about 12 to 15 minutes or until most of the water has evaporated. You will see small craters forming on top of the rice.
5. Cover tightly and reduce the heat to the lowest setting; simmer for another 5 to 6 minutes.
6. Remove from heat and let stand, covered, for about 5 minutes. Fluff with a fork before serving.

❈ Tri-Colored Rice

You can have a lot of fun with rice dishes. Prepare batches of Minty Rice, Tomato Rice, and Turmeric Rice (see the recipes in this chapter). Layer the rice or mound it on a plate for a spectacular presentation. Use the Minty Rice for a green layer, Turmeric Rice for yellow, and the Tomato Rice for a fiery red.

Spiced Semolina with Toasted Cashews
(Upma Kaju Wala)

Serves 4
Prep Time: 10 minutes
Cook Time: 30 minutes

Semolina is served here with toasted cashews. In South India, this is often served for breakfast. Serve sprinkled with fresh lemon juice.

1 tablespoon Clarified Butter (see recipe on page 15)
4 tablespoons unsalted cashew nuts
4 tablespoons vegetable oil
4 fresh curry leaves
½ teaspoon mustard seeds
1 small red onion, peeled and finely chopped
2 dried red chilies, broken
1 serrano green chili, minced
1 cup semolina
Table salt, to taste
2 cups hot water

1. In a small skillet, heat the butter. Add the cashews and toast them on medium heat until golden brown. Set aside.
2. In a medium skillet, heat the vegetable oil. Add the curry leaves and mustard seeds. When the mustard seeds begin to sputter, add the red onions and the red and green chilies; sauté for about 3 to 4 minutes.
3. Add the semolina and the salt; mix well.
4. Start adding the hot water, a little at a time. Stir the semolina constantly as the water is added. The semolina will begin to absorb the water. Continue until all the water has been added. Cover, lower the heat to medium low, and steam for about 5 minutes. The final consistency should be dry.
5. Remove from heat. Let the dish stand, covered, for about 10 minutes before serving. Top with the toasted cashews and serve.

✳ Clarified Butter and Religion
In India, clarified butter, or ghee, is used to light the cotton wicks of lamps. A symbol of wealth and opulence, it is used as an offering to the gods in many religious ceremonies.

CHAPTER 11
Lentil and Yogurt Dishes (Dal Aur Kadhi)

Creamy Split Peas
(Chana Dal)

Serves 4
Prep Time: 5 minutes, plus 1 hour to soak
Cook Time: 50 minutes

To reduce cooking times for this dahl (dal), use a pressure cooker. Serve this as a side with Simple Indian Bread (page 202).

1 cup chana dal or yellow split peas, well rinsed
Water, as needed
½ teaspoon turmeric powder
3 tablespoons vegetable oil, divided
1 teaspoon minced garlic
1 small red onion, minced
1 teaspoon cumin seeds
Table salt, to taste
¼ cup heavy cream

1. Soak the *chana dal* in 4 cups of water for 1 hour. Drain and set aside.
2. In a deep pan, combine the turmeric powder, 1 tablespoon of the vegetable oil, the garlic, and 4 cups of water. Bring to a boil. Add the *chana dal* and cook for 20 minutes, stirring occasionally. Reduce heat to medium, cover partially, and continue to cook for about 30 minutes or until the peas are very soft. Reduce the heat to a simmer for about 8 minutes or until most of the liquid has dried up. Remove from heat and use a wooden spoon to mix well. Set aside.
3. Heat the remaining vegetable oil in a medium-sized skillet. Add the cumin seeds. When they begin to sizzle (about 30 seconds), add the onions and sauté for 7 to 8 minutes or until the onions are brown.
4. Add this mixture to the *chana dal* and mix well. Add salt and mix. Add the heavy cream and mix well. Serve hot.

Cleaning Dahls

No matter what type of dahl you are cooking, rinse it well in 4 to 5 changes of water. This will get rid of any husks that might be in the dahl.

Simple Mung Bean Curry
(Tadka Dal)

1 cup yellow split mung beans
(yellow moong dal), well
rinsed
Water, as needed
½ teaspoon turmeric powder
4 tablespoons vegetable oil,
divided
1 teaspoon cumin seeds

1 small red onion, minced
1 serrano green chili, seeded
and minced
1 teaspoon grated ginger
1 small tomato, minced
Table salt, to taste
1 tablespoon minced cilantro
(optional)

Serves 4
Prep Time: 10 minutes
Cook Time: 50 minutes

Tadka in Indian cooking means "seasoning." This yellow dahl (dal) is a North Indian favorite. Serve atop steamed Indian basmati rice.

1. In a deep pan, combine 4 cups of water, the turmeric, and 1 tablespoon of the vegetable oil. Bring to a boil, then add the mung beans. Reduce the heat to medium-low and cook, uncovered and stirring occasionally, for 30 minutes or until the lentils are very soft. If the water starts to dry up, you can add another ½ cup of water. Remove from heat and set aside.

2. In a medium-sized skillet, heat 3 tablespoons of vegetable oil. Add the cumin seeds; when they begin to sizzle, add the red onions. Sauté for 7 to 8 minutes or until the onions are well browned.

3. Add the ginger, green chili, and tomatoes. Cook for another 8 minutes or until the tomatoes are soft.

4. Add the salt and cilantro and mix well. Add the onion mixture and mix well. Reheat gently and serve hot.

❄ Removing Gas

Some lentils contain gas-forming compounds. In order to reduce these, rinse them well. Never cook them in the soaking water—always use fresh water.

The Five-Lentil Delight
(Paanch Dalo Ka Sangam)

Serves 4
Prep Time: 10 minutes, plus 2 hours to soak
Cook Time: 55 minutes

Also called "Panchratan" or "The Five Jewels," this creamy dahl (dal) is a gourmet's delight. Serve with Simple Naan Bread (page 205).

4 tablespoons chana dal or yellow split peas, rinsed
4 tablespoons red split lentils (masoor dal), rinsed
4 tablespoons split black gram, or black lentils (safeed urad dal), rinsed
4 tablespoons pigeon peas (toor dal), rinsed
4 tablespoons green split mung beans (green moong dal), rinsed
Water, as needed

1 teaspoon turmeric powder
2 teaspoons table salt
5 tablespoons vegetable oil, divided
1 teaspoon cumin seeds
1 teaspoon Ginger-Garlic Paste (see recipe on page 13)
1 medium-sized red onion, minced
1 teaspoon red chili powder
½ teaspoon cumin powder
½ teaspoon Warm Spice Mix (see recipe on page 12)

1. Soak all the *dals* together in a deep pot with enough water to cover them well. Soak for about 2 hours. Drain and set aside.
2. In a deep pot, combine 6 cups of water, the turmeric powder, salt, and 2 tablespoons of the vegetable oil. Bring to a boil. Add all the drained *dals* and mix well. Bring to a full boil. Reduce heat to medium and cook, uncovered, for about 40 minutes or until the lentils are soft. If the water begins to dry out, add up to 1 cup more. (The consistency should be like a creamy soup.) Remove from heat and set aside.
3. In a medium-sized skillet, heat the remaining vegetable oil. Add the cumin seeds; when they begin to sizzle, add the Ginger-Garlic Paste. Sauté for 30 seconds and add the onions. Sauté for 7 to 8 minutes or until the onions are well browned.
4. Add the red chili powder, cumin powder, and spice mix; mix well.
5. Add the onion mixture to the *dals* and mix well. Serve hot.

Chickpea Curry
(Pindi Chane)

2 (14-ounce) cans chickpeas
4 tablespoons vegetable oil
2 teaspoons Ginger-Garlic Paste
 (see recipe on page 13)
1 large red onion, minced
1 teaspoon coriander powder
1 teaspoon pomegranate
 powder

½ teaspoon Warm Spice Mix
 (see recipe on page 12)
1 serrano green chili, seeded
 and minced
½ teaspoon red chili powder
Table salt, to taste
1 cup water

> **Serves 3–4**
> **Prep Time:** 10 minutes
> **Cook Time:** 15 minutes
>
> This time-saving recipe uses canned chickpeas (garbanzo beans), available at your local grocer. Serve with Fried Indian Bread (page 204).

1. Rinse the chickpeas well. Set aside.
2. In a deep pan, heat the vegetable oil. Add the Ginger-Garlic Paste and sauté for 1 minute, then add the onions; sauté for 7 to 8 minutes.
3. In quick succession, add the coriander powder, pomegranate powder, spice mix, green chili, red chili powder, and salt; mix well. Sauté for 30 seconds or until the spices begin to darken.
4. Add the chickpeas and mix well.
5. Add 1 cup of water and mix well. Lower the heat and simmer for about 8 minutes. Using a spoon, take out about 2 tablespoons of the chickpeas. Mash them and add them back to the pot; mix well. Remove from heat. Serve hot.

❊ Cauliflower Bites

Need something quick and yummy for those times when unexpected guests arrive? Break cauliflower into small florets. Heat oil in a deep fryer until it is almost smoking, then deep-fry the cauliflower florets, a few at a time, until they are dark brown in color and crisp. Remove from the oil using a slotted spoon and drain on a paper towel. Sprinkle with Chaat Spice Mix (page 14) and serve hot. These are the perfect accompaniment for drinks.

Indian Red Kidney Beans
(Rajmah)

Serves 4
Prep Time: 15 minutes
Cook Time: 20 minutes

Another time-saving recipe that uses canned beans. Serve it with Simple Basmati Rice (page 160) and a salad of your choice.

2 (14-ounce) cans red kidney beans
4 tablespoons vegetable oil
2 teaspoons Ginger-Garlic Paste (see recipe on page 13)
1 large red onion, minced
2 medium tomatoes, finely chopped
½ teaspoon turmeric powder
1 teaspoon red chili powder
Table salt, to taste
1 teaspoon coriander powder
1 teaspoon cumin powder
½ teaspoon Warm Spice Mix (see recipe on page 12)
Water, as needed

1. Rinse the kidney beans well and set aside.
2. In a deep pan, heat the vegetable oil on medium heat. Add the Ginger-Garlic Paste and sauté for about 20 seconds.
3. Add the onion and sauté for about 5 minutes or until well browned.
4. Add the tomatoes and sauté for about 8 minutes or until the oil begins to separate from the mixture.
5. Add the turmeric, red chili, salt, coriander, cumin, and spice mix; mix well. Add the red kidney beans and about ½ cup of water. Simmer for about 7 minutes. Remove from heat and serve hot.

☀ Storing Chutneys

Always cook and store chutneys in nonreactive pans and bowls. If cooked in other pots, the acid in the chutneys (from lemon juice, vinegar, etc.) will react to iron, copper, and brass, giving a nasty metallic taste to the chutney.

Creamy Red Lentils
(Masoor Ki Dal)

Water, as needed
½ teaspoon turmeric powder
1 teaspoon (or to taste) salt
4 tablespoons vegetable oil
1 cup red split lentils (masoor dal), well rinsed

½ teaspoon cumin seeds
2 garlic cloves, minced
½ teaspoon red chili powder

Serves 4
Prep Time: 10 minutes
Cook Time: 35 minutes

This dish tastes as beautiful as it appears. Serve with Dry Garlic Chutney (page 226) and hot Simple Naan Bread (page 205).

1. In a deep pot, combine 4 cups of water, turmeric powder, salt, and 2 tablespoons of the vegetable oil. Bring to a boil. Add all the lentils and mix well. Bring to a full boil. Reduce heat to medium and cook, uncovered, for about 25 minutes or until the lentils are soft. If the water begins to dry out, add up to ½ cup more. (The consistency should be like a creamy soup.) Remove from heat.
2. Using a spoon, mash the cooked lentils to a creamy consistency. Set aside.
3. In a medium pan, heat the remaining vegetable oil. Add the cumin seeds. When they begin to sizzle, add the garlic and red chili powder; sauté for about 20 seconds.
4. Remove from heat and pour over the lentils. Mix well and serve hot.

☀ A Change of "Season-ings"

Changing the final seasoning, or tadka, can completely change the taste of a dish. Take the Creamy Red Lentils above, for instance. Change the seasoning from cumin seeds to black mustard seeds and add a few fresh curry leaves, and taste the difference.

Creamy Black Gram Dahl
(Dal Makhani)

Serves 4
Prep Time: Soaking overnight
Cook Time: 1 hour and 10 minutes

This dal freezes well, but do not add the cream if you are planning on freezing it.

1 cup whole black gram, or black lentils (urad dal), rinsed
2 tablespoons dried red kidney beans
½ teaspoon turmeric powder
Water, as needed
4 tablespoons butter
1 teaspoon oil
1 teaspoon Ginger-Garlic Paste (see recipe on page 13)
1 cup tomato purée (canned or fresh)
1 teaspoon red chili powder
Table salt, to taste
4 tablespoons heavy cream

1. In enough water to cover, soak the *urad dal* along with the red kidney beans overnight. Drain and set aside.
2. In a heavy-bottomed pan, combine the turmeric and water; bring to a boil. Add the *urad dal* and red kidney beans and mix well. Cook on medium heat, uncovered and stirring occasionally, for about 1 hour. Check to see if the lentils are soft and if they are beginning to split. If not, continue cooking. If the lentils start to dry out, add up to 1 cup more of water. Remove from heat and set aside.
3. In a medium-sized skillet, heat the butter along with the oil. Add the Ginger-Garlic Paste and sauté for 30 seconds.
4. Add the tomatoes and cook for about 7 to 8 minutes or until the oil begins to separate from the mixture. (The tomatoes may splatter, so cover the skillet with a splatter guard or partially cover the mixture with a lid as it cooks.)
5. Add the red chili powder and salt; mix well. Remove from heat and pour over the *dal*; mix well. Just prior to serving, stir in the heavy cream. Serve hot.

❉ How Soft?

When cooking lentils, lift a few with a wooden spatula. Mash them between your fingers. If they mash easily, they are ready and cooked.

Black-Eyed Peas Curry
(Tarewale Lobhiya)

4 tablespoons vegetable oil
1 teaspoon Ginger-Garlic Paste
   (see recipe on page 13)
1 large red onion, minced
2 small tomatoes, finely
   chopped
½ teaspoon turmeric powder
1 teaspoon red chili powder

2 teaspoons coriander powder
Table salt, to taste
1 teaspoon tamarind pulp,
   concentrate
2 (14-ounce) cans black-eyed
   peas (lobhiya), rinsed
1 cup water
1 tablespoon minced cilantro

Serves 4
Prep Time: 10 minutes
Cook Time: 30 minutes

This dish is unusual
and quite delicious.
Serve with hot
Simple Naan Bread
(page 205) or your
favorite bread.

---

1. In a deep pan, heat the vegetable oil. Add the Ginger-Garlic Paste and sauté for about 30 seconds.
2. Add the onion and sauté for about 7 to 8 minutes or until well browned.
3. Add the tomatoes and sauté for another 8 minutes or until the oil begins to separate from the sides of the mixture.
4. Add the turmeric, red chili powder, coriander, and salt; mix well. Add the tamarind and mix well.
5. Add the black-eyed peas and mix well; sauté for 2 minutes.
6. Add the water and simmer on low heat for about 6 to 8 minutes, stirring occasionally.
7. Add the cilantro and cook for 1 minute. Remove from heat and serve hot.

❈ Edible Spoons?

Indian use their bread, torn into small pieces, as spoons to scoop up yummy lentils and gravies. Try it and see the difference it makes.

Split Pea Purée
(Andhra Patoli)

1 cup chana dal or yellow split peas, well rinsed
2 serrano green chilies
1 teaspoon cumin seeds
Water, as needed
4 tablespoons vegetable oil
½ teaspoon black mustard seeds

2 dried red chilies, roughly pounded
4 fresh curry leaves
1-inch piece fresh gingerroot, grated
¼ teaspoon turmeric powder
Table salt, to taste

1. In a food processor, grind together the *chana dal,* green chilies, and cumin seeds, along with 2 to 3 tablespoons of water, to make a coarse paste. You can add more water to aid the grinding process if necessary. Set aside.
2. In a large pan (with a lid), heat the vegetable oil. Add the mustard seeds. When they begin to sputter, add the red chilies, curry leaves, and gingerroot; mix well.
3. Add the *dal* paste, turmeric powder, and salt; mix well. Add about ¼ cup of water. Cover and cook on medium heat for 7 to 8 minutes
4. Uncover, stir well, and add another ¼ cup of water. Mix well and cover. Lower the heat and cook until the lentils are soft, about 5 to 6 minutes. Serve hot.

✳ Ginger Too Dry?
If your fresh ginger has dried up, soak it in some hot water for instant revitalization. As a rule, choose young gingerroot for the recipes in this book.

Gujarati Yellow Mung Beans
(Peele Moong Ki Dal)

Water, as needed
½ teaspoon turmeric powder
2 tablespoons vegetable oil
1 cup yellow split mung beans (yellow moong dal), rinsed
2 packed teaspoons jaggery or brown sugar
Table salt, to taste

3 tablespoons vegetable oil
½ teaspoon black mustard seeds
5–6 fresh curry leaves
Pinch of asafetida
2 dried red chilies, roughly pounded

Serves 4
Prep Time: 10 minutes
Cook Time: 45 minutes

This simple dal is a staple in the western Indian state of Gujarati. Serve garnished with minced cilantro.

1. In a deep pan, heat 4 cups of water, the turmeric, and vegetable oil on high heat. Bring to a boil.
2. Add the *moong dal*. Reduce the heat to medium. Cook, uncovered, for 30 minutes or until the *dal* is soft. If the *dal* begins to dry up, add up to ½ cup of hot water.
3. Remove from heat. Using a hand mixer or the back of a wooden spoon, mash the *dal* to a coarse purée. Add the jaggery and salt; mix well. Set aside.
4. Just before serving, heat the vegetable oil in a small pan. Add the mustard seeds. When they begin to sputter (about 30 seconds), in quick succession add the curry leaves, asafetida, and red chilies. Sauté for another 30 seconds.
5. Remove from heat and pour over the *dal*. Mix well and serve hot.

❈ Jaggery

Jaggery, or gur, as it is called in India, is a beautiful caramel-colored sugar. It comes from sugar cane juice and is often used in making Indian desserts.

Maharastrian Pigeon Pea Curry
(Ambat Varan)

Serves 4
Prep Time: 10 minutes, plus 1 hour to soak
Cook Time: 55 minutes

A tangy dish from the western Indian state of Maharastra, this is traditionally served with steamed rice sprinkled with 1 tablespoon of warmed ghee.

1 cup pigeon peas (toor dal), rinsed
Water, as needed
½ teaspoon turmeric powder
4 tablespoons vegetable oil
1 teaspoon minced garlic
A pinch of asafetida
½ teaspoon cumin seeds
½ teaspoon mustard seeds
1 teaspoon tamarind pulp concentrate
1 teaspoon sugar
Table salt, to taste

1. Soak the *toor dal* in enough water to cover, for 1 hour.
2. In a deep pan, combine 4 cups of water, the turmeric, and 2 tablespoons of the vegetable oil; bring to a boil.
3. Add the *toor dal* and stir. Lower heat to medium and cook, uncovered, for about 40 minutes or until the *dals* are soft. Mash them with the back of a wooden spoon to get a smooth consistency. Remove from heat and set aside.
4. In a small skillet, heat the remaining vegetable oil. Add the garlic and sauté for 30 seconds. In quick succession add the asafetida, cumin, and mustard seeds. When the mustard seeds begin to sputter, remove from heat and pour over the *toor dal*.
5. Return the *dal* to the stovetop and add the tamarind; mix well. Add the sugar and salt, and mix well. Add ½ cup of water and bring to a boil. Remove from heat and serve hot.

❊ Reducing the Cooking Time for Dahls

Soak dahls (dals) or lentils in hot water instead of cold water. Also, add salt, lemon juice, or tamarind only at the end of the cooking process for dahls. If you add it earlier, the dahl will take a lot longer to cook. Adding a little bit of oil and turmeric powder to dahls while boiling them will also considerably shorten the cooking process.

Split Pea and Cheese Curry
(Paneeri Chana Dal)

*1 cup chana dal or yellow
    split peas, well rinsed*
½ teaspoon turmeric powder
1 teaspoon red chili powder
*3 tablespoons vegetable oil,
    divided*

*1 cup fried Indian Cheese (see
    recipe on page 71)*
4 cups water
Table salt, to taste
1 teaspoon minced garlic
1 small red onion, minced

> **Serves 4**
> **Prep Time:** 10 minutes,
> plus 1 hour to soak
> **Cook Time:** 45 minutes
>
> A cozy combination
> of creamy chana dal
> and soft paneer
> (Indian Cheese), serve
> this with warm Simple
> Indian Bread (page
> 202). Garnish with
> minced cilantro.

1. Soak the *chana dal* in enough water to cover, for 1 hour. Drain and set aside.
2. In a deep pan, combine the turmeric powder, red chili powder, 1 tablespoon of the vegetable oil, the Indian Cheese, and water. Bring to a boil. Add the *chana dal* and cook, stirring occasionally. Reduce heat to medium, cover partially, and continue to cook for about 30 minutes or until the *dals* are very soft. Reduce the heat and simmer for about 8 minutes.
3. Remove from heat and add the salt; mix well with a wooden spoon. Set aside.
4. In a medium-sized pan, heat the remaining vegetable oil. Add the garlic and sauté for 30 seconds.
5. Add the onions and sauté for 7 minutes or until the onions are browned. Remove from heat and add to the *dal*; mix well. Serve hot.

❈ Paneer Substitutes

Use tofu as a substitute when a recipe calls for firm paneer. If you're not a fan of tofu, you can also use baked ricotta in its place. To bake the ricotta: Place ricotta cheese in an ovenproof dish. Bake at 350° for 45 minutes. Cut into small pieces.

Fried Lentil Balls Stir-Fry
(Moongodi Ki Subzi)

Serves 4
Prep Time: 10 minutes
Cook Time: 10 minutes

Use freshly prepared
Fried Mung Bean Balls
for this, as this recipe
will not taste good
with defrosted balls.

4 tablespoons vegetable oil
1 small red onion, peeled and
   thinly sliced
1-inch piece fresh gingerroot,
   peeled and julienned
1 recipe Fried Mung Bean
   Balls (see below)

¼ teaspoon turmeric powder
Table salt, to taste
2 generous tablespoons dried
   fenugreek leaves (kasoori
   methi)

1. In a large skillet, heat the vegetable oil. Add the onions and ginger and sauté for about 3 to 5 minutes or until the onions are soft.
2. Add the Fried Mung Bean Balls and sauté for 1 minute.
3. Add the turmeric, salt, and fenugreek; sauté for 2 minutes.

Fried Mung Bean Balls
(Moongodi)

Serves 4
Prep Time: 10 minutes
Cook Time: 30 minutes

These fritters freeze
well for use in curries
at a later date. To
defrost them, add
them to a bowl of
hot water.

1 cup yellow split mung beans
   (yellow moong dal), well rinsed
2 serrano green chilies
Table salt, to taste

1-inch piece fresh gingerroot,
   roughly chopped
Water, as needed
Vegetable oil for deep-frying

1. In a food processor, purée the *moong dal,* green chilies, salt, and ginger to a smooth paste. Add up to 1 tablespoon of water to aid in the grinding process, if necessary. Transfer the mixture to a bowl, then whisk the mixture to incorporate some air into it.
2. Heat the vegetable oil in a deep pan or a deep fryer to 375°. Place a few tablespoons of the mixture, 1 at a time, into the oil. Make sure you do not overcrowd the pan. Deep-fry the pieces until golden brown on each side, about 1 minute. Remove with a slotted spoon and drain on paper towels. Let the oil return to cooking temperature. Continue deep-frying until all the mixture is used. Serve immediately.

Lemony Black-Eyed Peas
(Nimbu Wala Lobhiya)

2 (14-ounce) cans black-eyed
   peas (lobhiya), rinsed
4 tablespoons fresh lemon juice
1 teaspoon black salt
1-inch piece fresh gingerroot,
   peeled and julienned

2 tablespoons minced cilantro
2 serrano green chilies, seeded
   and minced

Mix together all the ingredients in a bowl. Chill, covered, for 30 minutes. Serve cold.

> **Serves 4**
> **Prep Time:** 10 minutes,
> plus 30 minutes to chill
> **Cook Time:** None
>
> Lemon adds a zing to this simple salad. Serve this as a hearty salad or even as a side along with kebabs of your choice.

Black-Eyed Pea Fritters
(Lobhiya Ke Pakore)

2 (14-ounce) cans black-eyed
   peas (lobhiya), rinsed
2 tablespoons chickpea flour
1 tablespoon corn flour
1 teaspoon red chili powder

½ teaspoon turmeric powder
Table salt, to taste
2 serrano green chilies, seeded
Water, as needed
Vegetable oil for deep-frying

1. In a food processor, purée the black-eyed peas, chickpea flour, corn flour, red chili powder, turmeric powder, salt, and green chilies. Grind to a thick paste; add up to 2 tablespoons of water to aid in the grinding process if necessary. Transfer to a bowl.
2. Heat the vegetable oil in a deep pan or a deep fryer to 375°. Place a few tablespoons of the mixture, 1 at a time, in the oil. Deep-fry until golden brown on each side, about 1 minute. Remove with a slotted spoon and drain on paper towels. Let the oil return to temperature. Continue until all the mixture is used. Serve immediately.

> **Serves 4**
> **Prep Time:** 15 minutes
> **Cook Time:** 30 minutes
>
> Whip the batter with a spoon for a few minutes before deep-frying, for fritters that are perfectly crunchy outside and soft and moist on the inside.

Split Lentil Dumplings
(Urad Dal Ke Vade)

Serves 4
Prep Time: 10 minutes
plus 2 hours to
soak the dal
Cook Time: 30 minutes

These delightful
dumplings can be
served as cocktail
appetizers. Traditionally
they are served
drenched in yogurt and
topped with dollops
of Tamarind Chutney
(page 224).

*1 cup skinned and split black
    gram (also called white
    lentils), rinsed*
*½ teaspoon fenugreek seeds
    (methi)*
4 cups hot water

*1-inch piece fresh gingerroot,
    peeled and coarsely chopped*
2 serrano green chilies
Table salt, to taste
Vegetable oil for deep-frying

1. Soak the gram and fenugreek seeds together in the hot water for
   about 2 hours. Drain.
2. In a food processor, combine the soaked gram and fenugreek, ginger,
   chilies, and salt. Process to a smooth batter. Add up to 2 tablespoons
   of water if needed. Transfer to a bowl.
3. Heat the vegetable oil in a deep pan or a deep fryer to 375°. Place a
   few tablespoons of the mixture, 1 at a time, into the oil. Make sure
   you do not overcrowd the pan. Deep-fry the balls until golden brown
   all over, about 2 to 3 minutes. Remove with a slotted spoon and drain
   on paper towels. Let the oil return to temperature between batches.
   Continue until all the mixture is used. Serve hot.

❖ Cleaning Lentils

*Always check your lentils to make sure there are no tiny stones or
debris. Use a flat or shallow dish to spread out the lentils; this will
make it easier to spot the stones.*

Spicy Yogurt Curry
(Punjabi Kadhi)

*1 recipe Fried Mung Bean
   Balls (page 196)*
2 cups plain yogurt
4 cups water
4 tablespoons chickpea flour
1 teaspoon turmeric powder
1 teaspoon red chili powder

Table salt, to taste
2 tablespoons vegetable oil
*½ teaspoon black mustard
   seeds*
2 dried red chilies, broken
½ teaspoon cumin seeds

> **Serves 4**
> **Prep Time:** 10 minutes
> **Cook Time:** 45 minutes
>
> A staple in the North Indian state of Punjab, this dish is traditionally served with steamed Simple Basmati Rice (page 160) and Lentil Wafers (page 231).

1. Add the Fried Mung Bean Balls to 4 cups of *hot* water; soak for 5 minutes. Drain. Press each ball between the palms of your hands to squeeze out any water. Set aside.
2. Place the yogurt, 4 cups of water, chickpea flour, turmeric powder, red chili powder, and salt in a deep bowl. Using a hand blender or a spoon, blend well. Make sure that there are no lumps. Transfer to a deep pan.
3. Bring the yogurt mixture to a boil on medium heat, stirring constantly. Reduce the heat and continue cooking for another 20 to 30 minutes or until the mixture begins to thicken and gain a creamy consistency. Stir occasionally while cooking.
4. Add the soaked mung bean balls to the mixture and simmer for another 10 minutes. Remove from heat and set aside.
5. In a small skillet, heat the vegetable oil. Add the mustard seeds. When the seeds begin to sputter (about 30 seconds), add the red chilies and cumin seeds. Sauté for another 20 seconds. Remove from heat and pour over the yogurt mixture; mix well. Serve hot.

❁ Oily Fritters?
Oily fritters generally signal that the oil they were fried in was not hot enough. Allow the oil to heat to the required temperature between batches.

Yogurt Green Curry
(Hariyali Kadhi)

Serves 4
Prep Time: 5 minutes
Cook Time: 30 minutes

A variation on the classic Spicy Yogurt Curry (Punjabi Kadhi), serve this nutritious curry with Simple Basmati Rice (page 160).

1 (10-ounce) package chopped frozen spinach, thawed
1½ cups plain yogurt
4 tablespoons chickpea flour
2 tablespoons vegetable oil
Pinch of asafetida
2 dried red chilies, broken
1 teaspoon minced garlic
Water, as needed

1. Place the spinach in a deep pan and add enough water to cover. Boil until the leaves are cooked through, about 10 minutes. Remove from heat, drain thoroughly, and cool to room temperature. In a food processor, purée the spinach to a thick paste. Transfer to a deep bowl.
2. In a small bowl, add about 4 tablespoons of the yogurt and all of the chickpea flour. Mix well and make sure that there are no lumps. Add the rest of the yogurt and mix well. Add this mixture to the spinach purée; mix well.
3. In a deep pan, heat the vegetable oil. Add the asafetida, red chilies, and garlic; sauté for 30 seconds.
4. Add the spinach mixture to the seasoned oil. Add ½ cup of water and mix well. Cook on medium heat for about 15 minutes or until the mixture begins to thicken. Serve hot.

※ Stinking Spice

Asafetida is a stinky resin that is used for flavoring and as a digestive aid. Don't let the smell discourage you; it dissipates during the cooking process.

CHAPTER 12
Bread Basket (Roti Ki Tori)

Simple Indian Bread
(Chapati)

Serves 4
Prep Time: 15 minutes, plus 30 minutes for the dough to rest
Cook Time: 20 minutes

The chapati dough can be prepared up to a day in advance. Refrigerate the dough, and then let it come to room temperature before proceeding.

2 cups whole-wheat flour (atta), plus extra for dusting
1 teaspoon table salt
¾ cup warm water

Vegetable oil for greasing
2 teaspoons melted Clarified Butter (see recipe on page 15)

1. In a bowl, combine the flour and salt. Add the water slowly, kneading as you go. Make a soft dough, kneading for at least 10 minutes. The final dough should be soft and pliable. It should not be sticky; otherwise it will not roll out well.
2. Cover the dough with a damp cloth or plastic wrap and let it sit for 30 minutes.
3. Lightly dust a clean work surface with flour. Roll the dough into a log about 8 inches long. Cut into 12 equal portions and cover again with a damp cloth or plastic wrap.
4. Lightly dust the rolling surface with a bit more flour. Lightly grease your hands with oil. Take 1 portion and roll it into a ball between the palms of your hands, then flatten the ball. Place it on the prepared surface. Use a rolling pin to roll it out into a circle about 5 to 6 inches in diameter. Cover with a damp cloth or plastic wrap until ready to fry. Continue until all the portions are rolled out.
5. Heat a dry griddle on medium heat. Pick up a dough circle (keeping the remaining circles covered) and shake off any excess flour. Place it on the griddle. In about 1 minute, small blisters will begin to appear on the surface. Flip it over and cook on the other side for 1 minute.
6. Using a folded cloth to protect your fingers, press down the outer edges of the bread. This will encourage it to puff up. (If this does not happen, do not worry. It takes a good amount of practice to make the chapaties puff up.) Remove the chapati from the griddle and place in a paper towel or a cloth napkin and keep covered until ready to serve. Continue until all the chapaties are cooked
7. When you are ready to serve the chapaties, brush with a little bit of the butter. Serve hot.

Chickpea Flour Flatbread
(Missi Roti)

1 cup chickpea flour
1 cup whole-wheat flour (atta),
    plus extra for dusting
1½ teaspoons (or to taste)
    table salt
1 teaspoon carom seeds

½ teaspoon red chili powder
    (optional)
Water, as needed
Vegetable oil for greasing
4 tablespoons melted Clarified
    Butter (see recipe on page 15)

Serves 4
Prep Time: 30 minutes
Cook Time: 30 minutes

Chickpea flour and wheat flour are combined here to make this flavorful bread. Serve along with your favorite chutney.

1. In a bowl, combine the chickpea flour, wheat flour, salt, carom seeds, and red chili powder; mix well. Add water, a little bit at a time, kneading constantly. Continue kneading for at least 10 minutes or until you get a soft and pliable dough. The dough should not be sticky.

2. Cover the dough with a damp cloth or plastic wrap and let it sit for 30 minutes.

3. Lightly dust a clean surface with flour. Roll the dough into a log. Cut into 12 equal portions.

4. Lightly dust the rolling surface and rolling pin with a bit more flour. Lightly grease your hands with oil (or dust with flour). Take 1 portion of dough and roll it into a ball between the palms of your hands, then flatten the ball. Place it on the prepared surface. Use the rolling pin to roll it out into a circle about 5 to 6 inches in diameter. Cover with a damp cloth or plastic wrap until ready to fry. Continue until all the portions are rolled out.

5. Heat a dry griddle on medium heat. Pick up the circle of dough (keeping the remaining circles covered), shake off any extra flour, and place on the griddle. Small blisters will begin to appear on the surface in about 1 minute. Flip the dough over and cook on the other side for 1 more minute. Brush lightly with butter and flip over once more.

6. Remove the flatbread from the heat and place in a paper towel or a cloth napkin and keep covered until ready to serve. Continue until all the *rotis* are cooked. When you are ready to serve, brush with a little bit more of the butter. Serve hot.

Fried Indian Bread
(Bhatura)

Serves 4
Prep Time: 10 minutes, plus at least 4 hours for the dough to rest
Cook Time: 20 minutes

This puffy and crispy Indian bread tastes best when it is freshly prepared and eaten hot. It is traditionally served with Chickpea Curry (page 187).

2 cups all-purpose flour (maida), plus extra for dusting
½ teaspoon baking soda
1 teaspoon table salt
½ cup plain yogurt, whipped
Water, as needed
Vegetable oil for deep-frying and greasing

1. In a bowl, combine the flour, baking soda, and salt. Add the yogurt, slowly, and start kneading the dough. Add water as needed to form a smooth dough that is not sticky. The dough will be quite elastic.
2. Sprinkle some flour over the dough and continue to knead for at least 10 minutes.
3. Place the dough, covered, in a warm place for at least 4 hours.
4. Divide the dough into 14 equal parts. Lightly dust a clean work surface with flour.
5. Lightly grease your hands with oil. Take 1 portion of dough and roll it into a ball between the palms of your hands, then flatten the ball. Place it on the prepared surface. Use a rolling pin to roll it out into a thin disk about 5 to 6 inches in diameter. Cover with a damp paper towel until ready to fry. Continue until all the portions are rolled out.
6. In a deep pan or a deep fryer, heat the vegetable oil to 370°. Add a single disk at a time. It will begin to rise and puff up. Using the back of your slotted spoon, very lightly press the disk into the oil. Turn it over and fry for another 20 seconds or until golden brown. Using a slotted spoon, remove the fried bread from the oil and drain on paper towels. Continue until all the disks are fried. Serve immediately.

❋ Indian All-Purpose Flour

In Indian grocery stores you will find a fine white flour called maida. This is traditionally used to make Fried Indian Bread. This flour produces the right amount of elasticity in the dough to provide the spongy texture characteristic of the bread.

Simple Naan Bread
(Saada Naan)

¼ cup warm water
½ teaspoon sugar
1¼ teaspoons table salt
1 teaspoon dried active yeast
4 cups all-purpose flour (maida),
*   plus extra for dusting*

½ teaspoon baking powder
1 egg, beaten
½ cup plain yogurt, whipped
¼ cup warm milk
5 tablespoons melted Clarified
*   Butter (page 15)*

Serves 4
Prep Time: 20 minutes,
plus 2 hours to rise
Cook Time: 20 minutes

Naans are traditional Indian breads prepared in clay ovens or tandoors. Fiercely popular in Indian restaurants worldwide, these are easily prepared in the conventional oven.

1. Dissolve the sugar and ¼ teaspoon of the salt in warm water and add the yeast. Set aside for 10 minutes to allow the yeast to foam.
2. Place the flour, remaining salt, and baking powder in a large shallow bowl; mix well.
3. Add the egg and yogurt and begin to knead. Begin adding the yeast mixture and the warm milk and continue kneading until you have a soft dough. If you need more liquid, add a few tablespoons of warm water. Knead for at least 10 minutes or until you have a soft dough that is not sticky.
4. Cover the dough with a damp cloth and place in a warm place for 1½ to 2 hours or until the dough has doubled in volume
5. Adjust the racks in the oven so that the top rack is 5 inches away from the top element. Preheat oven to 400°. Lightly grease a large, heavy baking sheet or cast-iron griddle and set aside.
6. Lightly dust a clean work surface and rolling pin with flour. Knead the dough again on the floured surface for about 5 minutes. Divide it into 8 equal pieces and cover with a damp towel or plastic wrap.
7. Roll each piece into a ball and flatten it with your hands. Roll it out into an oval shape about 6 to 7 inches long. Using your hands, pull at both ends of the oval to stretch it a little. Continue until you have made 8 naans.
8. Brush each oval with the butter. Place the naans on the baking sheet and bake for 5 minutes. Turn on the broiler and broil for an additional 3 minutes or until golden brown. (Depending on the size of your baking tray, you may have to do the naans in 2 batches.) Serve warm.

Almond-Coated Naan Bread
(Badaami Naan)

Serves 4
Prep Time: 20 minutes,
plus 2 hours to rise
Cook Time: 20 minutes

A more royal version of the humble naan. You can also top it with grilled chicken, dried fenugreek, nigella seeds, or Indian Cheese (page 12).

¼ cup warm water
½ teaspoon sugar
1¼ teaspoons table salt
1 teaspoon dried active yeast
4 cups all-purpose flour (maida),
    plus extra for dusting
½ teaspoon baking powder

1 egg, beaten
½ cup plain yogurt, whipped
¼ cup warm milk
5 tablespoons melted Clarified
    Butter (page 15)
¼ cup almonds, slivered and
    blanched

1. Dissolve the sugar and ¼ teaspoon of salt in warm water and add the yeast. Put aside for 10 minutes to allow the yeast to foam.
2. Place the flour, remaining salt, and baking powder in a large, shallow bowl; mix well. Add the egg and yogurt and begin to knead. Begin adding the yeast mixture and the warm milk and continue kneading until you have a soft dough. If you need more liquid, add a few tablespoons of warm water. Knead for at least 10 minutes or until you have a soft dough that is not sticky.
3. Cover the dough with a damp cloth and put in a warm place for 1½ to 2 hours or until the dough has doubled in volume
4. Adjust the racks in the oven so that the top rack is 5 inches away from the top element. Preheat oven to 400°. Lightly grease a large, heavy baking tray or cast-iron griddle and set aside.
5. Lightly dust a clean work surface and a rolling pin with flour. Knead the dough on the prepared surface for about 5 minutes. Divide it into 8 equal pieces and cover with a damp towel or plastic wrap.
6. Roll each piece into a ball and flatten it with your hands. Roll it out into an oval shape about 6 to 7 inches long. Using your hands, pull at both ends of the oval to stretch it a little. Continue until you have made 8 naans. Brush each oval with the butter. Sprinkle with a few almonds. Lightly press the almonds into the dough.
7. Place the naans on the baking sheet and bake for 5 minutes. Broil for 3 more minutes or until golden brown. (Depending on the size of your sheet, you may have to bake in 2 batches.)

Mint-Flavored Bread
(Pudina Paratha)

2 cups whole-wheat flour
   (atta), plus extra for dusting
4 tablespoons semolina
2 tablespoons dried mint
1½ teaspoons (or to taste)
   table salt

8 tablespoons melted Clarified
   Butter (see recipe on
   page 15)
Water, as needed
Vegetable oil for greasing

Serves 4
Prep Time: 30 minutes,
plus 30 minutes to rest
Cook Time: 20 minutes

Serve with any raita of
your choice (see
Chapter 5) for a
complete meal.

1. In a bowl, combine the wheat flour, semolina, mint, salt, and 4 table-spoons of the butter. Add the water slowly, kneading the flour as you go. Make a soft dough, kneading for at least 10 minutes. The final dough should be soft and pliable. It should not be sticky; otherwise it will not roll out well.
2. Cover the dough with a damp cloth or plastic wrap and let it sit for 30 minutes.
3. Roll the dough into a log and cut it into 10 equal portions. Lightly dust a clean work surface with flour.
4. Lightly grease your hands with oil. Take 1 portion of the dough and roll it into a ball between the palms of your hands, then flatten the ball. Place it on the prepared surface. Use a rolling pin to roll it out into a disk about 5 to 6 inches in diameter.
5. Lightly brush the disk with the butter and fold it in half. Brush again with the butter and fold in half again to form a triangle.
6. Lightly flour the work surface again, and roll out the triangle into a triangle about 5 to 6 inches in diameter at the base.
7. Heat a griddle on medium. Brush it lightly with butter and add the *paratha* to the griddle. Cook for about 2 minutes or until the bottom of the *paratha* begins to blister. Brush the top surface lightly with butter and flip over. Cook for 2 minutes.
8. Remove the *paratha* from the griddle and place on a serving platter. Cover with a paper towel. Continue until all the *parathas* are rolled out and cooked. Serve hot.

Ground Meat—Stuffed Bread
(Kheema Ka Paratha)

2 cups whole-wheat flour (atta)
4 tablespoons semolina
1½ teaspoons table salt
6 tablespoons melted Clarified Butter
  (see recipe on page 15)

Water, as needed
½ recipe Peas and Minced-Meat
  Curry (page 121)
Vegetable oil for greasing

1. In a bowl, combine the wheat flour, semolina, salt, and 2 tablespoons of the butter. Add the water slowly, kneading as you go. Form into a soft dough, kneading for at least 10 minutes. The final dough should be soft and pliable, but not sticky. Cover the dough with a damp cloth or plastic wrap and let it sit for 30 minutes.

2. In a medium-sized skillet on high heat, warm the Peas and Minced-Meat Curry. Sauté until all the moisture has completely dried out. Remove from heat and allow to cool. Remove any whole spices and break up any large pieces of meat with a fork.

3. Roll the dough into a log. Cut into 8 equal portions. Lightly dust a clean work surface and a rolling pin with flour. Lightly grease your hands with oil. Take 1 portion of dough and roll into a ball between the palms of your hands, then flatten the ball. Place it on the prepared work surface, then roll it out into a circle about 5 to 6 inches in diameter.

4. Lightly brush the surface of the dough circle with the butter. Add 1 tablespoon of the minced-meat filling to the center. Bring the sides together and pinch them to seal, forming a ball. Flatten lightly and dust very lightly with flour.

5. Lightly dust the work surface with flour again, and roll out the flattened ball again until it is about 5 to 6 inches in diameter.

6. Heat a griddle on medium heat. Brush it lightly with butter and add the *paratha* to the griddle. Cook for about 2 minutes or until the bottom of the *paratha* begins to blister. Brush the top lightly with butter and flip over. Cook for 2 minutes.

7. Remove the *paratha* from the griddle and place on a serving platter. Cover with a paper towel. Continue until all the *parathas* are cooked.

Spinach Bread
(Palak Ka Paratha)

1 cup frozen, chopped spinach
2 cups whole-wheat flour
    (atta), plus extra for dusting
2 tablespoons semolina
1½ teaspoons table salt

6 tablespoons melted Clarified
    Butter (page 15)
Water, as needed
Vegetable oil for greasing

1. In enough water to cover, boil the spinach until wilted. Drain. Set aside to cool.
2. In a bowl, combine the spinach, wheat flour, semolina, and salt; mix well. Add 2 tablespoons of the butter. Add the water slowly, kneading the flour as you go. Make a soft dough, kneading for at least 10 minutes. The final dough should be soft and pliable. It should not be sticky; otherwise it will not roll out well.
3. Cover the dough with plastic wrap and let it sit for 30 minutes.
4. Roll the dough into a log and cut it into 10 equal portions. Lightly dust a clean work surface and rolling pin with flour.
5. Lightly grease your hands with oil. Take 1 portion and roll it into a ball between the palms of your hands, then flatten the ball. Place it on the prepared surface. Use the rolling pin to roll it out into a circle about 5 to 6 inches in diameter.
6. Lightly brush the surface of the dough circle with the butter and fold the circle in half. Brush again with the butter and fold in half again to form a triangle.
7. Lightly dust the work surface with flour again, and roll out the triangle of dough until the base of the triangle is about 5 to 6 inches wide.
8. Heat a griddle on medium heat. Brush it lightly with butter and add the *paratha* to the griddle. Cook for about 2 minutes or until the bottom of the *paratha* begins to blister. Brush the top lightly with butter and flip over. Cook for 2 minutes.
9. Remove the *paratha* from the griddle and place on a serving platter. Cover with a paper towel. Continue until all the *parathas* are rolled out and cooked. Serve hot.

Seasoned Bread
(Namak Mirch Ke Parathe)

Serves 4
Prep Time: 15 minutes, plus 30 minutes for the dough to rest
Cook Time: 20 minutes

This bread freezes well and will stay good frozen for up to three months. Serve with your favorite raita and a pickle of your choice.

2 cups whole-wheat flour (atta), plus extra for dusting
4 tablespoons semolina
1½ teaspoons (or to taste) table salt
1 teaspoon red chili powder
1 serrano green chili, seeded and finely minced
6 tablespoons melted Clarified Butter (page 15)
Water, as needed
Vegetable oil for greasing

1. In a bowl, combine the wheat flour, semolina, salt, red chili powder, green chili, and 2 tablespoons of the butter; mix well. Slowly add the water, kneading the flour as you go. Make a soft dough, kneading for at least 10 minutes. The final dough should be soft and pliable. It should not be sticky; otherwise it will not roll out well.
2. Cover the dough with a damp cloth and let it sit for 30 minutes.
3. Roll the dough into a log. Cut into 8 equal portions. Lightly dust a clean work surface and rolling pin with flour.
4. Lightly grease your hands with oil (or dust with flour). Take 1 portion of dough and roll it into a ball between the palms of your hands, then flatten the ball. Place it on the prepared surface. Use the rolling pin to roll it out into a circle about 5 to 6 inches in diameter.
5. Lightly brush the surface of the dough circle with the butter and fold the circle in half. Brush again with the butter and fold in half again to form a triangle.
6. Lightly flour the work surface again, and roll out the triangle of dough until the base of the triangle is about 5 to 6 inches wide.
7. Heat a griddle on medium heat. Brush it lightly with butter and add the *paratha* to the griddle. Cook for about 2 minutes or until the bottom of the *paratha* begins to blister. Brush the top lightly with butter and flip over. Cook for 2 minutes.
8. Remove the *paratha* from the griddle and place on a serving platter. Cover with a paper towel. Continue until all the *parathas* are rolled out and cooked. Serve hot.

Stuffed Bread
(Paratha)

*2 cups whole-wheat flour
(atta), plus extra for dusting
4 tablespoons semolina
1½ teaspoons table salt*

*6 tablespoons melted Clarified
Butter (page 15)
1 batch, your choice of filling*

Serves 4
Prep Time: 15 minutes,
plus 30 minutes for
the dough to rest
Cook Time: 30 minutes

Be careful when you
roll the bread; be
gentle so that the
filling does not break
out of the dough.
Serve with plain
yogurt.

1. In a bowl, combine the wheat flour, semolina, salt, and 2 tablespoons of the butter. Slowly add the water, kneading the flour as you go. Make a dough, kneading for at least 10 minutes. The final dough should be soft and pliable. It should not be sticky; otherwise it will not roll out well.

2. Cover the dough with a damp cloth or plastic wrap and let it sit for 30 minutes. While the dough is resting, prepare the filling of your choice.

3. Roll the dough into a log. Cut into 8 equal portions. Lightly dust a clean work surface with flour. Lightly grease your hands with oil (or dust with flour). Take 1 portion of dough and roll it into a ball between the palms of your hands, then flatten the ball. Place it on the prepared surface. Use the rolling pin to roll it out into a circle about 5 to 6 inches in diameter.

4. Lightly brush the surface of the dough circle with the butter and add 1 tablespoon of the filling to the center. Bring the sides together and pinch them together to seal, forming a ball. Flatten lightly and dust very lightly with flour.

5. Lightly dust the work surface with flour again, and roll out the flattened ball until it is about 5 to 6 inches in diameter.

6. Heat a griddle on medium heat. Brush it lightly with butter and add the *paratha* to the griddle. Cook for about 2 minutes or until the bottom of the *paratha* begins to blister. Brush the top lightly with butter and flip over. Cook for 2 minutes.

7. Remove the *paratha* from the griddle and place on a serving platter. Cover with a paper towel. Continue until all the *parathas* are cooked. Serve hot.

Potato Stuffing
(Aloo Ka Paratha)

Serves 4
Prep Time: 15 minutes, plus 30 minutes for the dough to rest
Cook Time: 30 minutes

If you tear up when chopping onions, try refrigerating them prior to use.

3 medium potatoes, peeled
Water, as needed
1 small red onion, peeled and finely minced
2 serrano green chilies, seeded and finely minced
1 tablespoon minced cilantro

1-inch piece fresh gingerroot, grated
1 teaspoon red chili powder
1 teaspoon Warm Spice Mix (page 12)
Vegetable oil for greasing

Boil the potatoes in enough water to cover for about 15 minutes. Drain. Put the potatoes in a bowl and mash them well with a fork. Add the onion, green chilies, cilantro, gingerroot, red chili powder, and spice mix; mix well. Set the filling aside to cool.

Cauliflower Stuffing
(Gobi Ka Paratha)

Serves 4
Prep Time: 15 minutes, plus 30 minutes for the dough to rest
Cook Time: 30 minutes

Be sure to squeeze out all the excess water from the grated cauliflower to keep the bread from tearing when you roll it.

Florets of 1 small cauliflower
Water, as needed
1 tablespoon minced cilantro
1-inch piece fresh gingerroot, grated

1 teaspoon red chili powder
1 teaspoon carom seeds
Vegetable oil for greasing

Using either the grater disk of a food processor or a box grater, grate the cauliflower. Squeeze handfuls of cauliflower over the sink to squeeze out any moisture. Place the cauliflower in a bowl. Add the cilantro, ginger, red chili powder, and carom seeds; mix well.

Green Peas Stuffing
(Hare Matar Ka Paratha)

1 cup peas (fresh or frozen and thawed)
Water, as needed
1 tablespoon minced cilantro
1 teaspoon red chili powder

Table salt, to taste
Vegetable oil for greasing

Boil the peas in water for 10 minutes or until tender. Drain well. Place the peas into a bowl along with cilantro, red chili powder, and salt; mash well.

❋ Cook Ahead Parathas

You can make parathas ahead of time to save some time later. Simply prepare the parathas as directed and fry them lightly until they are half cooked. Then refrigerate until you are ready to finish them. Fry them until done and serve!

Serves 4
Prep Time: 15 minutes, plus 30 minutes for the dough to rest
Cook Time: 30 minutes

Roll the bread gently so that the filling does not break out of the dough. Serve with plain yogurt.

Carom-Flavored Flatbread
(Ajwain Ka Paratha)

Serves 4
Prep Time: 15 minutes, plus 30 minutes for the dough to rest
Cook Time: 40 minutes

Carom, known for it legendary digestive properties, provides a savory flavoring to this bread. Serve with any raita of your choice (see Chapter 5).

2 cups whole-wheat flour (atta), plus extra for dusting
4 tablespoons semolina
1½ teaspoons (or to taste) table salt
1 teaspoon red chili powder
2 tablespoons dried fenugreek leaves, crumbled
1 tablespoon carom seeds
4 tablespoons melted Clarified Butter (see recipe on page 15)
Water, as needed
Vegetable oil for greasing

1. In a bowl, combine the wheat flour, semolina, salt, red chili powder, fenugreek leaves, carom seeds, and 2 tablespoons of the butter. Slowly add the water, kneading as you go. Make a soft dough, kneading for at least 10 minutes. The final dough should be soft and pliable. It should not be sticky; otherwise it will not roll out well.
2. Cover the dough with a damp cloth or plastic wrap and let it sit for 30 minutes.
3. Roll the dough into a log. Cut into 8 equal portions. Lightly dust a clean work surface and a rolling pin with flour.
4. Lightly grease your hand with oil (or dust with flour). Take 1 portion and roll into a ball between the palms of your hands, then flatten the ball. Place it on the prepared surface. Use the rolling pin to roll it out into a circle about 5 to 6 inches in diameter.
5. Lightly brush the surface of the dough circle with the butter and fold it in half. Brush again with the butter and fold in half again to form a triangle.
6. Lightly flour the work surface again, and roll out the triangle of dough until the base of the triangle is about 5 to 6 inches.
7. Heat a griddle on medium heat and brush it lightly with butter. Add the *paratha* to the griddle. Cook for about 2 minutes or until the bottom of the *paratha* begins to blister. Brush the top lightly with butter and flip over. Cook for 2 minutes.
8. Remove the *paratha* from the griddle and place on a serving platter. Cover with a paper towel. Continue until all the *parathas* are rolled out and cooked. Serve hot.

Onion Bread
(Pyaz Ka Paratha)

2 cups whole-wheat flour (atta),
  plus extra for dusting
4 tablespoons semolina
1½ teaspoons (or to taste)
  table salt
1 teaspoon red chili powder

1 medium-sized red onion,
  peeled and finely minced
6 tablespoons melted Clarified
  Butter (see recipe on page 15)
Water, as needed
Vegetable oil for greasing

Serves 4
Prep Time: 15 minutes,
plus 30 minutes for the
dough to rest
Cook Time: 40 minutes

Minced onions are
kneaded into the
dough to prepare this
delightful and savory
paratha. Serve with a
raita of your choice
(see Chapter 5).

1. In a bowl, combine the wheat flour, semolina, salt, red chili powder, onion, and 2 tablespoons of the butter. Slowly add the water, kneading as you go. Make a soft dough, kneading for at least 10 minutes. The final dough should be soft and pliable. It should not be sticky; otherwise it will not roll out well.
2. Cover the dough with a damp cloth or plastic wrap and let it sit for 30 minutes.
3. Roll the dough into a log and cut it into 10 equal portions. Lightly dust a clean surface and a rolling pin with flour.
4. Lightly grease your hands with oil (or dust with flour). Take 1 portion and roll into a ball between the palms of your hands, then flatten the ball. Place it on the prepared surface. Use a rolling pin to roll it out into a circle about 5 to 6 inches in diameter.
5. Lightly brush the surface of the dough circle with the butter and fold it in half. Brush with the butter and fold in half again to form a triangle.
6. Lightly flour the work surface again, and roll out the triangle until the base of the triangle is about 5 to 6 inches wide.
7. Heat a griddle on medium heat and brush it lightly with butter. Add the *paratha* to the griddle. Cook for about 2 minutes or until the bottom of the *paratha* begins to blister. Brush the top lightly with butter and flip over. Cook for 2 minutes.
8. Remove the *paratha* from the griddle and place on a serving platter. Cover with a paper towel. Continue until all the *parathas* are rolled out and cooked. Serve hot.

Puffed Bread
(Puri)

Serves 4
Prep Time: 10 minutes, plus 20 minutes for the dough to rest
Cook Time: 25 minutes

To enjoy these, serve them hot. Refrigerate rolled puris for about 15 minutes before frying; they will consume less oil and be crispier.

1 cup whole-wheat flour (atta)
1 cup all-purpose flour (maida), plus extra for dusting
1 teaspoon salt
2 tablespoons vegetable oil, plus more for deep-frying
Water, as needed

1. In a bowl, combine the wheat flour, all-purpose flour, salt, and the 2 tablespoons vegetable oil; mix well. Add the water slowly, kneading as you go. Continue to add a little water at a time and knead for about 4 to 5 minutes until you have a smooth dough that is not sticky. If the dough sticks to your fingers, add a little bit of vegetable oil and continue to knead.
2. Cover the dough with a damp cloth or a plastic cover and let rest for at least 20 minutes.
3. Divide the dough into 10 equal pieces. Roll into balls and cover with a damp cloth.
4. Heat vegetable oil in a deep fryer or a deep pan to 375°. Lightly flour a clean work surface and a rolling pin. Roll out each *puri* into a 3-inch circle.
5. Deep-fry 1 *puri* at a time. Lower it into the oil and use the back of a slotted spoon to press down lightly on the *puri*. This will make it puff up. Turn it over and fry for another 20 seconds or until golden brown.
6. Using a slotted spoon, remove the *puri* from the oil and drain on paper towels. Continue until all the *puris* are rolled out and fried. Serve immediately.

❋ Puris Too Oily?

Oily puris generally signal that the oil they were fried in was not hot enough. Allow the oil to heat to the required temperature between batches.

Puffed Bread with Peas
(Matar Ki Puri)

1 cup whole-wheat flour (atta)
1 cup all-purpose flour (maida),
plus extra for dusting
1 teaspoon salt
2 tablespoons vegetable oil,
plus more for deep-frying

Water, as needed
½ cup peas
1 tablespoon minced cilantro
¼ teaspoon red chili powder

Serves 4
Prep Time: 10 minutes,
plus 20 minutes for the
dough to rest
Cook Time: 25 minutes

A delicious variation
of the traditional puri,
serve these with any
pickle of your choice.

1. In a bowl, combine the wheat flour, all-purpose flour, the 1 teaspoon salt, and 2 tablespoons vegetable oil; mix well. Add the water slowly, and begin kneading. Continue to add a little water at a time and knead for about 4 to 5 minutes until you have a smooth dough that is not sticky. If the dough sticks to your fingers, add a little bit of vegetable oil and continue to knead.

2. Cover the dough with a damp cloth or a plastic cover and let rest for at least 20 minutes.

3. While the dough is resting, prepare the filling. Boil the peas in water for about 10 minutes or until tender. Drain. Place the peas into a bowl along with the cilantro, red chili powder, and salt to taste; mash well. Set aside.

4. Divide the dough into 10 equal pieces. Roll into balls. Keep them covered with a damp cloth.

5. Heat vegetable oil in a deep fryer or a deep pan to 375°. Lightly flour a clean work surface and a rolling pin. Roll out each *puri* into a 3-inch circle. Add 1 teaspoon of the pea filling to the center. Bring the sides together and pinch them to seal, forming a ball. Flatten lightly and dust very lightly with flour. Lightly flour the work surface again, and roll out the flattened ball until about 3 inches in diameter.

6. Deep-fry 1 *puri* at a time. Lower the *puri* into the oil and use the back of a slotted spoon to press down lightly on it. This will make it puff up. Turn it over and fry for another 20 seconds or until golden brown.

7. Using a slotted spoon, remove the *puri* from the oil and drain on paper towels. Continue until all the *puris* are rolled out and fried. Serve immediately.

Carom-Flavored Fried Bread
(Ajwain Puri)

Serves 4
Prep Time: 10 minutes, plus 20 minutes for the dough to rest
Cook Time: 25 minutes

This is a strongly flavored puri. Serve hot with any raita of your choice.

1 cup whole-wheat flour (atta)
1 cup all-purpose flour (maida), plus extra for dusting
1 teaspoon salt
1 teaspoon carom seeds
2 tablespoons vegetable oil, plus more for deep-frying
Water, as needed

1. In a bowl, combine the wheat flour, all-purpose flour, salt, carom seeds, and vegetable oil; mix well. Add water slowly and begin kneading. Continue to add a little water at a time and knead for 4 to 5 minutes until you have a smooth dough that is not sticky. If the dough sticks to your fingers, add a little bit of vegetable oil and continue to knead.
2. Cover the dough with a damp cloth or a plastic cover and let rest for at least 20 minutes.
3. Divide the dough into 10 equal pieces. Roll into balls. Keep them covered with a damp cloth as you begin to deep-fry.
4. Heat vegetable oil in a deep fryer or a deep pan to 375°. Lightly flour a clean work surface. Roll out each *puri* into a 3-inch disk.
5. Deep-fry 1 *puri* at a time. Lower the *puri* into the oil and use the back of a slotted spoon to press down lightly on it. This will make it puff up. Turn it over and fry for another 20 seconds or until golden brown. Serve hot.
6. Using a slotted spoon, remove the *puri* from the oil and drain on paper towels. Continue until all the *puris* are rolled out and fried. Serve immediately.

※ Mint Puri

Making mint puri is also very easy. Add 2 generous tablespoons of dried mint leaves to the Carom-Flavored Fried Bread recipe (above) in step 1, then follow the rest of the steps in the recipe.

Baked Fenugreek Bread
(Methi Ki Puri)

*1 cup whole-wheat flour (atta),
    plus extra for dusting
¼ cup semolina
2 heaping tablespoons dried
    fenugreek leaves
½ teaspoon turmeric powder
1 teaspoon red chili powder*

*Table salt, to taste
3 tablespoons Clarified Butter
    (see recipe on page 15)
Water, as needed
Vegetable oil for greasing*

**Serves 4
Prep Time:** 15 minutes
Cook Time: 20 minutes

This bread keeps for 2 days stored in an airtight container. You can even serve this instead of chips with a dip of your choice.

1. Place the whole-wheat flour, semolina, fenugreek leaves, turmeric, red chili powder, salt, and 1 tablespoon of the butter in a bowl; mix well. Add water slowly, kneading the flour into a smooth dough. The dough should be a bit firm, pliable, and not sticky.
2. Lightly grease your hands with oil, and divide the dough into 10 equal portions. Roll each portion into a ball.
3. Preheat oven to 300°. Grease a baking sheet with the remaining butter. Lightly dust a clean work surface and a rolling pin with flour.
4. Roll each dough ball into a 3- to 3½-inch circle. Prick each rolled-out *puri* all over with a fork. Continue until all the *puris* are rolled out.
5. Place a few *puris* on the baking sheet and bake for about 10 minutes. Turn and bake for 2 to 3 minutes or until the *puris* are golden brown and cooked through. (Keep the uncooked *puris* covered with a damp cloth.)
6. Remove the *puris* from the oven and place on a serving platter. Serve at once.

❋ Fresh or Dried Herbs
Most Indian cooks, particularly those in India, will not use dried herbs. Dried herbs are much stronger than fresh ones. As a general rule, you need three times the quantity if you are using fresh herbs in place of dried ones.

Mixed Flour Bread
(Thalepeeth)

3 tablespoons chickpea flour
4 tablespoons rice flour
4 tablespoons whole-wheat flour
1 small red onion, peeled and
   minced
2 tablespoons minced cilantro
1 teaspoon turmeric powder
$\frac{1}{2}$ teaspoon red chili powder

Table salt, to taste
Pinch of asafetida
$\frac{1}{2}$ teaspoon carom seeds,
   crushed
Water, as needed
2 tablespoons vegetable oil

1. In a bowl, mix together all the ingredients *except* the vegetable oil. Add water, a little bit at a time, to make a very thick batter. Mix well and make sure your batter does not have any lumps.
2. Heat a medium-sized nonstick skillet on medium heat. Coat very lightly with vegetable oil.
3. Using a ladle, add about 4 tablespoons of batter to the center of the skillet (similar to a pancake). Add a few drops of vegetable oil to the sides of the bread. Lower the heat and cover for about 2 minutes. This will enable the bread to cook in its own steam.
4. Uncover and flip over. Cook until well browned on both sides, about 2 to 3 minutes.
5. Remove from heat and place on a paper towel. Continue until all the batter is used. Serve hot.

❈ Storing Chapaties

Chapaties are a classic Indian flatbread, served at almost every meal. They do take some practice to make, so don't worry if they are not perfectly round or do not puff up; they will still taste good. Chapaties can be prepared and frozen for up to 1 month. When you are ready to serve them, place them on a paper towel and microwave for a minute or so until soft.

Indian Corn Flatbread
(Makki Di Roti)

2 cups corn flour (makki ka atta)
1 teaspoon table salt
Warm water, as needed
Vegetable oil for greasing

4–5 tablespoons melted
Clarified Butter (see recipe
on page 15)

Serves 4
Prep Time: 10 minutes
Cook Time: 20 minutes

Originally from the Indian state of Punjab, this bread is served with Punjabi Mustard Greens (page 72) and freshly made white butter.

1. In a bowl, combine the flour and the salt; mix well. Begin adding water, a little bit at a time, to make a soft dough. Knead for 2 to 3 minutes. The dough should be soft and not sticky.
2. Lightly grease your hands with oil. Divide the dough into 8 equal balls.
3. To prepare the *rotis*, place a ball between 2 pieces of plastic wrap, or wax paper. Using a rolling pin, roll out the dough into a circle about 3 to 4 inches in diameter and around ¼ inch thick. (This is not a thin bread.) Continue until all the *rotis* are rolled out.
4. Heat a griddle on medium heat. Brush it lightly with the melted butter. Place a flattened *roti* on the griddle. In about 1 or 2 minutes, the bottom of the *roti* will start to blister. Brush the surface of the *roti* with more butter. Flip it over and cook for 1 minute or until crisp.
5. Place the *roti* on a serving platter lined with a paper towel or cloth napkin. Continue until all the *rotis* are cooked. Serve hot.

☀ Droopy Naans

Naans get their traditional teardrop shape from the way the dough actually droops when it is applied to the extremely hot walls of the Tandoor.

CHAPTER 13

Chutney, Pickles, and Papads (Kuch Saath Me)

Mint-Cilantro Chutney
(Pudine Dhaniye Ke Chutney)

Yields ½ cup
Prep Time: 10 minutes
Cook Time: None

Use this as a dipping sauce, salad dressing, or as a topping for grilled meats or seafood.

1 packed cup cilantro
½ packed cup mint
2 serrano green chilies, roughly
    chopped

2 fresh garlic cloves
Table salt, to taste
2 tablespoons fresh lemon
    juice

Blend all the ingredients in a food processor to a smooth paste. To aid in the blending process, you can add 1 tablespoon of water if needed. Chill for about 30 minutes. Serve as a dipping sauce. This chutney will keep, refrigerated, for 4 days.

Tamarind Chutney
(Imli Ki Chutney)

Yields 2 cups
Prep Time: 35 minutes
Cook Time: 10 minutes

If you find it hard to chop dates, soak them in hot water for 10 minutes before using. This chutney will keep in the freezer for up to 6 months.

1 cup tamarind pulp
2 cups hot water
½ cup jaggery or brown sugar
1 teaspoon red chili powder

Table salt, to taste
½ cup dates, pitted and
    chopped

1. In a glass bowl, soak the tamarind pulp in the hot water for 30 minutes. Strain through a fine-meshed sieve into a bowl. Discard any residue in the sieve.
2. Add the jaggery, red chili powder, and salt to the bowl and mix well. Add the dates and purée the entire mixture in a blender. Transfer the mixture to a nonreactive cooking pan.
3. Heat on low until the chutney reaches a custardlike consistency, about 7 to 8 minutes.
4. Remove from heat and let cool to room temperature. Refrigerate for up to a week until needed.

Green Chili and Coconut Chutney
(Hari Mirch Aur Nariel Ke Chutney)

1 cup shredded coconut
4 serrano green chilies
1-inch piece fresh gingerroot,
   peeled
1 tablespoon fresh lemon juice
1 tablespoon minced cilantro
1 tablespoon plain yogurt
   (optional)

Water, as needed
1 tablespoon vegetable oil
½ teaspoon mustard seeds
2 dried red chilies, roughly
   pounded
4 fresh curry leaves

Yields 1 cup
Prep Time: 5 minutes
Cook Time: 5 minutes

This chutney tastes best when it is made fresh, but refrigerated it will keep for 4 days. Serve as a topping for grilled fish.

1. In a blender, purée the coconut, green chilies, ginger, lemon juice, cilantro, yogurt, and ½ cup of water to a smooth paste. Transfer to a nonreactive container with a lid and set aside.
2. In a small skillet, heat the vegetable oil. Add the mustard seeds, red chilies, and curry leaves. In less than 1 minute the mustard seeds will start to sputter. Remove from heat and pour over the coconut chutney.
3. Mix well. Refrigerate, covered, until needed.

❈ The Roots of Chutney

Chutney is the English term of the Indian word chatni. In India, chutneys are generally made fresh daily, in small quantities. They add pizzazz to any meal. They can be sweet, sour, tangy, savory, fresh, or preserved. Fresh chutneys have a bright flavor and are usually thin, smooth sauces. Cooked chutneys have a deeper, broader flavor.

Dry Garlic Chutney
(Lasan Ki Chutney)

Yields 1 cup
Prep Time: 10 minutes
Cook Time: 5 minutes,
plus 10 minutes to cool

Sprinkle this chutney
on warm steamed rice
or atop lightly but-
tered toast. This
keeps well in the
refrigerator for up to
1 week.

1 cup unsweetened desiccated
coconut
12 fresh garlic cloves, peeled

1 teaspoon red chili powder
Table salt, to taste

1. In a medium-sized skillet, roast the coconut and the garlic for about 3 to 4 minutes on low heat. The coconut and the garlic will begin to darken and release their aroma. Remove from heat and allow to cool for about 10 minutes.
2. Transfer the mixture to a blender and add the red chili powder and salt. Blend until you have a coarse powder.
3. Transfer to a container. Cover, and refrigerate until needed.

Saffron Mayonnaise
(Kesari Mayonnaise)

Yields 1 cup
Prep Time: 5 minutes,
plus 30 minutes to chill
Cook Time: None

This recipe is so fla-
vorful, you need just a
tiny bit to dress your
foods. Try this on
grilled salmon.

1 cup mayonnaise
¼ teaspoon Roasted Saffron
(see recipe on page 16)

1 teaspoon crushed red pepper
Table salt, to taste

In a bowl, combine all the ingredients; mix well. Let the mixture chill, covered, in the fridge at least 30 minutes before serving. It will keep for up to 1 week in the refrigerator.

❋ Buying Saffron

Look for Iranian or Spanish saffron. It should be deep red in color. You should be able to see the threads clearly; if it is powdered it is not of good quality. A rule of thumb, 1 ounce of saffron is about 4 tablespoons. In India saffron (the spice and the color) has tremendous religious significance.

Carrot Chutney
(Gajar Ki Chutney)

1½ cups shredded carrot
1 teaspoon grated gingerroot
Water, as needed
1 teaspoon red chili powder

Table salt, to taste
1 tablespoon liquid honey
2 tablespoons fresh lemon
  juice

In a deep pan, bring the carrots, ginger, and 1 cup of water to boil. Reduce heat and cook until the carrots are tender, about 3 to 4 minutes. Drain and let cool for about 20 minutes. Add the red chili powder, salt, honey, and lemon juice; mix well. Refrigerate until needed.

> **Yields 1 cup**
> **Prep Time:** 10 minutes
> **Cook Time:** 5 minutes, plus 20 minutes to cool

> Serve this as an accompaniment to any meal for an added punch. Keeps for 2 to 3 days in the refrigerator.

Green Chili Pickle
(Hari Mirch Ka Achaar)

2 teaspoons fennel seeds
2 teaspoons black mustard seeds
4 teaspoons dried mango
  powder

25 serrano green chilies
4 tablespoons vegetable oil
4 tablespoons fresh lemon juice

1. In a medium-sized skillet, heat the fennel and black mustard seeds. When the seeds begin to sizzle (less than 1 minute), remove from heat. Allow them to cool for about 10 minutes. Using a spice grinder, grind the spices to a powder. Add the mango powder. Set aside.
2. Slit the green chilies. (If you like heat, do not seed the chilies.) Using the tip of your knife, add some of the spice mixture to each of the chilies.
3. Heat the vegetable oil in a skillet. Add the chilies and sauté for 3 to 5 minutes or until the chilies are softened. Remove from heat. Add the lemon juice. Cool to room temperature, about 15 minutes. Transfer to an airtight jar and refrigerate until ready to serve.

> **Yields 1 cup**
> **Prep Time:** 20 minutes
> **Cook Time:** 5 minutes, plus 25 minutes to cool

> There are innumerable variations of this pickle. This will keep for 1 week in the refrigerator.

Shredded Mango Pickle
(Aam Ka Achaar)

Yields ½ cup
Prep Time: 10 minutes
Cook Time: 10 minutes, plus 1 day to let the pickle marinate

Traditionally this is made with diced mango; my recipe uses shredded. This is quite hot; reduce the amount of red chili powder to taste.

4 tablespoons vegetable oil
1 teaspoon mustard seeds
½ teaspoon onion seeds or wild fennel seeds (optional)
1 cup green mango, coarsely shredded (with peel)
2 tablespoons red chili powder
1 teaspoon asafetida powder
Salt, to taste

1. Heat the vegetable oil in a medium-sized skillet. Add the mustard seeds and onion seeds. As soon as the seeds begin to sputter, remove from heat and cover the pan. Set aside.
2. In a clean, dry jar (with a cover), combine the mango, red chili powder, salt, asafetida, and the seasoned oil from step 1; mix together using a dry spoon.
3. Store the jar, covered, in a warm place for 1 day. Shake it intermittently to allow the spices to mix well. Refrigerate until needed.

Mango-Saffron Chutney
(Kairi Kesar Ki Chutney)

Yields 2 cups
Prep Time: 10 minutes, plus 1 hour to stand
Cook Time: 10–15 minutes, plus 20 minutes to cool

Don't use a nonstick skillet here, as the sugar won't carmelize.

2 cups green mango, peeled and coarsely shredded
1 cup sugar
2 teaspoons grated gingerroot
2 dried red chilies, pounded
A pinch of salt
¼ teaspoon saffron, soaked in 4 tablespoons hot water for 10 minutes

1. In a glass bowl, combine the mango and the sugar; mix well. Let it stand for about 1 hour.
2. Heat a small skillet on medium. Add the mango-sugar mixture. Lower the heat and cook for 10 to 12 minutes or until the mangoes become very soft and the sugar begins to turn a light brown.
3. Add the ginger, red chilies, and salt; mix well. Strain the saffron and discard any residue. Add the saffron-infused water and mix well. Simmer for 1 minute. Remove from heat and let cool for about 20 minutes. Cover and refrigerate until needed.

Goan Shrimp Pickle
(Mole De Camarao)

6 tablespoons vegetable oil, divided

2 cups medium shrimp, peeled and deveined

8 curry leaves

2 serrano green chilies, minced

1 tablespoon minced garlic

6 dried red chilies, roughly pounded

2 small red onions, peeled and minced

6 tablespoons white vinegar

½ teaspoon turmeric powder

Table salt, to taste

> **Yields 2 cups**
> **Prep Time:** 10 minutes
> **Cook Time:** 20–25 minutes, plus 20 minutes to cool

> You can increase the quantity of this and serve it as a side dish. It will keep for up to 1 week refrigerated.

1. Heat 3 tablespoons of the vegetable oil in a medium-sized skillet. Add the shrimp and sauté for 3 to 4 minutes or until no longer pink. Transfer the shrimp to a bowl.
2. In the same skillet, heat the remaining vegetable oil. Add the curry leaves, green chilies, garlic, red chilies, and onions; sauté for 7 to 8 minutes or until the onions are well browned.
3. Add the vinegar, turmeric, and salt. Bring to a slow boil. Reduce heat.
4. Add the shrimp and simmer on very low heat for about 8 minutes.
5. Remove from heat and cool to room temperature, about 20 minutes. Transfer to a dry bowl. Refrigerate, covered, until needed.

❈ Choosing Mangoes

When buying mangoes, feel the fruit. It should yield to gentle pressure. It should also be very fragrant. To ripen mangoes, place them in a brown paper bag for a few days.

Sesame Chutney
(Til Ki Chutney)

Yields 1 cup
Prep Time: 5 minutes
Cook Time: 10 minutes, plus 10 minutes to cool

Serve this with any warm Indian bread of your choice (see Chapter 12). This chutney keeps for 1 week, refrigerated.

1 cup white sesame seeds
3 fresh garlic cloves
5 (or to taste) serrano green chilies, seeded
Table salt, to taste
2 tablespoons fresh lemon juice

Water, as needed
1 tablespoon vegetable oil
1 dried red chili, whole
¼ teaspoon mustard seeds

1. In a small skillet on low heat, roast the sesame seeds for 2 to 3 minutes. Stir constantly. When the seeds begin to darken, remove from heat. Cool for about 10 minutes.
2. In a food processor, combine the sesame seeds, garlic, green chilies, salt, and lemon juice. Grind to a fine paste. You may add up to 2 tablespoons of water to aid in the processing if needed. Transfer the chutney to a bowl. Set aside.
3. Heat the vegetable oil in a small skillet. Add the red chili and the mustard seeds. In less than 1 minute, the seeds will begin to sputter. Remove from heat and pour over the prepared chutney. Refrigerate, covered, until ready to use.

☀ Sesame Seeds

Sesame seeds are popular not only in Asia but also in the Middle East. Middle Eastern tahini, a sweet creamy sauce made from sesame seeds, is becoming very popular in North America. Because of the high oil content, sesame seeds tend to become rancid very quickly, so make sure you use fresh seeds.

Lentil Wafers
(Papads)

6 lentil wafers

Serves 4
Prep Time: None
Cook Time: Few minutes

Cook these just prior to serving, as they taste best freshly made. Buy prepackaged papads from your local Indian grocer to save time.

Approach 1: Using tongs, hold the wafer over a low flame. Roast them until they start to change color and small black spots begin to appear on the surface. Continue until all the *papads* are roasted. Serve.

Approach 2: Microwave each wafer for about 1 minute or until it begins to crisp all over and change color. Serve.

Approach 3: Heat vegetable oil in a deep fryer to 350°. Deep-fry a single wafer at a time for less than 1 minute or until the wafer becomes crisp. Drain on a paper towel and serve hot.

☀ Move Over, Popcorn

Top your favorite papad with diced onions, green chilies, and Chaat Spice Mix (page 14), for a perfect movie-time snack. If you love popcorn, cook as you would normally, then serve sprinkled with Chaat Spice Mix.

South Indian Ginger Chutney
(Allam Pachadi)

Yields 1 cup
Prep Time: 15 minutes
Cook Time: 10 minutes, plus 20 minutes to cool

Serve this wonderful chutney as a topping for grilled fish. Or simply use as a flavorful dipping sauce. Keeps for 1 week in the refrigerator.

1 tablespoon tamarind pulp, soaked in ¼ cup hot water for 10 minutes
1 tablespoon vegetable oil
2 dried red chilies
¼ teaspoon fenugreek seeds
½ teaspoon mustard seeds
½ cup grated gingerroot
2 tablespoons sugar
1 teaspoon salt

1. Using a fine-meshed sieve, strain the tamarind pulp over a bowl. Discard any residue in the sieve. Set aside.
2. Heat the vegetable oil in a small skillet and add the red chilies, fenugreek seeds, and the mustard seeds. When the seeds begin to sputter (about 30 seconds), add the gingerroot. Sauté for about 2 minutes.
3. Add the strained tamarind pulp, sugar, and salt; simmer for about 5 minutes. Remove from heat and cool for about 20 minutes.
4. Transfer to a blender or food processor and blend to a smooth paste.
5. Transfer to a bowl. Cover and refrigerate until needed.

Quick Pink Ginger Pickle
(Gulabi Adrak)

Yields 1 cup
Prep Time: 10 minutes, plus 5 to 6 hours to stand
Cook Time: None

This is a standard pickle in most North Indian homes.

¾ cup julienned ginger
½ teaspoon red chili powder
3–4 large serrano green chilies, slit
1 cup rice vinegar

Combine all the ingredients in a dry glass jar. Cover and let stand in the sun for about 5 to 6 hours. Refrigerate until needed. This will keep for up to 3 weeks.

Quick Carrot Pickle
(Jhatpat Gajar Ka Achar)

2 cups diced carrots
½ cup fresh lemon juice
Salt, to taste

½ teaspoon red chili powder
½ teaspoon black mustard
   seeds, roughly pounded

Combine all the ingredients in a dry glass jar. Cover and let stand in the sun for about 5 to 6 hours. Refrigerate until needed.

✴ Handling Pickles

Always use dry spoons to handle pickles or they will spoil. Moisture is the biggest enemy of pickles. Also, always store them in airtight jars to prevent spoilage.

Yields 2 cups
Prep Time: 10 minutes, plus 5 to 6 hours to stand
Cook Time: None

Serve as an accompaniment to any meal. Keeps for 3 days in the refrigerator.

Pineapple Chutney
(Ananas Ki Chutney)

1 (14-ounce) can pineapple
   chunks, drained
1 tablespoon grated fresh
   gingerroot
4 tablespoons sugar
1 tablespoon vegetable oil

½ teaspoon fennel seeds
½ teaspoon cumin seeds
2 dried red chilies, roughly
   pounded
Pinch of salt to taste

1. In a bowl, combine the pineapple, ginger, and sugar. Set aside.
2. In a small skillet, heat the vegetable oil. Add the fennel, cumin, and red chilies. Sauté for about 1 minute or until the spices begin to sizzle.
3. Remove from heat. Pour over the pineapple-ginger mixture and mix well. Transfer to a food processor and grind to a coarse paste.
4. Transfer to a covered container and refrigerate until needed.

Yields 1 cup
Prep Time: 5 minutes
Cook Time: 5 minutes

Serve this chutney with pork, turkey, or as a topping for vanilla ice cream. This chutney will keep for 3 to 4 days, refrigerated.

Papaya Chutney
(Papite Ki Chutney)

Yields 1 cup
Prep Time: 10 minutes
Cook Time: 15 minutes

Do not use a ripe papaya for this, as it will not taste as good. This will keep refrigerated for about 3 days.

2 tablespoons vegetable oil
½ teaspoon cumin seeds
½ teaspoon fenugreek seeds
1 teaspoon fennel seeds
½ teaspoon mustard seeds
2 cups green papaya, peeled and grated

1 tablespoon grated fresh gingerroot
¼ cup sugar
½ cup water
Table salt, to taste

1. In a medium-sized skillet, heat the vegetable oil. Add the cumin, fenugreek, fennel, and mustard seeds. As soon as the seeds begin to sizzle (about 1 minute), add the papaya.
2. Add the gingerroot and sugar; mix well. Add the water and simmer on low heat until the papaya is soft, about 10 minutes. Add salt to taste. Remove from heat. Cool and refrigerate until needed.

Date Pickle
(Khajoor Ka Achar)

Yields 1 cup
Prep Time: 5 minutes
Cook Time: 8 minutes

This pickle will last, refrigerated, up to 6 months. Serve alongside your favorite kebabs.

2 tablespoons tamarind pulp, soaked in ½ cup hot water for 10 minutes
2 cups pitted dates
1 teaspoon red chili powder
3 teaspoons coriander powder

2 teaspoons cumin powder
2 teaspoons fennel seeds, roughly pounded
Salt, to taste
4 tablespoons sugar

1. Using a fine-meshed sieve, strain the tamarind pulp over a bowl. Discard any residue in the sieve. Set the strained pulp aside.
2. In a deep pan, boil the dates in water to cover until tender, about 8 minutes. Drain.
3. Add the dates to a food processor and coarsely grind. Transfer to a bowl.
4. Add the tamarind paste, red chili powder, coriander, cumin, fennel, salt, and sugar to the dates; mix well. Transfer to a glass jar. Cover and refrigerate until needed.

Raw Mango Chutney
(Kacche Aam Ki Chutney)

*1 medium-sized green mango,
    peeled and cubed*

*6 dried red chilies
Pinch of salt*

Purée all the ingredients in a food processor. Add 1 tablespoon of water if needed to aid in the process. Serve.

❈ Tarty Starter

Slice tart green mangoes; sprinkle with Chaat Spice Mix (page 14) or black salt. Serve with cocktails as a snazzy appetizer.

Yields 1 cup
Prep Time: 5 minutes
Cook Time: None

Keeps for 2 to 3 days, refrigerated.
Serve as a dressing for grilled fish.

Mint Chutney
(Pudine Ki Chutney)

*2 packed cups fresh mint
1-inch piece fresh gingerroot,
    peeled and coarsely
    chopped
3 tablespoons lemon juice*

*3 serrano green chilies, seeded
    and coarsely chopped
1 small red onion, peeled and
    coarsely chopped*

Combine all the ingredients in a food processor. Blend to a fine paste. Transfer to a bowl. Refrigerate, covered, until ready to serve.

Yields 1 cup
Prep Time: 5 minutes
Cook Time: None

One of the most popular Indian chutneys. A perfect dipping sauce, this even makes a unique salad dressing. This tastes best freshly made.

Green Chili Chutney
(Hari Mirch Ki Chutney)

Yield 1 cup
Prep Time: 10 minutes
Cook Time: None

Very spicy and robust. Use as a salad dressing over fresh vegetables. Don't forget to seed the chilies if you want a milder taste.

20 serrano green chilies, stemmed and coarsely chopped
½ packed cup cilantro
4 tablespoons fresh lemon juice
1 teaspoon sugar
1 teaspoon salt

In a blender, blend together all the ingredients to a fine paste. Transfer to a covered container. Refrigerate until needed.

✳ Fruit for Dinner?

Green chili, a fruit, is eaten raw with dinner in most North Indian households. (Yes, seeds and all.) If you decide to try it, ensure that the chili is properly washed and I would suggest removing the seeds at first. Drizzle with a bit of lemon juice and see if you like it!

Chili Garlic Sauce
(Mirch Aur Lasan Ki Sauce)

Yields ¼ cup
Prep Time: 5 minutes
Cook Time: 10 minutes, plus 10 minutes to cool

A perfect accompaniment to Indian Chinese dishes, this sauce keeps for up to a week in the refrigerator.

2 tablespoons vegetable oil or sesame oil
4 dried red chilies
6 fresh garlic cloves, minced
2 tablespoons white vinegar
¼ cup canned tomato sauce
Pinch of sugar

1. Heat the vegetable oil in a small skillet. Add the red chilies and sauté for about 1 minute or until they begin to change color. Remove the chilies from the skillet and drain on a paper towel. Reserve the oil in the skillet.
2. Add the garlic to the skillet and sauté for 30 seconds. Add the vinegar and tomato sauce and bring to a slow boil.
3. Remove from heat. Add the sugar and let cool for about 10 minutes.
4. In a spice grinder, grind the fried red chilies to a fine powder. Add to the tomato sauce; mix well. Refrigerate, covered, until ready to use.

South Indian Gun Powder
(Mullaga Podi)

½ cup pigeon peas (toor dal)
½ cup chana dal or yellow
   split peas
½ cup split black gram, or black
   lentils (safeed urad dal)

Pinch of asafetida
4 fresh curry leaves
6 dried red chilies
2 teaspoons table salt

1. In a medium-sized skillet, roast all the ingredients *except* the salt, stirring constantly. In 1 minute or so the *dals* will begin to change color. Remove from heat.
2. Cool for about 20 minutes. Transfer to a spice grinder and grind to a fine powder. Add the salt and mix well. Transfer to a dry jar. Cover and keep until needed. Sprinkle on steamed rice and add 1 tablespoon of hot ghee as a garnish. You can even use it to marinate vegetables, *paneer*, and meats. This will keep for up to 3 months.

> **Yields 1 cup**
> **Prep Time:** None
> **Cook Time:** 15 minutes, plus 20 minutes to cool
>
> This recipe comes from the Indian state of Tamil Nadu. A spicier version has earned the name "Gun Powder" for the heat that it adds.

Peanut Chutney
(Moongphali Ki Chutney)

1 cup salted roasted peanuts
½ teaspoon cumin powder
½ teaspoon red chili powder
1 tablespoon jaggery or palm
   sugar

2 fresh garlic cloves, peeled
   (optional)
Pinch of table salt

In a spice grinder, grind all the ingredients until powdered. As soon as the powder starts to moisten, stop grinding. Transfer to a dry bowl. Cover until ready to use.

> **Yields 1 cup**
> **Prep Time:** 5 minutes
> **Cook Time:** None
>
> Serve this with grilled chicken or even just as a spread on toast. The chutney has a shelf life of about 2 weeks without refrigeration.

Roasted Eggplant Chutney
(Bhune Baigan Ki Chutney)

Yields 1 cup
Prep Time: 10 minutes
Cook Time: 1 hour,
15 minutes, plus 20
minutes to cool

Serve this as a
topping for grilled
portobellos, broiled
salmon, or even
simple steamed rice.
This chutney keeps for
1 week, refrigerated.

1 (1-pound) eggplant
4 tablespoons vegetable oil,
  divided
1 tablespoon tamarind pulp,
  soaked in ⅓ cup hot water
  for 10 minutes
2 tablespoons unsweetened
  desiccated coconut

2 dried red chilies
1 teaspoon minced garlic
2 medium tomatoes, finely
  chopped
Table salt, to taste

1. Preheat oven to 475°.
2. Smear the eggplant with 2 tablespoons of the vegetable oil and place
   it on a foil-lined baking tray. Roast until the eggplant is soft and the
   skin is charred, about 45 to 50 minutes. Remove from the oven and
   let cool.
3. Peel off and discard the skin. Mash the eggplant into a smooth pulp.
   Set aside.
4. Using a fine-meshed sieve, strain the tamarind pulp over a bowl.
   Discard any residue in the sieve. Put the strained pulp in the bowl
   and set aside.
5. Heat a small skillet and roast the red chilies and coconut, stirring
   constantly. In less than 1 minute, the red chilies and coconut will
   begin to change color. Remove from heat and cool for about
   5 minutes. Set aside.
6. In a medium-sized skillet, heat the remaining vegetable oil. Add the
   minced garlic and sauté for about 30 seconds. Add the tomatoes and
   sauté for about 7 minutes or until the tomatoes are cooked.
7. Add the eggplant pulp. Mix well and cook, uncovered, for 8 to 9 minutes or until the eggplant is completely cooked.
8. Add the red chilies mixture and strained tamarind; mix well. Remove
   from heat and allow to cool for about 20 minutes.
9. In a blender, blend the chutney to a smooth paste. Transfer to a
   bowl. Refrigerate, covered, until ready to use.

CHAPTER 14
Sweet Talk (Meeti Meeti Batien)

Rice Pudding
(Kheer)

3 cups whole milk
1 cup heavy cream
¼ cup basmati rice, rinsed
¾ cup sweetened condensed milk

¼ cup coconut milk (optional)
¼ teaspoon saffron threads

1. Add the whole milk and cream to a deep pan. Bring to a boil on medium heat. Stir constantly to prevent scorching.
2. Reduce the heat to medium-low. Add the rice and mix well; cook for about 20 minutes or until the milk has reduced and you obtain a creamy custardlike consistency. Stir frequently while cooking.
3. Add the condensed milk and mix well. Cook for another 5 minutes. If you are adding coconut milk, add it at this point and cook for another 5 minutes.
4. Crush the saffron threads between your fingers, and add to the rice pudding.
5. Remove from heat. Serve hot or cold. To serve cold, refrigerate, covered, for at least 2 hours before serving.

❈ Avoid Spilling Milk
Rub a little butter on the rim of the pot you are using to boil milk. When the milk begins to boil and reaches the buttered rim, it will settle back down and not boil over the pot.

Blancmange
(Phirni)

3 tablespoons ground almonds
6 tablespoons rice flour
2 cups whole milk
1 cup heavy cream
¾ cup sweetened condensed
   milk

¼ teaspoon (or less, to taste)
   cardamom powder
1 tablespoon rose water
   (optional)

Serves 4
Prep Time: 10 minutes
Cook Time: 40 minutes

Blancmange is a simple pudding that was first devised during the Middle Ages, probably in England.

1. In a deep, heavy-bottomed pan, combine the ground almonds, rice flour, whole milk, and heavy cream. Bring to a boil on high heat. Reduce heat to medium and cook, stirring constantly, for about 20 minutes or until the rice mixture obtains a creamy consistency.
2. Add the condensed milk and cook for another 10 minutes.
3. Add the cardamom and rose water and mix well. Remove from heat. Serve hot or cold.

Mango Cream
(Aamraas)

15 ounces sweetened mango
   pulp
½ cup whole milk
4 tablespoons heavy cream,
   whipped

4 tablespoons sweetened
   condensed milk

Serves 4
Prep Time: 5 minutes, plus 30 minutes to chill
Cook Time: None

Serve as a cold dessert soup garnished with mint leaves. Or serve it as a sauce over vanilla ice cream.

Combine all the ingredients in a bowl. The consistency will be sauce-like. Mix well and chill for at least 30 minutes. Serve.

☀ Sweetened Mango Pulp
Although Alphonso mangoes (the most famous of Indian mangoes) are not available here in the States, you can buy canned Alphonso mango pulp at your Indian grocer. If you use fresh mango pulp for this recipe, strain it first to remove any fibers.

Semolina Pudding
(Sooji Ka Halwa)

4 tablespoons Clarified Butter (see recipe on page 15)
1 cup semolina
3 cups hot water
1 cup sugar

1. In a large saucepan, heat the butter.
2. Add the semolina, and cook over low heat. Stir constantly and cook for about 15 minutes or until the semolina is well browned.
3. Add the water and continue cooking on low heat until all the water is absorbed, about 10 minutes. Stir constantly.
4. Add the sugar and mix well. Continue to cook for about 3 minutes. Cover and cook for another 3 to 4 minutes.
5. Remove from heat. Allow to cool for about 20 minutes. Serve.

Saffron Yogurt Pudding
(Kesari Shrikhand)

2 cups Hung Yogurt (see recipe on page 14)
1/4 teaspoon Roasted Saffron (see recipe on page 16)
1/4 cup (or to taste) sugar

Place all the ingredients in a bowl and mix well. You can do this with a spatula or a handheld blender. Adjust sugar to taste. Chill for about 30 minutes, then serve.

Date Halwa
(Khajoor Ka Halwa)

2 tablespoons Clarified Butter
(see recipe on page 15)
1–1¼ cups finely chopped
pitted dates

2 tablespoons heavy cream
2 tablespoons slivered almonds

Heat the butter in a medium-sized pan. Add the dates and sauté for 30 seconds. Add the cream and mix well. Remove from heat. Add the slivered almonds. Serve immediately.

❋ Dates
If using the dates sold in a block, soak them in hot water for 10 minutes, drain, and then chop. If using loose dates, cut them with kitchen shears or chop them with a sharp knife dipped in hot water.

Serves 4
Prep Time: 5 minutes
Cook Time: 5 minutes

A power-packed dessert, serve this along with some hot Indian tea (see Chapter 4).

Opo Squash Pudding
(Dudhi Ka Halwa)

1 cup peeled and grated opo
squash
2 cups whole milk
4 tablespoons milk powder

¾ cup sweetened condensed
milk
¼ teaspoon Roasted Saffron
(see recipe on page 16)

1. Take a few handfuls of the opo squash at a time and squeeze out all the excess water. Place the squash in a deep pan.
2. Add the milk and milk powder to the pan; mix well. Bring to a boil on high heat, stirring constantly.
3. Reduce heat and continue to cook until you obtain a creamy consistency, about 35 minutes.
4. Add the condensed milk and cook for 10 more minutes.
5. Remove from heat, add the saffron, and serve warm.

Serves 4
Prep Time: 10 minutes
Cook Time: 45 minutes

This simple pudding can be made a day in advance. Serve warm garnished with roasted unsalted cashews and raisins.

Sweetened Yogurt
(Mishti Doi)

Serves 4
Prep Time: None
Cook Time: 40 minutes,
plus 4 hours to set,
and time to chill

This dish from the
eastern Indian state
of Bengal can be
steamed or baked.

1 (14-ounce) can sweetened
   condensed milk
2 cups Hung Yogurt (page 14)
   or plain yogurt

Pinch of cardamom powder
   (optional)

1. Preheat the oven to 275°.
2. Blend together all the ingredients and place in an ovenproof dish.
   Place in the oven and bake for 40 minutes.
3. Turn off the oven and leave the dish in the oven for another 4 hours.
   To check for doneness, insert a toothpick into the dish; if it comes
   out clean, the dish is done. Refrigerate, covered, overnight.
4. Alternatively, once you blend the ingredients, place them in a small
   bowl. Cover with aluminum foil. Steam it in a pot of boiling water for
   20 minutes or until the yogurt is set. Serve chilled.

Cheese Dessert
(Bengali Sandesh)

Yields 12 pieces
Prep Time: 5 minutes
Cook Time: 15–20
minutes

Serve as is or drizzled
with a puréed rasp-
berry sauce.

¼ pound ricotta cheese
4 heaping tablespoons milk
   powder

4 tablespoons sweetened condensed milk
Sugar, to taste (optional)

1. Blend together all the ingredients using a hand blender or by hand
   until you get a smooth paste. Taste the mixture. If you like your
   dessert sweeter, add sugar.
2. In a medium-sized nonstick pan, over very low heat, heat the cheese
   mixture, stirring constantly. Cook for about 15 to 20 minutes or until
   the mixture begins to leave the sides of the pan.
3. Remove from heat and transfer to a lightly buttered serving tray. Allow
   to cool for about 1 hour.
4. Cut into 12 portions. Mold into desired shapes of your choice and serve.

Mango Cheesecake
(Aam Ka Cake)

¼ cup water

1 envelope unflavored gelatin

2 cups Indian Cheese (see recipe on page 12), crumbled

1 cup ricotta cheese

4 tablespoons sweetened mango pulp

2 tablespoons sweetened condensed milk

1 cup heavy cream, whipped

1 (15-ounce) can Alphonso mango slices, drained, or fresh mango slices, coarsely chopped

> **Serves 4**
> **Prep Time:** 15 minutes, plus 2 hours to chill
> **Cook Time:** 5 minutes
>
> I love sprinkling some toasted coconut on this dessert to bring the tropics home in the sub-zero temperatures of the East Coast winter.

1. Heat the water on low in a small pan, sprinkle the gelatin on top, and heat until the gelatin completely dissolves. Set aside.
2. In a bowl, combine the Indian Cheese, ricotta cheese, mango pulp, and condensed milk. Mix well and make sure that there are no lumps. A handheld blender works well for this.
3. Slowly add the gelatin to the cheese mixture; mix well.
4. Fold in the whipped cream, and pour into a lightly buttered 6-cup mold. Chill until firm, about 2 hours.
5. When ready to serve, invert the mold onto a serving platter and top the cheesecake with the Alphonso mango.

❋ Using Paneer in Desserts

If you are using store-bought paneer (Indian Cheese), grate it while still cold, using either the grater disk of a food processor or a box grater. Let it come to room temperature before attempting to combine it with the other ingredients. When using homemade paneer, (see recipe on page 12), crumble and mash the paneer by hand to a smooth consistency before using; this will make it easier to blend with the other ingredients.

Creamy Milk Pudding
(Basoondi)

1 cup ricotta cheese
1 cup whole milk
1 cup heavy cream
½ cup (or more, to taste) sugar

1 (14-ounce) can crushed pineapple, drained and chilled

1. In a bowl, combine the ricotta cheese, milk, cream, and sugar. Mix well by hand or with a hand blender. Taste to check sweetness and add more sugar if needed.
2. Transfer the mixture to a heavy-bottomed pan. Heat on low for about 40 minutes, stirring frequently. This mixture needs to cook on a very low heat. The mixture will become creamy and have a very pale yellow color. The final consistency should be that of a creamy custard.
3. Remove from heat. Cool to room temperature, about 1 hour.
4. Fold in the chilled pineapple and serve.

❈ Vark, or Silver Foil

You will often notice Indian sweets are covered with what appears to be shining silver. It is what it appears to be—silver! Silver is beaten into very thin sheets and used as a decorative ingredient in desserts. It is edible and provides a majestic touch to dishes. It is not easily available—check with your Indian grocer.

Tapioca Pudding
(Sabudana Kheer)

¼ cup tapioca
½ cup water
1½ cups whole milk
4 tablespoons sweetened
   condensed milk

Sugar, to taste (optional)
½ teaspoon cardamom seeds

> **Serves 4**
> **Prep Time:** 1 hour
> **Cook Time:** 25 minutes,
> plus 1 hour to chill
>
> A light dessert, serve this garnished with chopped fruit of your choice.

1. In a large bowl, soak the tapioca in the water for about 1 hour. Drain.
2. In a deep pan on medium heat, cook the tapioca and milk for about 20 minutes or until the tapioca is cooked through.
3. Add the condensed milk and mix well. Taste to check for sweetness. Add sugar if needed.
4. Add the cardamom seeds. Cook for 5 minutes.
5. Remove from heat. Chill for about 1 hour. Serve.

Mango Mousse
(Aam Ka Meetha)

¼ cup water
1 packet unflavored gelatin
1 (15-ounce) can Alphonso
   mango slices, drained

2 tablespoons sugar
1 cup heavy cream
1 egg white
Whipped cream, for garnish

> **Serves 4**
> **Prep Time:** 5 minutes,
> plus time to chill
> **Cook Time:** None
>
> A specialty of the new Indian generation. Since fresh Alphonso mangoes are not available in the United States, I use the canned version here.

1. Add the water to a small pan on low heat. Dissolve the gelatin slowly. Set aside.
2. In a blender, blend the mango slices, sugar, and cream. Add the gelatin to the mango mixture and mix well. Set aside.
3. Whip the egg white until it forms peaks. Then fold it into the mango mixture. Transfer to a serving bowl and chill. Garnish with whipped cream before serving.

Apple Kheer
(Saeb Ki Kheer)

Serves 4
Prep Time: 10 minutes
Cook Time: 25 minutes

This is best served chilled. Garnish with silver foil (optional).

2 (red delicious) apples, cored
*   and peeled*
6 tablespoons sugar

2 cups whole milk
½ cup heavy cream

1. Grate the apples and place in a medium-sized, nonstick pan. Add the sugar and cook on low heat until the sugar has dissolved.
2. Add the milk and cream. Bring to a boil on medium heat, stirring constantly.
3. Lower the heat and continue stirring. Cook until the mixture reaches a creamy consistency, about 10 minutes.
4. Remove from heat and pour into a serving bowl. Cover and chill. Serve.

Cheese Pudding
(Paneeri Kheer)

Serves 4
Prep Time: 5 minutes
Cook Time: 1 hour, plus 5 hours to cool and chill

This recipe comes to you from my great-grandmother's kitchen. She calls this her dil khus kheer, or "heart happy pudding"! Serve chilled.

1 cup Indian Cheese (see
*   recipe on page 12), grated*
3 cups whole milk

½ cup heavy cream
½ cup (or more, to taste)
*   sugar*

1. In a bowl, combine the Indian Cheese, milk, cream, and sugar. Mix well by hand or with a hand blender. Taste to check sweetness; add more sugar if needed.
2. Transfer the mixture to a heavy-bottomed pan. Heat on very low heat for about 40 to 60 minutes, stirring constantly. The mixture will become creamy and have a very pale yellow color. The final consistency should be that of a thick custard.
3. Remove from heat and let cool to room temperature, about 1 hour. Then chill for at least 4 hours.

Vermicelli Pudding
(Seviyan Ki Kheer)

4 tablespoons Clarified Butter
  (see recipe on page 15)
  or butter
½ cup broken vermicelli
2 cups whole milk
4 tablespoons sweetened
  condensed milk

1 tablespoon raisins
1 tablespoon slivered almonds
¼ teaspoon Roasted Saffron
  (see recipe on page 16)

Serves 2–3
Prep Time: 5 minutes
Cook Time: 30 minutes,
plus 30 minutes to cool

Roasted vermicelli is
used to make this aro-
matic pudding. Serve
warm in decorative
bowls, garnished with
slivered cashews.

1. Heat a medium-sized nonstick pan on medium. Add the butter. Add the vermicelli and sauté for 1 minute or until it turns brown. Remove from heat and set aside.
2. In a deep pan, combine the milk and condensed milk. Mix well and bring to a boil. Reduce heat to medium and cook for about 15 minutes or until the milk reaches a creamy consistency. Stir constantly.
3. Add the vermicelli, raisins, and almonds. Mix well and cook for another 10 minutes or until the vermicelli is soft.
4. Remove from heat. Add the saffron and mix well. Allow to cool to room temperature (about 30 minutes) before serving.

❈ Nimish

Nimish is one of the most unusual and ethereal Indian desserts. It is prepared by churning boiled milk until foam forms on top. This foam is collected and served in terra-cotta pots. It is believed that the milk needs to be placed outside overnight and there has to be dew for this dish to achieve perfection.

Fruit Salad
(Phal Ka Salaad)

<table>
<tr><td>

Serves 4
Prep Time: 15 minutes, plus 20 minutes to chill
Cook Time: None

Use your choice of seasonal fruits for this. I often make a variation using berries alone. Serve chilled and garnished with fresh mint.

</td></tr>
</table>

1 cup strawberries, roughly chopped
1 cup melon chunks
1 cup papaya chunks
1 cup Hung Yogurt (see recipe on page 14)
¼ teaspoon Roasted Saffron (see recipe on page 16)
1 tablespoon sweetened condensed milk

1. Combine the strawberries, melon, and papaya in a bowl. Set aside.
2. Whip together the yogurt, saffron, and condensed milk; mix well. Pour the yogurt sauce over the fruits. Chill for about 20 minutes. Serve.

Carrot Pudding
(Gajar Ka Halwa)

Serves 4
Prep Time: 15 minutes
Cook Time: 1 hour

Quintessential India, serve this warm, garnished with your choice of unsalted nuts. This dish freezes well.

3 cups whole milk
½ cup heavy cream
6 tablespoons sweetened condensed milk
3 cups grated carrots
4 generous tablespoons milk powder
4 tablespoons butter
¼ cup slivered almonds

1. In a bowl, combine the milk, cream, and condensed milk; mix well. Transfer to a deep, heavy-bottomed nonstick pan, and bring to a boil.
2. Add the carrots and mix well. Cook on medium heat for about 40 minutes, stirring constantly.
3. When most of the liquid has evaporated, add the milk powder and butter. Mix well and continue to cook for another 10 minutes, stirring constantly. When the mixture begins to draw away from the pan, add the almonds. Cook, stirring constantly, for another 5 minutes. Serve hot.

Instant Saffron Ice Cream
(Kesari Kulfi)

2 (8-ounce) cans (or cartons)
   table cream
1 (12-ounce) can evaporated
   milk

1 (14-ounce) can sweetened
   condensed milk
½ teaspoon crushed saffron

Combine all the ingredients in a bowl and mix well. Pour into molds
(should make about 16 small or 8 large servings). Cover and freeze
overnight. Serve.

Serves 6–8
Prep Time: 2 minutes,
plus overnight to freeze
Cook Time: None

If you cannot find
table cream, use
heavy cream. Serve
this bathed in Mango
Cream (page 241).

Pineapple Cake
(Ananas Ka Cake)

1 (1-pound) pound cake
½ cup pineapple juice
   (reserved from the drained
   pineapple)
1 cup whipping cream, whipped

¼ cup canned crushed
   pineapple, drained and
   chilled (juice reserved)

Slice the pound cake and set each slice on an individual serving
plate. Pour 2 to 3 tablespoons of pineapple juice over each slice.
Add a dollop of cream to the slices. Top each with 1 tablespoon of
crushed pineapple and serve immediately.

Serves 4
Prep Time: 10 minutes
Cook Time: None

Although not "tradi-
tionally" Indian, this
cake is very popular
on Indian restaurant
menus. This is an
instant version of the
cake, utilizing store-
bought ingredients.

Mango Yogurt Pudding
(Amrakhand)

Serves 4
Prep Time: 5 minutes,
plus 30 minutes to chill
Cook Time: None

A variation on Saffron Yogurt Pudding (page 242), this is traditionally served with hot Puffed Bread (page 216).

2 cups Hung Yogurt (see recipe on page 14)
½ cup sweetened canned mango pulp

2 tablespoons (or to taste) sugar

Place all the ingredients in a bowl and mix well. You can do this with a spatula or a handheld blender. Adjust sugar to taste. Chill for about 30 minutes, then serve.

❋ Storing Mango Dishes

Always store dishes prepared with mangoes in nonmetallic containers, because mango can discolor metallic containers.

Almond Pudding
(Badam Ki Kheer)

Serves 4
Prep Time: 15 minutes,
plus 2 hours to soak
Cook Time: 20 minutes

Serve garnished with silver foil (optional). You can add a few drops of amaretto flavoring if you like.

2 cups water
¼ cup blanched almonds
¼ cup unsalted cashews

2 cups whole milk
6 tablespoons (or to taste) sugar

1. Bring the water to a boil. Remove from heat.
2. Add the almonds and cashews to the boiled water. Leave immersed in the water for at least 2 hours.
3. Drain the almonds and cashews and transfer to a blender. Add 1 cup of the milk and blend to a coarse paste.
4. In a deep pan, combine the rest of the milk and sugar; mix. Taste and add more sugar if needed. Add the nut paste.
5. Bring to a boil, stirring constantly. Reduce heat to medium and cook for 10 to 20 minutes or until the pudding is very creamy. Allow to cool for about 30 minutes. Serve.

Cream Rose Fudge
(Gulabi Malai Laddoo)

1 cup ricotta cheese, drained of any whey
1 cup Indian Cheese (see recipe on page 12), crumbled
1 (12-ounce) can sweetened condensed milk
2 tablespoons rooh afza or 2 teaspoons rose water
1–2 drops pink food color (optional)

> **Yields 10–12 pieces**
> **Prep Time:** 5 minutes
> **Cook Time:** 15 minutes, plus 30 minutes to cool

> Rooh afza is a fragrant syrup available at your Indian grocer. These keep for 3 days refrigerated.

1. In a bowl, combine all the ingredients and mix well by hand or using a hand blender.
2. Heat a medium-sized nonstick pan. Add the mixture and cook on low heat, stirring constantly, for about 15 minutes or until the mixture dries up and begins to pull away from the sides of the pan.
3. Remove from heat and transfer to a platter. Allow it to cool, for 30 minutes.
4. Divide into 12 pieces and roll each piece into a small ball. Serve.

Trifle

1 (4-serving-size) packet straw-berry jello
1 (4-serving-size) packet instant vanilla pudding
1 (1-pound) sponge cake
1 cup orange juice
1 cup mixed unsalted nuts, chopped
Whipped cream, for garnish

> **Serves 4**
> **Prep Time:** Time to prepare pudding and jello, plus 20 minutes to chill
> **Cook Time:** None

> This recipe uses instant mixes to save time, and it still makes a delightful dessert.

1. Prepare the jello according to the directions on the packet. Cut into small pieces; set aside.
2. Prepare the pudding according to directions on the packet; set aside.
3. Cut the sponge cake into small pieces of equal size. Place the cake pieces in a deep, decorative glass bowl and layer the jello over it. Then pour the juice over the jello. Finally, layer the pudding over the jello.
4. Chill for about 20 minutes. Sprinkle with the nuts and garnish with whipped cream. Serve.

Sweet Bread
(Meeti Roti)

Serves 4
Prep Time: 15 minutes, plus 30 minutes for the dough to rest
Cook Time: 40 minutes

Serve this unique dessert along with Indian tea. I usually cut this up into strips that are easy to pick up by hand.

2 cups whole-wheat flour (atta), plus extra for dusting
4 tablespoons semolina
4 tablespoons fine sugar or jaggery
1 teaspoon fennel seeds
6 tablespoons melted Clarified Butter (see recipe on page 15)
Water, as needed
Vegetable oil for greasing

1. In a bowl, combine the wheat flour, semolina, sugar, fennel seeds, and 4 tablespoons of the butter. Slowly begin to add the water, kneading as you go. Make a soft dough, kneading for at least 10 minutes. The final dough should be soft and pliable. It should not be sticky; otherwise it will not roll out well.
2. Cover the dough with a damp cloth or plastic wrap and let it sit for 30 minutes.
3. Roll the dough into a log. Cut into 10 equal portions. Lightly dust a clean work surface and a rolling pin with flour.
4. Lightly grease your hands with oil. Take 1 portion of dough and roll it into a ball between the palms of your hands, then flatten the ball. Place it on the prepared surface. Use the rolling pin to roll it out into a circle about 5 to 6 inches in diameter.
5. Lightly brush the circle with the butter and fold in half. Brush again with the butter, and fold in half again to form a triangle.
6. Lightly flour the work surface again, and roll out the triangle of dough until the base of the triangle is about 5 to 6 inches wide.
7. Heat a griddle on medium heat and brush it lightly with butter. Add the triangle of dough to the griddle. Cook for about 2 minutes or until the bottom of the bread begins to blister. Brush the top lightly with butter and flip over. Cook for 2 minutes.
8. Remove the bread from the griddle and place on a serving platter. Cover with a paper towel. Continue until all the *rotis* are rolled out and cooked. Serve hot.

Orange Cream
(Malai Santra)

2 (10-ounce) cans mandarin
   oranges
4 tablespoons heavy cream

Pinch of dried mint
¼ teaspoon Roasted Saffron
   (see recipe on page 16)

Drain the mandarin oranges; reserve the syrup. Layer the oranges on a decorative platter. Mix together the heavy cream, mint, and saffron. Add 1 tablespoon of the reserved syrup and mix well. Pour over the oranges. Chill for about 20 minutes. Serve.

Serves 4
Prep Time: 5 minutes, plus 20 minutes to chill
Cook Time: None

In India, cooks prepare this with the cream that forms on top of boiling milk. Try this with your favorite fruit.

Watermelon Ice
(Kalinger Ka Gola)

3 cups watermelon chunks,
   seeds removed

4 tablespoons sugar
4 tablespoons heavy cream

Put all the ingredients in a blender and blend until smooth. Transfer to popsicle molds. Add a stick to each mold. Chill overnight before serving.

Serves 4
(8 large popsicles)
Prep Time: 10 minutes, plus overnight to chill
Cook Time: None

Growing up, I loved golas, or crushed ice popsicles, which you could buy from vendors pushing rattling carts along city roads.

Instant Fruit Cream
(Jaaldi Phal Malai)

Serves 6–8
Prep Time: 10 minutes
Cook Time: None

Try your favorite ice cream and fruits to create this simple dessert. Serve in decorative bowls topped with whipped cream and cherries.

3 cups French vanilla ice cream, softened
2 (15-ounce) cans fruit cocktail, drained

¼ cup slivered almonds
1 drop pink food coloring (optional)

Combine all ingredients in a bowl and serve.

✳ Litchi

You will find canned or fresh litchis at your local Indian grocers. Drain the canned litchis and serve chilled. Fresh litchis are covered by a leathery rind that is pink to strawberry red in color and rough in texture. The edible portion, or aril, is white, translucent, firm, and juicy.

Honey Yogurt
(Shahad Wale Dahi)

Serves 4
Prep Time: 5 minutes, plus 30 minutes to chill
Cook Time: None

This refreshing recipe is best served chilled. You can use plain yogurt for this if you like. I prefer the creamier texture of Hung Yogurt.

3 cups Hung Yogurt (see recipe on page 14)
4 tablespoons honey
¼ teaspoon Roasted Saffron (see recipe on page 16)

2 tablespoons raisins, for garnish

Combine the yogurt, honey, and saffron in a bowl; mix well. Chill, covered, for about 30 minutes. Serve topped with raisins.

Cardamom Cookies
(Eliachi Ke Biscut)

1 cup all-purpose flour
½ cup sugar
½ teaspoon cardamom powder
4 tablespoons chilled Clarified
   Butter (see recipe on
   page 15)

1 large egg
1 tablespoon milk

Yields 24 (2-in.) cookies
Prep Time: 20 minutes,
plus 2 hours to chill and
20 minutes to stand
Cook Time: 10 minutes

Tea time is very popular in India. Biscuts, or biscuits, are served along with a steaming hot cup of Grandma's Chai (page 46).

1. In a large bowl, sift together the flour, sugar, and cardamom; mix well.
2. Cut in the butter until the mixture resembles coarse crumbs.
3. In a small bowl, whisk together the egg and the milk; add to the flour mixture. Stir until a soft dough forms. (The dough will be crumbly.) Pat it together into a ball and flatten slightly. Wrap in plastic and chill for at least 2 hours.
4. Take the dough from the refrigerator and let it sit for about 20 minutes or until it is just workable.
5. Preheat oven to 375°.
6. Roll out the dough between 2 sheets of wax paper or plastic wrap to about ¼-inch thickness. Cut into desired shapes with a knife or a cookie cutter.
7. Bake on an ungreased cookie sheet for 5 to 8 minutes or until the edges turn golden brown. Remove to a cooling rack. Store in an airtight container until ready to serve.

❋ Pineapple Sauce

Here is another wonderful sauce for topping ice cream, fruits, or yogurt: In a blender, purée 1 cup of pineapple chunks, 1 tablespoon of fresh grated ginger, 2 tablespoons honey, and a few mint leaves. Chill and serve.

CHAPTER 15

A Royal Feast (Raj Khana)

Chicken Kebabs
(Sindhi Murgh Kebabs)

¾ cup water
1 tablespoon soya sauce
1 teaspoon red chili powder, divided
2 tablespoons brandy
1 pound ground chicken
1 large red onion, peeled and finely chopped
3 serrano green chilies, seeded and finely chopped
1-inch piece fresh gingerroot, peeled and grated
2 garlic cloves, minced
Table salt, to taste
2 teaspoons coriander powder
1 tablespoon minced cilantro
1 teaspoon Warm Spice Mix (see recipe on page 12)
2 tablespoons vegetable oil

1. In a bowl, combine ¼ cup of the water, the soya sauce, ½ teaspoon of the red chili powder, and the brandy. Set the sauce aside.
2. In another bowl, combine the chicken, onion, green chilies, ginger, garlic, salt, coriander, cilantro, Warm Spice Mix, and remaining red chili powder; mix well. Divide into 8 equal portions and roll into small round balls.
3. In a deep pan, bring the remaining water to a boil. Add the kebabs to the water. Reduce the heat and cook for about 3 to 4 minutes on each side. The kebabs will begin to darken as they absorb the water. Remove the kebabs from the water and place on a paper towel.
4. Heat a medium-sized nonstick skillet. Add the oil to it. Add the kebabs and sauté until golden brown.
5. Add the sauce. Mix well and cook for another minute. Serve with Mint Chuntey (page 235).

✹ Ceremonial Food

Kheer, or pudding, is served in India during many religious ceremonies as an offering to the gods. During the research for this book, I also discovered that rice kheer in particular is served in some parts of western India at funerals.

Lemon Chicken
(Nimbu Wali Murgh)

2 tablespoons butter
1 tablespoon oil
4 skinless bone-in chicken
   thighs
Juice of 2 lemons

¼ cup water
2–3 teaspoons Warm Spice Mix
   (see recipe on page 12)
Table salt, to taste

> **Serves 4**
> **Prep Time:** 10 minutes
> **Cook Time:** 35 minutes
>
> You can use your choice of chicken cuts—adjust the cooking time accordingly. Serve warm, garnished with minced cilantro and thinly sliced lemons.

1. In a large nonstick skillet, heat the butter and oil. Add the chicken and cook for 3 to 4 minutes per side or until each side is well browned.
2. Add the lemon juice and water. Reduce heat to medium, cover, and cook until the chicken is done, about 7 minutes (depending on the thickness of the cut).
3. Remove the cover and increase the heat to high. Add the spice mix and salt. (If you like your dish milder, add only 2 teaspoons of garam masala.) Mix well. Cook until all the water has dried off. Serve hot.

✳ Salting Chicken

Don't salt chicken before you cook it. The salt forces the juices out and impedes browning. Instead, salt the chicken toward the end of the cooking process.

Royal Rice
(Shahi Chawal)

Serves 4
Prep Time: 10 minutes,
plus 3 hours to soak
Cook Time: 20 minutes

This spectacular dish can be served garnished with raisins.

¼ cup dried dates, pitted and chopped
¼ cup dried apricots, pitted and chopped
1 cup whole milk
1 cup cream
3 tablespoons vegetable oil
4 tablespoons cashews

4 tablespoons slivered almonds
2 green cardamom pods, bruised
1 bay leaf
1 black cardamom pod
2 cups basmati rice, rinsed
Table salt, to taste
2 cups water

1. Place the dates and apricots in a bowl. Add the cream and milk, and let soak for 3 hours.
2. In a deep pan, heat the vegetable oil. Add the cashews and sauté for 20 seconds. Add the almonds and green cardamom; sauté for another 20 seconds.
3. Add the bay leaf, black cardamom, and rice; sauté for 1 minute.
4. Add the salt, water, and the apricot-date mixture. Bring to a boil.
5. Reduce heat. Cover and cook until the rice is done, about 15 minutes. Serve hot.

❉ Frying Nuts

When frying almonds, cashews, or other nuts at the same time, first fry the cashews, then the almonds, as the almonds will discolor the oil.

Minty Potato Salad
(Pudine Wale Aloo)

*4 medium potatoes, peeled
and cubed
Juice of 1 lemon
1 cup fresh mint
¼ cup fresh cilantro
2 fresh garlic cloves, crushed
Table salt, to taste
1 tablespoon vegetable oil*

*Water, as needed
½ cup canned chickpeas
(garbanzo beans)
1 small red onion, peeled and
chopped
1 small cucumber, peeled and
chopped*

Serves 4
Prep Time: 10 minutes
Cook Time: 15 minutes,
plus time to chill

This chilled dish can
be served as a salad
or a hearty appetizer.
Serve garnished with
diced cherry toma-
toes and slit green
chilies.

1. Boil the potatoes, in enough water to cover, for 7 to 8 minutes or until tender. Drain and set aside.
2. In a blender or food processor, blend together the lemon juice, mint, cilantro, garlic, salt, and vegetable oil. Add a few tablespoons of water to aid in blending. The final consistency should be that of a salad dressing. Set aside.
3. In a bowl, combine the potatoes, garbanzo beans, red onion, and cucumber. Pour the dressing over the potato mixture. Chill and serve.

✴ Oil-Free Green Chili Pickle

Here is a simple recipe to create a healthy green chili pickle: Mince green chilies; add salt, red chili powder, a pinch of turmeric, and lemon juice (enough to cover the chilies). Let it sit for about 2 hours. Your tangy pickle is ready to eat.

Rose Lemonade
(Gulabi Nimbu Pani)

Serves 4
Prep Time: 5 minutes
Cook Time: None

This lemonade is perfect to serve on hot summer nights. Serve this chilled, garnished with pink rose petals.

4 cups cold water
Juice of 2 large lemons
4 tablespoons sugar
1 teaspoon rose water

In a blender, blend all the ingredients until the sugar is dissolved. Serve over crushed ice.

Mango Ice Cream
(Aam Ki Kulfi)

Yields about 16 pieces
Prep Time:
Overnight to freeze
Cook Time: None

Topped with fresh mango chunks and mint sprigs, this dessert is a gourmet's delight.

2 (8-ounce) cans table cream or half-and-half
1 (12-ounce) can evaporated milk
1 (14-ounce) can sweetened condensed milk
1 cup canned mango pulp

Combine all the ingredients in a bowl and mix well. Pour into your choice of ice cream molds (should make about 16). Cover and freeze overnight. Serve.

Appendices

Appendix A
Glossary

Appendix B
Suggested Menus

Appendix C
Additional Resources

Appendix A

Glossary

anise seed *(sauf)*: These small, oval-shaped seeds have a strong licorice flavor and belong to the celery family. They are used to flavor curries, desserts, and drinks. They can be substituted for fennel.

asafetida *(hing)*: Also known as the stinking spice, this resin has a strong pungent smell. The smell totally disappears once the spice is cooked. It adds a garlic flavor to the recipe.

bay leaf *(tej patta)*: Leaves of the laurel tree, these add a delicate, sweet flavor to dishes. These are not a substitute for curry leaves. Remove from the final dish before serving.

black cardamom pods *(moti* or *bari eliachi)*: These are about ½ inch in size and black in color. They have a woody smell and provide a strong and nutty flavor to the dish. Remove from the dish before serving.

black peppercorns *(kali mirch)*: Berries of the pepper plant, black peppercorns have a strong peppery taste. They can be used whole or crushed.

black salt *(kala namak)*: This grayish, light pink salt has a strong tangy flavor. It is often used to add zest to a recipe. It is not a substitute for regular table salt. It does have a characteristic aroma that disappears when it is added to a dish.

carom seeds *(ajwain)*: These tiny seeds are said to be very strong digestive aids. They are very similar to thyme in flavor. Gently crush them (with a rolling pin) prior to use; this will help release their fragrance and flavor.

chana dal: Very similar in appearance to yellow split peas, *chana dal* are a bit larger in size. Since they are hard to digest, these lentils are generally cooked with asafetida, as it aids in digestion.

chickpea flour *(besan)*: This flour is made from chickpeas and is used as a thickener in curries or to prepare desserts. Also called gram flour.

cilantro *(hara dhaniya)*: Fresh cilantro, also known as Chinese parsley, has a lemony flavor and is a highly aromatic herb. It is used liberally as a garnish for most North Indian dishes. Dried coriander powder is not a substitute for fresh cilantro. Best when fresh, dried leaves are virtually flavorless.

cinnamon stick *(dalchini)*: Cinnamon comes from the inner bark of an evergreen tree. It is used in most dishes here in the whole stick form. It imparts a strong sweet flavor to the dish. Remove from the dish before serving.

cloves *(laung)*: These dried flower buds of an evergreen tree pack quite a punch. Bitter in taste, they are added to sweet and savory dishes.

coconut milk *(nariel ka doodh)*: Coconut milk is prepared by soaking the flesh of the coconut in hot water. Do not substitute coconut water.

coconut, desiccated *(sukha nariel)*: Dried coconut flakes used in many sweet and savory dishes. Make sure you do not select the sweetened variety unless specifically indicated in the recipe.

coriander seeds *(dhaniya)*: These lemony seeds are used whole or ground in Indian cooking.

cumin seeds *(jeera)*: One of the most versatile spices in the world, cumin adds a musk-like flavor to dishes. It can be used whole or ground. Buy the *safeed jeera*, or brown cumin seeds, for the recipes in this book. The black cumin seeds, *shahi jeera*, are more exotic and not used here.

curry leaves *(kari patta)*: These small pointed leaves are very fragrant and add a unique lemony flavor to dishes. Bay leaves are not a substitute.

fennel *(sauf)*: These small oval-shaped seeds are very similar to anise seeds. They are used whole or in powdered form to flavor curries. Similar in appearance to cumin seeds, they have a strong licorice-like taste.

fenugreek leaves, dried *(kasoori methi)*: Highly aromatic, these dried leaves are often used to flavor curries. Use sparingly, as too much will add a lot of bitterness to the dish.

fenugreek seeds *(methi dana)*: These small, flat brown seeds are very bitter tasting. The bitterness disappears during the cooking process. They are used in South Indian cooking. These seeds are also commonly used for pickling.

green cardamom pods *(choti eliachi)*: Cardamom is often called the Queen of Spices. These green pods are used in both sweet and savory dishes. Each green pod can contain up to 20 black, sticky seeds. Crush the pod before using it to help release the fragrance. Cardamoms are also chewed raw as breath fresheners.

jaggery *(gur)*: Thick boiled sugar cane juice, it has a unique sweet taste. Brown sugar can be used as a substitute.

kokum: There is no English name for this fruit and no substitute for its taste. This purple fruit is sold in its dried form in Indian grocery stores.

mango powder *(amchur)*: Made from dried green mangoes, it is used to add a tangy taste to dishes. In a pinch, you can use lemon juice.

mint *(pudina)*: A strong aromatic herb, it is used in preparation of chutneys, curries, and drinks.

mustard seeds *(rai)*: These tiny, round black seeds are generally sizzled in hot oil at the beginning of a dish preparation. They add a toasty flavor to the dish.

pigeon peas *(toor dal)*: These pale yellow *dals* are used extensively in South Indian cooking. Sold as oily or dry, pick the dry variety for the recipes in this book. Also called cajan peas or dahl.

pomegranate powder *(anardana)*: This powder is used to add sourness to a dish. Prepared from dried pomegranates, it is sold in a powdered form.

poppy seeds *(khus khus)*: Indian poppy seeds are white in color and are used to provide a rich nutty flavor to dishes.

pulses: Refer to any of a wide variety of dried beans, split peas, and lentils. Pulses are a staple in India.

red chilies, whole dried and powder (*sukhi lal mirch*): These dried whole red chilies are used to add heat to a dish. You can grind them to create the powder or buy prepared red chili powder. Cayenne pepper can be used as a substitute.

red lentils (*masoor dal*): These skinless red split lentils turn a creamy yellow when cooked. They are also sold with the skin on (brownish in color).

rose water (*gulabi jal*): Rose water is used sparingly to add a touch of elegant flavor. It is sold in bottles and should be refrigerated after opening.

saffron (*kesar*): This very expensive spice has a flavor so unique that it cannot be substituted. Use about 3 strands per person in a recipe, as a general rule. The world's best saffron comes from Spain and from India's Kashmir valley. It adds a beautiful amber hue to dishes.

sesame seeds (*til*): These small cream-colored seeds are used to add a nutty flavor to dishes. They turn rancid quickly, so make sure you taste them before using.

split black gram (*safeed urad dal*): Also called a split black lentil, this pulse is usually used to make fritters and curries. It has a sticky consistency when ground or cooked. When the black skin is removed, revealing the white interior, this lentil is referred to as a "white lentil" or "skinned and split black gram"; without the skin, it has a milder taste.

tamarind (*imli*): Sold as concentrate or in dried blocks, tamarind is used to add a sourness to dishes.

turmeric (*haldi*): Turmeric comes from a rhizome. It has a warm aroma and provides Indian dishes with the characteristic yellow color. In ancient India, turmeric was valued for its antiseptic properties.

whole black gram (*urad dal*): Small round and black, these lentils take a long time to cook and soften.

yellow fal (*peeli moong dal*): A tiny yellow lentil, it cooks quickly and has a very creamy texture when soft.

Suggested Menus

Sunday Brunch

APPETIZER: Crunchy Bread Fritters (page 32)

BEVERAGE: Coconut and Tomato Soup (page 51)

ENTRÉE: Parsi-Style Eggs (page 112)

SIDE DISH: Indian-Style Coleslaw (page 54)

STARCH: Mint-Flavored Bread (page 207)

DESSERT: Creamy Milk Pudding (page 246)

Indian Chaat Party

APPETIZER: Potato Cutlets (page 35)

BEVERAGE: Mint-Ginger Cooler (page 41)

ENTRÉE: Chickpea Curry (page 187)

STARCH: Fried Indian Bread (page 204)

DESSERT: Instant Saffron Ice Cream (page 251)

Summer Cookout

APPETIZER: Corn Fritters (page 30)

BEVERAGE: Mango Yogurt Drink (page 42)

ENTRÉE: Ginger-Flavored Lamb Chops (page 127)

SIDE DISH: Green Beans with Coconut (page 88)

STARCH: Lemon Rice (page 165)

DESSERT: Mango Mousse (page 247)

An Elegant Dinner

APPETIZER: Chicken Tikka (page 24)

BEVERAGE: Fizzy Rose Drink (page 40)

ENTRÉE: Shrimp in Coconut Milk (page 133)

SIDE DISH: Fried Okra (page 79)

STARCH: Garlic Rice (page 172)

DESSERT: Mango Cheesecake (page 245)

Ladies' Luncheon

APPETIZER: Cucumber Cup Coolers (page 18)

BEVERAGE: Maharastrian Buttermilk (page 44)

ENTRÉE: Salmon in Saffron-Flavored Curry (page 154)

SIDE DISH: Potato and Yogurt Salad (page 59)

STARCH: Simple Basmati Rice (page 160)

DESSERT: Cheese Pudding (page 248)

High Tea

APPETIZER: Onion Rings (page 36)

BEVERAGE: Grandma's Chai (page 46)

ENTRÉE: Chicken Tikka (page 24)

SIDE DISH: Punjabi Onion Salad (page 66)

DESSERT: Honey Yogurt (page 256)

Quick Family Dinner

APPETIZER: Curried Mixed Nuts (page 38)

BEVERAGE: Rose-Flavored Yogurt Drink (page 40)

ENTRÉE: Sizzling Tandoori Chicken (page 93)

SIDE DISH: Carrot and Tomato Salad (page 62)

STARCH: Simple Basmati Rice (page 160)

DESSERT: Mango Cream (page 241)

Indian Chinese Night

APPETIZER: Indian Cheese Manchurian (page 21)

BEVERAGE: Fresh Lime Soda (page 41)

ENTRÉE: Lollipop Chicken (page 90)

SIDE DISH: Vegetable Fried Rice (page 174)

DESSERT: Rice Pudding (page 240)

Diwali Dinner (Indian Festival Dinner)

APPETIZER: Indian Cheese Tikka (page 23)

BEVERAGE: Saffron Lemonade (page 43)

ENTRÉE: Indian Red Kidney Beans (page 188)

SIDE DISH: Cheese and Spinach Curry (page 71)

STARCH: Malabari Coconut Rice (page 177)

DESSERT: Mango Ice Cream (page 264)

An Autumn Dinner

APPETIZER: Sweet Potatoes with Tamarind (page 22)

BEVERAGE: Minty Yogurt Drink (page 45)

ENTRÉE: Butter Chicken (page 94)

SIDE DISH: Punjabi Mustard Greens (page 72)

STARCH: Indian Corn Flatbread (page 221)

DESSERT: Saffron Yogurt Pudding (page 242)

Appendix C

Additional Resources

Stores for Your Indian Food Needs

ALABAMA

Asian Groceries

504 G Jordan Lane

Huntsville, AL 35805

Tel: 205-539-5100

ALASKA

Bombay House

1401 Old Glenn Highway

Eagle River, AK 99577

Tel: 907-696-6055

ARIZONA

India International Foods

5054 E. McDowell Road

Phoenix, AZ 85008

Tel: 602-273-6777

CALIFORNIA

Dana Bazar

5113 Mowry Avenue

Fremont, CA 94536

Tel: 510-742-0555

Raj Imports

1933 S. Broadway, Suite 371

Los Angeles, CA 90007

Tel: 213-748-3510

COLORADO

Taste of India

4820 Flintridge Drive

Colorado Springs, CO 80918

Tel: 719-598-3428

CONNECTICUT

India Spice & Gift Shop

3295 Fairfield Avenue

Bridgeport, CT 06605

Tel: 203-384-0666

DELAWARE

Spice Mahal

3621 Kirkwood Highway

Wilmington, DE 19808

Tel: 302-994-8144

DISTRICT OF COLUMBIA

Saras Food Market

3008 Q Street NW

Washington, D.C. 20017

Tel: 202-223-7972

FLORIDA

Bombay Super Bazaar

2008 Northeast 164th Street

Miami, FL 33162

Tel: 305-582-2566

Patel Brothers

7400 Southland Blvd

Orlando, FL 32809

Tel: 407-438-0766

GEORGIA

Taj Mahal Imports

1612 Woodcliff Drive NE

Atlanta, GA 30329

Tel: 404-321-5940

ILLINOIS

Asian Market

1014 West Leland Avenue

Chicago, IL 60640

Tel: 773-334-1970

INDIANA

International Bazaar

4225 Lafayette Road

Indianapolis, IN 46254

Tel: 317-299-4628

IOWA

International Groceries

7517 Douglas Avenue, Suite 16

Urbandale, IA 50322

Tel: 515-278-1522

KANSAS

Patel Foods

119th St. Metcalf Ave

Overland Park, KS 66212

Tel: 913-696-1950

KENTUCKY

Sagar India Market

3340 Holwyn Road

Lexington, KY 40503

Tel: 606-296-9573

LOUISIANA

India Imports

3200 Georgia Avenue

Kenner, LA 70065

Tel: 504-443-1504

MARYLAND

Patel Brothers

2080 University Blvd

E Langley Park, MD 20783

Tel: 301-422-1555

MASSACHUSETTS

International Market

365 Somerville Avenue

Boston, MA 02143

Tel: 617-776-1880

MICHIGAN

Bombay Grocers

3022 Packard Street

Ann Arbor, MI 48108

Tel: 734-971-7707

MINNESOTA

Patel Groceries

1848 Central Avenue NE

Minneapolis, MN 55418

Tel: 612-789-8800

MISSOURI

Taj Emporium

1400 Fellows Place

Columbia, MO 65201

Tel: 573-442-5201

NEBRASKA

Indian Grocery

3029 S. 83rd Plaza

Omaha, NE 68124

Tel: 402-391-0844

NEVADA

India Food & Spices

1166 E. Twain Avenue

Las Vegas, NV 89109

Tel: 702-733-0640

NEW HAMPSHIRE

East West Foods

295 DW Highway

Nashua, NH 03060

NEW JERSEY

Panchvatee Food Mart

1700 Oak Tree Rd

Edison, NJ 08820

Tel: 732-549-5631

NEW MEXICO

India Kitchen

49-12 Calle Del Cielo NE

Albuquerque, NM 87111

Tel: 505-884-2333

NEW YORK

Asia Food Market

71½ Mulberry

New York, NY 10016

Tel: 212-962-2020

NORTH CAROLINA

Patel Bros

4434-5 Creedmoor Road

Raleigh, NC 27612

Tel: 919-510 0085

OHIO

Patel Brothers

6876 Pearl Rd.

Middleburg Heights, OH 44134

Tel: 440-885-4440

OKLAHOMA

Spices of India

2020 North Macarthur Blvd.

Oklahoma City, OK 73127

Tel: 405-942-7813

OREGON

India Foods

125 West 11th Avenue

Eugene, OR 97401

Tel: 503-646-0592

PENNSYLVANIA

International Food & Spices

4203 Walnut Street

Philadelphia, PA 19104

Tel: 215-222-4480

RHODE ISLAND

India Imports, Inc.

3 Davol Square

Providence, RI 02904

Tel: 401-521-3283

SOUTH CAROLINA

Indian Grocers, Inc.

1417 Laurens Road, #B

Greenville, SC 29607

Tel: 864-232-9889

TENNESSEE

Taj International Foods

7334 Lee Highway

Chattanooga, TN 37421

Tel: 423-892-0259

TEXAS

India Grocers

6606 Southwest Freeway

Houston, TX 77074

Tel: 713-266-7717

UTAH

Eastern Groceries

1616 W. 3500 South

West Valley City, UT 84119

Tel: 801-975-7805

VIRGINIA

Shivam Music & Spices

11139 Lee Highway

Fairfax, VA 22030

Tel: 703-591-5116

WASHINGTON

India Bazaar

20936 108th SE

Kent, WA 98031

Tel: 253-850-8906

WEST VIRGINIA

Taste of India

1011 Quarrier St.

Charleston, WV 25301

Tel: 304-342-2642

WISCONSIN

Indian Groceries & Spices

10633 W. North Avenue

Milwaukee, WI 53226

Tel: 414-771-3535

Web Sites You Can Shop

Namaste.com

Finest online Indian products and services.

www.namaste.com

Ethnic Grocer

This site sells not only Indian products but also spices and herbs used in other global cuisines.

www.ethnicgrocer.com

India Food Company

Great prices on herbs and spices.

www.indiafoodco.com

Kundan Foods

Online since 1979, they provide some of the freshest spices and food products.

www.kundanfoods.com

India Plaza

An Indian portal, offering herbs, spices, recipes, jewelry, and much more.

www.indiaplaza.com

Spice Store

A mail-order/online site that orders spices straight from India.

www.spices-store.com

Spices Galore

Here, you'll find a variety of not only hard to find spices, but sauces, marinades, East Indian specialties, and Indian groceries.

www.spicesgalore1.com

Index

THE EVERYTHING SERIES!

BUSINESS

Everything® **Business Planning Book**
Everything® **Coaching and Mentoring Book**
Everything® **Fundraising Book**
Everything® **Home-Based Business Book**
Everything® **Leadership Book**
Everything® **Managing People Book**
Everything® **Network Marketing Book**
Everything® **Online Business Book**
Everything® **Project Management Book**
Everything® **Selling Book**
Everything® **Start Your Own Business Book**
Everything® **Time Management Book**

COMPUTERS

Everything® **Build Your Own Home Page Book**
Everything® **Computer Book**
Everything® **Internet Book**
Everything® **Microsoft® Word 2000 Book**

COOKBOOKS

Everything® **Barbecue Cookbook**
Everything® **Bartender's Book, $9.95**
Everything® **Chinese Cookbook**
Everything® **Chocolate Cookbook**
Everything® **Cookbook**
Everything® **Dessert Cookbook**
Everything® **Diabetes Cookbook**
Everything® **Indian Cookbook**
Everything® **Low-Carb Cookbook**
Everything® **Low-Fat High-Flavor Cookbook**

Everything® **Low-Salt Cookbook**
Everything® **Mediterranean Cookbook**
Everything® **Mexican Cookbook**
Everything® **One-Pot Cookbook**
Everything® **Pasta Book**
Everything® **Quick Meals Cookbook**
Everything® **Slow Cooker Cookbook**
Everything® **Soup Cookbook**
Everything® **Thai Cookbook**
Everything® **Vegetarian Cookbook**
Everything® **Wine Book**

HEALTH

Everything® **Alzheimer's Book**
Everything® **Anti-Aging Book**
Everything® **Diabetes Book**
Everything® **Dieting Book**
Everything® **Herbal Remedies Book**
Everything® **Hypnosis Book**
Everything® **Massage Book**
Everything® **Menopause Book**
Everything® **Nutrition Book**
Everything® **Reflexology Book**
Everything® **Reiki Book**
Everything® **Stress Management Book**
Everything® **Vitamins, Minerals, and Nutritional Supplements Book**

HISTORY

Everything® **American Government Book**
Everything® **American History Book**
Everything® **Civil War Book**
Everything® **Irish History & Heritage Book**

Everything® **Mafia Book**
Everything® **Middle East Book**
Everything® **World War II Book**

HOBBIES & GAMES

Everything® **Bridge Book**
Everything® **Candlemaking Book**
Everything® **Casino Gambling Book**
Everything® **Chess Basics Book**
Everything® **Collectibles Book**
Everything® **Crossword and Puzzle Book**
Everything® **Digital Photography Book**
Everything® **Easy Crosswords Book**
Everything® **Family Tree Book**
Everything® **Games Book**
Everything® **Knitting Book**
Everything® **Magic Book**
Everything® **Motorcycle Book**
Everything® **Online Genealogy Book**
Everything® **Photography Book**
Everything® **Pool & Billiards Book**
Everything® **Quilting Book**
Everything® **Scrapbooking Book**
Everything® **Sewing Book**
Everything® **Soapmaking Book**

HOME IMPROVEMENT

Everything® **Feng Shui Book**
Everything® **Feng Shui Decluttering Book, $9.95 ($15.95 CAN)**
Everything® **Fix-It Book**
Everything® **Gardening Book**
Everything® **Homebuilding Book**

All Everything® books are priced at $12.95 or $14.95, unless otherwise stated. Prices subject to change without notice.
Canadian prices range from $11.95–$31.95, and are subject to change without notice.

Everything® **Home Decorating Book**
Everything® **Landscaping Book**
Everything® **Lawn Care Book**
Everything® **Organize Your Home Book**

EVERYTHING®
KIDS' BOOKS

All titles are $6.95
Everything® **Kids' Baseball Book,
3rd Ed.** ($10.95 CAN)
Everything® **Kids' Bible Trivia Book**
($10.95 CAN)
Everything® **Kids' Bugs Book** ($10.95 CAN)
Everything® **Kids' Christmas Puzzle &
Activity Book** ($10.95 CAN)
Everything® **Kids' Cookbook** ($10.95 CAN)
Everything® **Kids' Halloween Puzzle &
Activity Book** ($10.95 CAN)
Everything® **Kids' Joke Book** ($10.95 CAN)
Everything® **Kids' Math Puzzles Book**
($10.95 CAN)
Everything® **Kids' Mazes Book**
($10.95 CAN)
Everything® **Kids' Money Book**
($11.95 CAN)
Everything® **Kids' Monsters Book**
($10.95 CAN)
Everything® **Kids' Nature Book**
($11.95 CAN)
Everything® **Kids' Puzzle Book**
($10.95 CAN)
Everything® **Kids' Riddles & Brain
Teasers Book** ($10.95 CAN)
Everything® **Kids' Science Experiments
Book** ($10.95 CAN)
Everything® **Kids' Soccer Book**
($10.95 CAN)
Everything® **Kids' Travel Activity Book**
($10.95 CAN)

KIDS' STORY BOOKS

Everything® **Bedtime Story Book**
Everything® **Bible Stories Book**
Everything® **Fairy Tales Book**
Everything® **Mother Goose Book**

LANGUAGE

Everything® **Inglés Book**
Everything® **Learning French Book**
Everything® **Learning German Book**
Everything® **Learning Italian Book**
Everything® **Learning Latin Book**
Everything® **Learning Spanish Book**
Everything® **Sign Language Book**
Everything® **Spanish Phrase Book,**
$9.95 ($15.95 CAN)

MUSIC

Everything® **Drums Book (with CD),**
$19.95 ($31.95 CAN)
Everything® **Guitar Book**
Everything® **Playing Piano and
Keyboards Book**
Everything® **Rock & Blues Guitar
Book (with CD),** $19.95
($31.95 CAN)
Everything® **Songwriting Book**

NEW AGE

Everything® **Astrology Book**
Everything® **Divining the Future Book**
Everything® **Dreams Book**
Everything® **Ghost Book**
Everything® **Love Signs Book,** $9.95
($15.95 CAN)
Everything® **Meditation Book**
Everything® **Numerology Book**
Everything® **Palmistry Book**
Everything® **Psychic Book**
Everything® **Spells & Charms Book**
Everything® **Tarot Book**
Everything® **Wicca and Witchcraft Book**

PARENTING

Everything® **Baby Names Book**
Everything® **Baby Shower Book**
Everything® **Baby's First Food Book**
Everything® **Baby's First Year Book**
Everything® **Breastfeeding Book**

Everything® **Father-to-Be Book**
Everything® **Get Ready for Baby Book**
Everything® **Getting Pregnant Book**
Everything® **Homeschooling Book**
Everything® **Parent's Guide to
Children with Autism**
Everything® **Parent's Guide to Positive
Discipline**
Everything® **Parent's Guide to Raising
a Successful Child**
Everything® **Parenting a Teenager Book**
Everything® **Potty Training Book,**
$9.95 ($15.95 CAN)
Everything® **Pregnancy Book, 2nd Ed.**
Everything® **Pregnancy Fitness Book**
Everything® **Pregnancy Organizer,**
$15.00 ($22.95 CAN)
Everything® **Toddler Book**
Everything® **Tween Book**

PERSONAL FINANCE

Everything® **Budgeting Book**
Everything® **Get Out of Debt Book**
Everything® **Get Rich Book**
Everything® **Homebuying Book, 2nd Ed.**
Everything® **Homeselling Book**
Everything® **Investing Book**
Everything® **Money Book**
Everything® **Mutual Funds Book**
Everything® **Online Investing Book**
Everything® **Personal Finance Book**
Everything® **Personal Finance in Your
20s & 30s Book**
Everything® **Wills & Estate Planning
Book**

PETS

Everything® **Cat Book**
Everything® **Dog Book**
Everything® **Dog Training and Tricks
Book**
Everything® **Golden Retriever Book**
Everything® **Horse Book**
Everything® **Labrador Retriever Book**
Everything® **Puppy Book**
Everything® **Tropical Fish Book**

All Everything® books are priced at $12.95 or $14.95, unless otherwise stated. Prices subject to change without notice.
Canadian prices range from $11.95–$31.95, and are subject to change without notice.

REFERENCE

Everything® **Astronomy Book**
Everything® **Car Care Book**
Everything® **Christmas Book, $15.00**
($21.95 CAN)
Everything® **Classical Mythology Book**
Everything® **Einstein Book**
Everything® **Etiquette Book**
Everything® **Great Thinkers Book**
Everything® **Philosophy Book**
Everything® **Psychology Book**
Everything® **Shakespeare Book**
Everything® **Tall Tales, Legends, &**
Other Outrageous
Lies Book
Everything® **Toasts Book**
Everything® **Trivia Book**
Everything® **Weather Book**

RELIGION

Everything® **Angels Book**
Everything® **Bible Book**
Everything® **Buddhism Book**
Everything® **Catholicism Book**
Everything® **Christianity Book**
Everything® **Jewish History &**
Heritage Book
Everything® **Judaism Book**
Everything® **Prayer Book**
Everything® **Saints Book**
Everything® **Understanding Islam**
Book
Everything® **World's Religions Book**
Everything® **Zen Book**

SCHOOL & CAREERS

Everything® **After College Book**
Everything® **Alternative Careers Book**
Everything® **College Survival Book**
Everything® **Cover Letter Book**
Everything® **Get-a-Job Book**
Everything® **Hot Careers Book**

Everything® **Job Interview Book**
Everything® **New Teacher Book**
Everything® **Online Job Search Book**
Everything® **Resume Book, 2nd Ed.**
Everything® **Study Book**

SELF-HELP/ RELATIONSHIPS

Everything® **Dating Book**
Everything® **Divorce Book**
Everything® **Great Marriage Book**
Everything® **Great Sex Book**
Everything® **Kama Sutra Book**
Everything® **Romance Book**
Everything® **Self-Esteem Book**
Everything® **Success Book**

SPORTS & FITNESS

Everything® **Body Shaping Book**
Everything® **Fishing Book**
Everything® **Fly-Fishing Book**
Everything® **Golf Book**
Everything® **Golf Instruction Book**
Everything® **Knots Book**
Everything® **Pilates Book**
Everything® **Running Book**
Everything® **Sailing Book, 2nd Ed.**
Everything® **T'ai Chi and QiGong Book**
Everything® **Total Fitness Book**
Everything® **Weight Training Book**
Everything® **Yoga Book**

TRAVEL

Everything® **Family Guide to Hawaii**
Everything® **Guide to Las Vegas**
Everything® **Guide to New England**
Everything® **Guide to New York City**
Everything® **Guide to Washington D.C.**
Everything® **Travel Guide to The**
Disneyland Resort®,
California Adventure®,

Universal Studios®, and
the Anaheim Area
Everything® **Travel Guide to the Walt**
Disney World Resort®,
Universal Studios®, and
Greater Orlando, 3rd Ed.

WEDDINGS

Everything® **Bachelorette Party Book,**
$9.95 ($15.95 CAN)
Everything® **Bridesmaid Book, $9.95**
($15.95 CAN)
Everything® **Creative Wedding Ideas**
Book
Everything® **Elopement Book, $9.95**
($15.95 CAN)
Everything® **Groom Book**
Everything® **Jewish Wedding Book**
Everything® **Wedding Book, 2nd Ed.**
Everything® **Wedding Checklist,**
$7.95 ($11.95 CAN)
Everything® **Wedding Etiquette Book,**
$7.95 ($11.95 CAN)
Everything® **Wedding Organizer,**
$15.00 ($22.95 CAN)
Everything® **Wedding Shower Book,**
$7.95 ($12.95 CAN)
Everything® **Wedding Vows Book,**
$7.95 ($11.95 CAN)
Everything® **Weddings on a Budget**
Book, $9.95 ($15.95 CAN)

WRITING

Everything® **Creative Writing Book**
Everything® **Get Published Book**
Everything® **Grammar and Style Book**
Everything® **Grant Writing Book**
Everything® **Guide to Writing**
Children's Books
Everything® **Screenwriting Book**
Everything® **Writing Well Book**

Available wherever books are sold!
To order, call 800-872-5627, or visit us at everything.com